"As a mom of a transgender daughter, I wish this labor of love existed when my child began her journey. *He's Always Been My Son* is a heartstring-pulling story from the perspective of a mom, and it's filled with input from other family members and friends that make this book an essential guide for anyone who loves a transgender youth."

—*Jeanette Jennings, President/Founder, Transkids Purple Rainbow Foundation, featuring with her family on the television docu-series "I Am Jazz"*

"So many loving parents have shared in print their stories of parenting a transgender child, but *He's Always Been My Son* does what no other book has…capturing the essential truth that it takes a village to grow a thriving gender creative child."

—*Diane Ehrensaft PhD, Director, Mental Health, Child and Adolescent Gender Center, UCSF, and author of* Gender Born, Gender Made *and* The Gender Creative Child

"A wonderful balance between a mother's love for her son and resources available to families who are navigating a similar journey."

—*Roz Gould Keith, President/Founder, Stand with Trans, Creator, Ally Moms, parent of a transgender teen*

of related interest

Straight Expectations
The Story of a Family in Transition
Peggy Cryden, LMFT
With Janet E. Goldstein-Ball, LMFT
ISBN 978 1 78592 748 5
eISBN 978 1 78450 537 0

The Gender Agenda
A First-Hand Account of How Girls and
Boys Are Treated Differently
Ros Ball and James Millar
Foreword by Marianne Grabrucker
ISBN 978 1 78592 320 3
eISBN 978 1 78450 633 9

Can I tell you about Gender Diversity?
A guide for friends, family and professionals
CJ Atkinson
Illustrated by Olly Pike
ISBN 978 1 78592 105 6
eISBN 978 1 78450 367 3

Trans Voices
Becoming Who You Are
Declan Henry
Foreword by Professor Stephen Whittle, OBE
Afterword by Jane Fae
ISBN 978 1 78592 240 4
eISBN 978 1 78450 520 2

All You Need Is Love
Celebrating Families of All Shapes and Sizes
Shanni Collins
ISBN 978 1 78592 251 0
eISBN 978 1 78450 534 9

HE'S ALWAYS BEEN MY SON

—A mother's story about raising her transgender son—

Janna Barkin

Jessica Kingsley *Publishers*
London and Philadelphia

First published in 2017
by Jessica Kingsley Publishers
73 Collier Street
London N1 9BE, UK
and
400 Market Street, Suite 400
Philadelphia, PA 19106, USA

www.jkp.com

Library of Congress Cataloging in Publication Data
A CIP catalog record for this book is available from the Library of Congress

British Library Cataloguing in Publication Data
A CIP catalogue record for this book is available from the British Library

ISBN 978 1 78592 747 8
eISBN 978 1 78450 525 7

Printed and bound in Great Britain

Dedicated to my children, my greatest teachers. To Amaya, my son, who is transgender, and who is wise beyond his years; this book exists because of him. To Emily, my firstborn, my daughter with a wide-open heart; she has always celebrated Amaya for being exactly who he is. And to Travis, my stepson and father to our granddaughters, who is creative and courageous.

This book is also dedicated to my husband, Gabriel, my best friend, my partner in love and life. I could not have written this book without his support. His unwavering confidence in me got me to the finish line. His editorial and creative input was invaluable.

Last but never least, I dedicate this book to my mom, Linda Sue Masia, and my dad, Aaron Masia—may he rest in peace, and may his memory always be for a blessing. I am forever grateful for their love, support, and guidance. They set the foundation for who I am today.

CONTENTS

AMAYA'S BLESSING

To the readers of this book

At the age of three, I began wearing "boys' clothes." By the time I was in the first grade my hair was cut short, never to be long again. In the seventh grade (when puberty was in full effect, not only for myself, but for my fellow classmates as well), I became increasingly aware of my developing chest. It wasn't until I was 14 and in the eighth grade that I started connecting the dots between these things.

At that point I decided to reach out to my parents. I sent an email—yes, an email—to my mother (the author of this book) expressing my discomfort. I knew her response would be positive and supportive, because that's the type of person she is. But still, it was extremely nerve-racking for me. Little did I know that sending that email would be one of the best decisions of my life.

It is hard for me to fathom that parents would be mad, disappointed, or have feelings of resentment when a transgender child expresses their authentic selves and entrusts their parents with that information. The sad truth, however, is that this happens all too often. Knowing this, I am even more grateful to have the support and unconditional love that I have from my parents. I could not be more proud of my mother for writing her story and sharing the knowledge she has gained in the hope of educating and supporting other parents as they undergo a similar journey.

So, with great excitement, I approve of the words my mother has written and I cannot wait to see the impact they have!

Sincerely,
Amaya Barkin

INTRODUCTION

There was not one *ah-hah!* moment when I knew my child was transgender. Early in the life of our youngest child, my husband, Gabriel, and I were keenly aware that Amaya was not your typical girl, or even your average "tomboy." The signs were always there, from the way he insisted upon being dressed, to the so-called "boy" toys he consistently chose to play with, to the way he carried himself and moved his body. My understanding and acceptance developed over a long period of time and tracked closely with my child's understanding and acceptance of himself.

Before we go on, an important note about pronouns and gender-specific words:

- To be clear, I will use male pronouns for Amaya consistently throughout this book, even though our family and community used female pronouns for Amaya until he asked us to switch at age 14.

- Likewise, I will use the appropriate male, female, or gender-neutral pronouns for all other people in this book, with respect to each individual's gender identity.

- Also, readers should note that I will use gender-neutral words (*they, them,* and *their*) instead of gender-specific words (*he/she, her/him,* or *her/his*) when I refer to singular people. For instance, I may refer to "a child who expresses *their* gender variance."

When I first started looking for information and support to help me understand my child, I was lucky to find some valuable resources. At the time there were scant few voices and websites that provided information and perspectives about parenting a transgender child. I was unaware of the budding phenomenon called "blogging," and today's abundant online blogosphere was in its infancy. Now there are many great resources available on the Internet and elsewhere. Sadly, the world is also full of a lot of misinformation, fear, hate, and ignorance.

My purpose in writing this book is to share and spread information, love, acceptance, and empathy. Every child deserves to be loved and supported unconditionally. Being transgender is just one more beautiful normal variation of being human.

Aside from my own deep connection to my transgender son, here are some other challenges faced by transgender people and their families that inspire me to write this book:

- Lesbian, Gay, Bisexual, Transgender, Queer or Questioning (LGBTQ) youth have among the highest suicide rates in the nation. While more studies are needed, currently it is believed that at least 25 percent of transgender youth have attempted suicide, and rates as high as 41 percent have been cited.[1]

- The Human Rights Campaign (HRC) conducted a groundbreaking study in 2012 in which 10,000 LGBTQ identified youth ages 13–17 were surveyed. The results: 42 percent said that the community in which they live is not accepting of LGBT people; 26 percent said their biggest problems were "not feeling accepted by their family/trouble at school/bullying," and "fear to be out/open."[2]

My husband and I are all so grateful to all of our extended family, to our wide circle of friends, and to all those within our greater community who have accepted and even embraced our son's transition. My family and I know we are fortunate in this regard, as many transgender youth do not experience this level of acceptance. I know we live in "a bubble within a bubble within a bubble" here in Northern California, as some might say, and I recognize our good fortune. There are many who don't have the support or resources that our family has, and I know part of my work is to advocate for those who are marginalized most.

It is my goal that the story I tell, as well as the memories and messages included in this book that were written by my close family and friends, provide consistently positive, uplifting, educational guidance to other families as well as to educators, counselors, transgender people, or anyone else interested in this issue. To support this goal, I have also included: resource information for legal and other assistance; notes on some of the latest research on gender; lists of non-profit and other organizations that support transgender youth and families; lists of medical and other health professionals skilled in working with trans youth; and information about online and local support groups for parents and their children.

I make this offering to parents, family members, and others who want to learn more about what it is like to *parent*, *advocate for*, and above all *love* a transgender child. It is my dear wish that sharing our story, we will open hearts and minds and help to bring about greater acceptance and equal treatment of all transgender and gender non-conforming/gender-expansive people.

I write to support, inspire, educate, and celebrate!

WHAT DOES THAT MEAN? A GLOSSARY FOR THIS BOOK

The words we use to describe others and ourselves are important. Words we use to describe *ourselves* tell the world who we are and how we want to be seen. Words we use to describe *others* tell them what we think about who they are, based on what we have discerned from their own words and behavior as well as information from other inputs (peers, cultural norms, environmental factors, etc.).

Here are some words I use to describe myself:

- I am a mom.

- I am a teacher.

- I am cisgender.

These are words I might use to describe my youngest child:

- He is my son.

- He is a student.

- He is transgender.

Given that words are vital for understanding someone's gender identity, it is important that I pause here to define some of the key terms used in this book. The terms below are significant and relevant to my family's story, and I will use these terms throughout these pages. For a more in-depth exploration of terms and definitions, there is a plethora of resources available online including the websites I used as primary references for the glossary included in this book, hosted by Gender Spectrum,[3] and the University of California at San Francisco (UCSF) Child and Adolescent Gender Center.[4]

By the way, did you know that Facebook, until just recently, had over 58 choices for gender? Now, they have said the choices are unlimited![5]

WHAT IS GENDER?

Gender has three components:

1. *Gender biology:* What we typically mean when we use the term "sex" to describe the gender of the newborn. Body parts, DNA, chromosomes, hormones, brain functions; the body a person is born with. (In the United States and the United Kingdom, and pretty much everywhere, the gender marked on a birth certificate is based only on the genitalia visible at birth.)

2. *Gender expression:* The way one presents to the outside world. This includes choices in clothes, style, hair, activities, communication style.

3. *Gender identity:* A person's deeply felt inner sense of who they are.

More terms to know:

- *Sex:* This refers to the label, male or female, noted at the time of birth based on visible genitalia; also sometimes known as birth sex, natal sex, bio-sex or assigned sex.

- *Intersex:* A gender identity used to describe someone whose visible genitalia at birth may include some combination of male and female genitalia such as vulva, clitoris, penis, or testicles, or someone who was born with ambiguous genitalia.

- *Gender binary:* A construct that recognizes only two distinct categories: male and female. Both cisgender (see below) and transgender (see below) people can have a gender identity that is binary.

- *Gender spectrum:* A construct that describes gender as a continuum, with male characteristics toward one end and female characteristics toward the other, with many gender identities existing on a spectrum between the two ends.

- *Cisgender:* A term used to identify people whose gender identity and natal sex are congruent. Put simply, this describes people who feel inside that their gender matches their natal sex, the gender marker they have carried since it was marked on their birth certificate.

- *Transgender:* Typically used to refer to someone whose gender identity is the opposite of their natal sex. Sometimes the word transgender is used more broadly to encompass anyone who does not identify as gender binary. People may identify as transgender whether or not they have had—or plan to have—any medical interventions. (Examples of medical interventions include sex reassignment or genital surgery, chest surgery, and hormonal treatments.) To be clear, a person who has had any or all of these interventions may not identify as transgender.

- *Trans:* An abbreviation for *transgender;* these two words are sometimes used interchangeably. In addition, trans is used by some people as a catch-all phrase to include all those whose gender identity and/or gender expression does not align with the gender marked on their birth certificate.

- *MTF:* Abbreviation of "male to female." This is a gender identity that describes someone who was assigned male gender at birth and has now transitioned to female.

- *FTM:* Abbreviation of "female to male." A gender identity that describes someone who was assigned female gender at birth and has now transitioned to male.

- *Non-binary:* An umbrella term used for gender identities that are not exclusively male/female. People who identify as non-binary may feel both male and female, or neither, or some combination of all of these.

- *Gender queer:* For some people the Q in LGBTQ stands for *queer.* Gender queer is a broad term that describes people whose gender identity does not fit into conventional gender norms. In addition, the word *queer* is sometimes used today as a political statement: People who do not fit into the gender binary construct have long been the brunt of many a derogatory insult, and the word queer evolved as a slur when used in reference to LGBTQ people. Identifying as gender queer can be a way for some people to identify with the struggle for acceptance and equality for those who do not conform to the dominant gender norms in our society—a reclaiming or celebration of the word and concept. Queer is not a derogatory term if used to describe someone who self identifies as queer.

- *Gender questioning:* For some people the Q in LGBTQ stands for *questioning*. This describes a process a person may go through when confused or unsure about their own internal sense of gender identity. Sometimes the term is used to describe their gender identity when questioning their gender identity.

- *Gender fluid:* Some people experience their gender identity as fluid in that it flows or shifts rather than being set or static.

- *Agender:* A person who is without gender or feels no connection to any gender. Someone who feels neither male nor female and/or does not want to be seen as either by others.

- *Gender expansive or gender creative:* These broad terms are often used to describe someone who may not fit into typical male/female stereotypes of behavior or expression in one or more ways. These individuals often challenge the expectations around gender within their community. Other similar terms include *gender non-conforming* and *gender variant.*

- *Transboy:* A child who was assigned a female sex at birth and has a boy gender identity.

- *Transgirl:* A child who was assigned a male sex at birth and has a girl gender identity.

- *Bio-boy:* An individual who was born with boy parts and assumed to be a boy at birth (ABAB).

- *Bio-girl:* An individual who was born with girl parts and assumed to be a girl at birth (AGAB).

- *Cross-dresser:* Someone who enjoys dressing in clothing stereotypically worn by the opposite sex. People who are cross-dressers may or may not be transgender.

- *Gender dysphoria:* A profound, persistent state of unease or dissatisfaction, anxiety, or depression that occurs when a person's's internal sense of who they are does not align with the sex assigned at birth. Until recently, gender dysphoria was known as "gender identity disorder," and the diagnosis was classified by the American Psychiatric Association (APA) as a psychological disorder. However, being transgender or gender non-conforming is no longer considered a mental disorder; "gender identity disorder" was removed from the APA's *Diagnostic and Statistical Manual of Mental Disorders* (*DSM*) in 2013.

- *Transition:* The process a person goes through to align aspects of their life to be consistent with their gender identity. Transition broadly encompasses the many changes a person makes in order to affirm and live consistently with their gender identity. Transition can happen on several different levels including:

- *Social transition:* Changes to social identifiers may encompass pronouns, name, clothing, hairstyle, and many other outward-facing expressions in one's day-to-day life and interactions with others.

- *Legal transition:* Individuals may seek to change government-issued documents such as birth certificates, driver's licenses, and passports in order to have their legal status align with their gender identity.

- *Medical transition:* An individual may use medicine such as hormone blockers or cross-sex hormones to align their physical characteristics with their gender identification.

- *Surgical transition:* Some people choose to modify their body surgically via addition or removal of gender-associated physical traits. This can include (but is not limited to) the alteration of genitalia, facial reconstruction, and/or laser hair removal.

- *Gender confirmation surgery:* Also known as GCS, this is the surgical procedure in which an individual's genitalia is altered to correspond to the opposite of their sex assigned at birth. Formally known as sex reassignment surgery or SRS.

- *Bottom surgery:* This is another term used to describe GCS.

- *Top surgery:* The surgical procedure that includes removal of the breasts and creation of a male chest.

- *Transsexual:* Refers specifically to a person who has had gender confirmation surgery and has transitioned to the opposite of the sex they were assigned at birth. This is an older term that some people still use to describe themselves, but many trans people prefer the word *transgender*.

- *Sexual orientation:* We describe *sexual orientation* in terms of whom someone is attracted to. *Heterosexual* (attracted to opposite gender), *homosexual* (attracted to same gender), and *bisexual* (attracted to both men and women) are commonly known sexual orientations. There are other orientations that are perhaps less known, such as *pansexual* (attracted to all or any gender, a.k.a. to "people, not parts"), and *asexual* (not attracted to anyone, and/or not interested in sex). *Gender identity* is different from *sexual orientation*, although they are interrelated; it has been said that "sexuality" is who you want to go to bed *with* and "gender" is who you want to go to bed *as*. Some people argue that this is an oversimplification. Developmentally, a child typically has a core sense of gender at a younger age than the age at which they become aware of their sexual orientation (or sexuality in general).

- *Misgender:* To misgender someone is to use the pronouns, adjectives, or a name corresponding to the wrong gender, whether by accident or on purpose.

There are also many terms that are outdated, considered offensive, or are otherwise no longer acceptable when talking about gender today. Here are some examples of what *not* to say:

- **Gender identity disorder:** This term was used until recently in the *DSM* to describe what is now known as *gender dysphoria*. The APA changed the term in 2013 because the old definition implied that being transgender or having confusion about one's gender was a disorder or a disease that needed a diagnosis and cure. Now the *DSM* lists gender dysphoria as a diagnosis, and being transgender is no longer considered a mental illness. On the contrary, being transgender is now recognized as a normal variation of human experience, and the needs of those with gender dysphoria can be addressed appropriately with this diagnosis.

- **Tranny:** A word considered by many people today to be an insult (as it is has so often been employed) intended to deride or diminish transgender people. Although some people may use this word due to mere ignorance of its pejorative context, it is often used when "stereotyping" someone, and often compared to the "N-word" to illustrate the impact that using the word could have on its target victims.

- **Transvestite:** Sometimes used as a broad slur toward transgender or gender non-conforming people. However, to be clear, most dictionaries define a transvestite simply as someone who dresses in some way like the opposite sex, usually only in particular situations. (Of note, the definition in *Merriam*

Webster's Dictionary online includes a quote declaring that most cross-dressers are likely not transgender.) The term "cross-dresser" is more commonly used today, and use of the word transvestite is considered outdated and inappropriate.

A note: These are common definitions today, but if anyone chooses to use a word on this "what *not* to say" list in order to describe themselves, that is their choice, and it should be respected when referring to that person.

Now let's go back to those words I used to describe myself above: I am a teacher. I am a mom. I am cisgender. Regarding that last one, saying I am *cisgender* means that in my core, I know myself to be a woman (that's my gender identity), and I was determined female at birth because I was born with a vagina (that's the gender written on my birth certificate, also called *natal sex*, or the sex assigned at birth). My gender identity and natal sex are congruent, so I define myself as female. I was born this way.

Here are the words I used above to describe my youngest child: He is my son. He is a student. He is transgender. As defined above, *transgender* is a gender identity for someone whose inner core sense of who they are does not align with, or is the opposite of, the sex that was determined at birth. My child was born with female genitalia, so my child was assigned female at birth. (That's his natal or birth sex.) My son has a deeply felt sense of self that is male. (That's his gender identity.) He defines himself first and foremost as male, and he is also transgender. He was born that way.

NAVIGATION GUIDE

There is no one way to be transgender, and there is no single trajectory for all transgender people's lives. Each person is unique, and each person's experience is unique.

Until very recently most trans people did not transition until they were adults. Today we are seeing more and more children transition at younger and younger ages. This raises a significant series of questions for parents: How can they navigate and understand the trajectory of their kids' lives, and what role should they play to support children who exhibit or express gender-expansive behavior? Although there are a rapidly increasing amount of resources available, there is no single guidebook or checklist a parent can follow. I hope my book will be a resource for parents and others who seek support or information, as well as those who just need to know they are not alone on their journey.

This book is divided into parts that follow chronologically with my child's ages and stages. Just as we describe the process of human development in stages (such as early childhood, tween years, teenage years, and finally adulthood), it can be said that there are certain stages a transgender person may go through on their way to living fully as their true selves. The stages of transition that I outline here may or may not match up with all trans people's experiences. Each person's experience will take its own form.

Here are the stages I observed in my son's transition, which may or may not apply to other people's transitions as well:

- *Before Years:* This is the period before there is any incongruence between a person's assigned gender and either their inner sense of gender identity or their outward expression. For my son, this period lasted from birth until he was about two-and-a-half years old.

- *Early Years:* The early years encompasses the age period wherein a child may show some early signs of incongruence relative to gender identity and expression. Children during this period (which lasted roughly from preschool days through the first years of elementary school in our child's experience) often have a developing inner sense of who they are. A child during this stage may exhibit preferences that would be stereotypically assigned to the opposite gender, regardless of whether they are too young to express it verbally or not. For example, a boy at age two may insist verbally that "he" is a girl, or a girl may start to refuse to wear dresses. Parents or others may notice the young person does not behave in gender-typical ways. The child may be referred to as "tomboy" or "girly boy." There may be a feeling that the child will "grow out of it." My son was in this stage until he was about seven.

- *Tween Years:* These are the years between those Early Years and Transition. Incongruence is present but nothing is clear, neither for the child nor the parents. A child may not be aware of their incongruence. Or perhaps they now have a growing inner awareness of self that is (or is not) expressed outwardly. Or there *is* outward expression, but seemingly no inner understanding or awareness as yet. There can be confusion for the young person and others around them. There may be experimentation (trying on personalities, for instance), isolation, and frustration. There may be questions, some of them unasked. The young person or the parents may reach out for support to doctors, teachers, therapists, clergy, family, friends. For our child, this phase lasted from ages 6–13.

- *Transition Years:* At this stage a maturing person is actively beginning to affirm their gender identity and is taking steps to live and move about in the world as their affirmed, true gender. A person in transition is purposeful in their actions and asks that others honor and respect their requests relative to their social transition, including clothing and hair choices, name changes, personal pronoun changes, changes to legal identity documents, and use of the bathroom or locker room of one's affirmed gender. Our child went through transition between the ages of 14 and 17.

- *Complete:* A complete person has made the necessary adjustments to live comfortably as their authentic, affirmed selves relative to gender identity and expression. It is up to each individual to decide when their transition can be considered complete, and a feeling of being complete may change in the future for some individuals. Some may never feel complete with their transitions. Amaya was able to say he felt complete sometime around age 17.

• *Now:* The current state. (Complete...for now.)

As a childhood educator (I have taught at and directed preschools for many years), I note that the stages I defined above for my child's transition toward living as his true self correspond with well-established psychological childhood development stages. For example, when my child was very young, before age three, he didn't express any sense of self other than what we projected upon him. These were our "Before Years." By the time he was three, the age at which humans develop the concept of a "self" that is separate from "others," our child began to express his predilection for all things *boy*. He was beginning to experience a sense of self and he wanted to express that feeling outwardly. These "early years" of his childhood development, as often defined, were in step with the "Early Years" stage I noted above on his journey toward transition. When he went through puberty, he was very much caught in an in-between phase; he was a girl (as we knew him then) who looked like a boy who was growing breasts. These were his "tween years" of psychological development, and also the "Tween Years" of his gender journey. Food for thought.

This book is told from my point of view as a mom to a transgender child who underwent these stages of transition in order to live as his true, authentic self. Some of the chapters were written by my husband, Gabriel, by Amaya's siblings, by other family members, and by some dear friends. I hope my story—really, *his* story, *our* story—inspires you, supports you, informs you, or even just entertains you. Naturally, I'll start from the beginning, from the "Before Years" long before our "Now" was something I would ever imagine…

— *Part 1* —

THE BEFORE YEARS

People who are gender non-conforming most often have a time in their life when they and those closest to them (usually their parents) are unaware of any incongruence regarding gender. We could say that these Before Years are a time in which there are no obvious signs that a child identifies with any gender other than the gender assigned at birth. For many trans people, these Before Years encompass a very brief period in their life. For some trans people, there wasn't really much *before* at all; while they might not have expressed it outwardly in any way, some say they always had an inner sense that their gender identity was different than the way the world saw them. Sadly, without a societal construct that allows children to feel safe to express this inner knowing, many trans people say that as children, they pushed their feelings aside or hid them from even those closest to them.

Some children announce at a very young age that their gender identity is something different from that assigned at birth. Such was the case for Jazz Jennings, a well-known transgender teen who is 16 as of this writing. (By complete coincidence, my mother and Jazz's grandmother happen to be close friends. They met when they lived in the same apartment complex when they were very young, and they've kept in touch ever since. Small world.) Jazz came to national prominence in the United States when she was interviewed by Barbara Walters on ABC's news magazine program *20/20* at age six, and she later starred with her family in a reality show on the TLC network. Way back when she was just 18 months old, Jazz began insisting to her family that she was a girl, and she has not wavered since. At age five, she was the first child in the United States to share her social transition with the public and attend public school registered as her affirmed gender (girl) rather than that of her natal sex on her birth certificate (male). Though she attended school as a girl, her birth certificate and school records showed "male" until fifth grade. Jazz's experience is just one story; other children may not experience any disconnect relative to gender identity until they are older. Some may feel something is different about them but not know how to express it outwardly. There are many ways.

During the before years of Amaya's life, until he was about three years old, my husband, Gabriel, and I were under the logical impression that we had a little girl, and so we treated our child as such. Gabriel and I did not parent specifically in a gender-neutral way, but we certainly provided all of our kids with a variety of choices. Before he turned three, Amaya sometimes wore jeans, and other times dresses. He had all types of toys available to play with, including balls, dolls, cars, blocks, Lego, and stuffed animals. Amaya was a happy, easygoing child, and he did not protest about any of the choices we made regarding clothing or toys.

Looking back now, I can see that even during those early years, there were remarkable moments that perhaps foreshadowed Amaya's expression of gender variance later on. Here on the following pages is a collection of stories that illustrate this.

DREAM BABY

While writing this book, I pulled out the prenatal dream journal in which I'd recorded my dreams during my pregnancy with Amaya in 1997 (he was born in January 1998). When I read some of the things I'd written, I was taken by some of the prophetic dreams I'd described.

First, I wrote this in my prenatal dream journal on November 12, 1997, just two weeks after my father Aaron died. I was six-and-a-half months pregnant with Amaya:

> I dreamed we had a boy. It was an easy labor, we slept through most of the labor and the baby came out really fast. We really wanted to name it Ezra Joe but remembered its name is Aaron Joe.
>
> I nursed him and was squirting him (with milk?) and he didn't like it, but he was smiling at me and he said, "I don't have a penis." I said, "Yes you do."

About a month later, I wrote in my journal that I dreamed about a girl baby. But the very next night I dreamed about a boy:

> Aunt Belinda [my father's sister] delivered him to us at home, like a package.

And then, early in my ninth month of pregnancy, I wrote this:

> Dreamed I thought you were a boy, but I saw and felt
> your vagina, and said, "Look she's a girl," needing to
> convince your dad.

Finally, on January 1, 1998, I made my final entry in that particular journal:

> All right, we just don't know! What are you? A BABY.
> We can't wait to meet you! I can't believe how soon
> it is. We are ready and not at the same time.
>   We love you!

Amaya was born 25 days later.

SHE HAD ONE JOB

Amaya was born at home in 1998. My husband, Gabriel, and our daughter, Emily, were with me as Amaya came into this world. Emily, who had also been birthed at home, was just a few months past her fifth birthday.

My family and I were well cared for at Amaya's birth. We were attended by our midwives, Shannon and Jennie, and by our dear friends, Lisa, Kendra, and Randi. Randi was seven months pregnant herself at the time.

As I labored in our bedroom during the early morning hours, Kendra played with Emily. When Randi arrived, she took a turn being with Emily, and they went to a nearby park to play for a while. Gabriel and Lisa and the midwives supported me as the morning continued and labor progressed. I remember that Lisa and Gabriel had their hands on me while Kendra sang and prayed and minded the video camera. And I remember leaning on Jennie while Shannon rested.

Things progressed smoothly, and pretty soon it was time to push. Around that time, Randi and Emily returned from the park. It had started to drizzle. (Blessed rain from above. More on that later.)

As I did my labor thing, Emily, attended by our friends, came in and out of the room with the attention span of a girl her age. She really wanted to be at the birth, and we had given her an important role: she was the one among us designated to name the sex of the newborn upon arrival. (I say "sex" because we used that word then, but now I would use the word "gender.") Emily would announce to the world if it was a girl or boy – it was her "One Job!" (Unlike many pregnant women, I did not want to know the gender of the children I carried when I was pregnant. During both of my pregnancies, I wanted to bond with the Being without knowing very much about the baby at all. I am so grateful I trusted this intuition and developed this connection with my babies.)

I labored in my bed as Jennie and Shannon prepared for the imminent birth of our baby. Gabriel was at my side holding my hand and Randi was at my head. Lisa was at my foot on one side and the midwives were on the other. Finally, it was time. We called for Emily and Kendra to come in from Emily's bedroom where they were playing, and I remember seeing Emily standing with Lisa at the foot of the bed as she watched me push.

With a few pushes, the baby was born and the midwives quickly brought it into my arms all wrapped up.

Gabriel said, "Everyone remember, it is EMILY'S JOB to say if it's a boy or a girl!" I peeked, and I know what I saw: girl parts. I was elated! I noticed Gabriel saw the same thing that I did. But we kept quiet because Emily had One Job!

And she looked closely at the little babe and said, "I think…it's a boy!"

All of us adults in the room figured she just didn't identify the parts correctly. It sure is a lot to take in. My husband gently corrected Emily, saying, "I think maybe it's a girl." And we all agreed, even Emily upon further inspection, that Emily must have thought she saw something that just wasn't there.

But, the truth is that Emily had One Job! And she did it well. We just didn't know it at the time.

AMAYA'S NAME

Amaya Jael Masia Barkin:

- *Barkin:* Paternal family name
- *Masia:* Maternal family name
- *Jael:* In honor of my maternal grandfather, Joe
- *Amaya:* In honor of my father, Aaron.

The death of my father when I was six months pregnant with my second child shocked me, and I grieved deeply. In the midst of my grief, I also came to a crisis of conscience.

In the tradition of our family, it was almost a given that this baby should be named for my father. Though my husband and I were not then (and are not now) practicing Jews, religiously speaking, the traditions of my ancestry were important to us. In Judaism, one strong tradition is to name a child after someone who has died. The choice should be someone who lived a "good" life, who was a good person, a mensch. It is considered a blessing to give a child the name of a beloved family member.

Given the timing of his death and my child's impending birth, tradition loomed strong. If I bore a boy he would be named Aaron, and a girl would have a name starting with an "A."

However, another very important tradition in Judaism is the ritual of circumcision. Gabriel and I already knew we were not going to circumcise our child. We had already had the conversation with my family when I was pregnant with our daughter several years earlier. I knew my father absolutely wished us to carry on the traditions of our family; he had made his position quite clear, and the issue was important to him. But he and my mother also were aware of our feelings. (I will note here that the decision to circumcise our oldest child, Travis, was in the hands of his birth mother, who raised him until he came to live with us at age 14.)

These two traditions tore at my heart. The added challenge, and one more piece of the puzzle, was the idea of having a son named Aaron. In my grief following my father's death, this did not make sense; I did not want to have a son named Aaron because I did not want the truth of my father's death to be real.

Still, I knew I would name a boy after my father. And yet, I knew I would not circumcise that boy. I just could not reconcile these two facts. How could I name a child after my father to honor him, and yet *not* honor one of his deepest-held beliefs? I was conflicted.

My midwife helped me to understand and find peace with the decisions we would ultimately make. She said to me, "You must do what you know is to be true for you in your heart. And, you can honor your father in other ways."

This helped. But with all this in my mind and heart, I prayed to the universe: "Please send me a girl."

I shared this prayer with no one.

Finally, it happened. I went into labor, and I bore a girl. Among many other things I thought and felt that morning immediately after the birth, I was relieved. I would not have to face my dilemma regarding circumcision. Equally relieving was the blunt realization that my father's death would not be underscored by naming my child Aaron. With my husband's blessing and support for any name I chose, I named the baby Amaya Jael.

TO SNIP OR NOT TO SNIP?

by Gabriel Barkin, Amaya's father

When Janna was pregnant with our first child together, her parents asked us about circumcision. As observant Jews, it was important for them to know we had no plans to be all "hippie" about it (okay, that's my word, not theirs) and let our son, should he be a boy, avoid the scalpel. What to do?

We were not glad they asked about this. Our easy agreement as expecting parents was to eschew this unnecessary operation if it turned out we had a boy. Both Janna and I felt the procedure was medically unnecessary—and for me, my position also sprung from my own sense that as a male, I may have been missing out on something, sensation-wise, as a hoodless adult. Right or wrong, that's where we stood.

Also, neither my wife nor I were observant Jews as adults, and we felt little compulsion to foster this tradition, which had a bit more potential impact than, say, lighting Hanukah candles or attending a Seder. Indeed, a few small tugs and pangs of ancestral persuasion stirred inside our hearts, and I considered whether I would be challenged by having my son look different than me "down there," but that scant feeling was easily overshadowed by our desire to forego foreskin removal and spare our child the potential trauma and attendant challenges that possibly would accompany the cut. We joked about our role in the evolving Jewish pantheon; we would "end the madness."

To be clear, we had decided to be traditionalists in some fashion; we would avoid finding out the sex of our child until he or she arrived in our arms. So we knew, with a bit of dread, that this conversation with my wife's parents would continue to be uncomfortable and would feel unresolved until either a baby girl arrived or a baby boy arrived and was summarily snipped. Janna's father in particular seemed loath to let this debate go. I imagine he felt we were being rash and immature, though he generally respected our lifestyle and decisions, as far as we could tell, in most other areas.

In some measure, my wife and I began to hope for a girl in earnest, just to avoid this grandparental challenge. So there was the usual "which do I want?" conversation and low-level conflict that expectant parents experience, compounded and made less fun by this minor but present rift between us and the 'rents.

We received a letter from my in-laws one day about midway through Janna's pregnancy (it was not unusual for them to send us letters—this was back in the dark ages before we all had email and texting and internet connections), explaining their position. I recall in particular that they argued that we were limiting our child's choice to be Jewish by refusing circumcision at birth. We countered that any adult male who wanted to convert could opt for the procedure, so we were in fact allowing for more choice. Still, it was clear that we were at loggerheads. We knew the decision was totally up to us, but we felt sad that we were having conflict about this and we certainly were not fond of disappointing Janna's parents.

I can't recall if we ever mentioned this to my parents at the time. They were both raised as observant Jews, but were not in the least observant as adults, and I was not raised with any more than a bit of rudimentary Sunday School Jewish learning. Still, we thought best not to discuss any of this with them. We figured my mom would probably be fully supportive, but my dad was an unknown. (I may be misremembering this—I think it's possible we did discuss it with my mother, and she advised never telling my father. Perhaps I'll ask her about this in retrospect someday soon.)

Our child Emily arrived a few months after we received the letter. The night before her birth, we had a "visitor" while Janna was laboring at home. (Both of the kids we had together were born at home.) It was nothing really—simply that a ceiling light that had never worked at all in our entire time living in that home flickered and came on all by itself as Janna and I walked slowly by during one of her contractions. I felt a warm touch of love and reassurance in that moment of unexpected light. Moreover, in that instant, I thought suddenly and sharply of a very dear friend named Emily who had died a few years earlier. I'm not the type of person who goes around feeling spirits and seeing ghosts, and yet this was a profound sensation. I knew it was Emily, somehow. Our girl, born the next morning as a white-tailed doe ate leaves just a few feet outside our bedroom window, was given her name by both of her parents before we even spoke it aloud to each other; when I opened my mouth to speak it, Janna beat me to the punch by saying, "Let's call her Emily Deva."

I don't remember exactly when it was, but I'm pretty sure it was within an hour or two after the birth that Janna and I realized we had passed through the gauntlet of our circumcision conversation with her parents, and we'd arrived at the end of the journey in one piece. I can imagine there was a point where we both said, "Phew!"

I don't recall discussing circumcision at all five years later when Janna was pregnant with Amaya, our second child together. Certainly, any conversation we had on the topic was eclipsed when Janna's father Aaron died during her sixth month of pregnancy. Janna was devastated. Our entire circle of family and friends, close and extended, was distraught. My mother's father had also died during one of her pregnancies (her firstborn, my brother Vic), and she felt a deep sympathetic kinship with Janna. The tears flowed in torrents.

Janna and I knew this child would be named in memory of Aaron and we hoped for our child to reflect his spirit. We stayed in the "A's" when we perused baby name books—"A for Aaron" if it's a boy, but what if it's a girl?

Janna has written elsewhere about Emily's job at Amaya's birth. At five years old, the big sister's role was to announce the sex of the newborn. We adults in the room were quiet as she looked; we know what we saw, anatomically speaking. But Emily said, "I think it's a boy."

I said, "No, I think it's a girl," trying not to make her feel bad for being wrong.

But now, looking back: Who was wrong?

Oh, and at some point, I imagine we again paused to reflect on the circumcision thing, and there was probably another "Phew!" And today, knowing Amaya as I do, it figures: young man that he is with a strong sense of ethics, it occurs to me that it would be just like him at birth to try to find a way to find a unique approach to resolve the family quarrel over whether to have him undergo the procedure. To circumcise or not to circumcise if it's a boy? Honor Grandpa's memory or stay firm on principle? Well, how about if there's another way to look at this...?

There is a lot of Grandpa Aaron in Amaya. He has Grandpa's calm demeanor, his sense of logic and reason, and his big heart. Aaron was a rock in his community, the steel in his family, a mensch, someone people could rely upon. Like Aaron, Amaya has the strength, courage, dignity, and respect for others that reflect the best of masculinity's qualities. What else matters? The rest is merely (fore)skin.

�֎

NOTES FROM A NAMING CEREMONY

When Amaya was eight days old, we held a naming ceremony in our home, inviting family and friends to come meet the baby and offer their wishes for a healthful and happy life. We asked people to write their wishes for Amaya.

Here are two strikingly appropriate messages from that day, written by Amaya's paternal grandparents (emphasis added):

For Amaya—
May your life be filled with constant discovery—of self, of life, of community, of world—and *always feel free to change that which you can change*.

Grandma Elaine

Amaya Jael,
I wish you happiness, and love, which I am sure you will have, and also the *daring and courage to become whatever you want to be*, which may be difficult and arduous at times, and even cost you some of that happiness that will come so easily, but may *in the end be worth more than you think at first*.

Your Grandfather George

THE POWER OF THREE

Gabriel and I raised three children together: Travis, Emily, and Amaya. Travis, our oldest, is Gabriel's son and my stepson. Though I have known him since he was two, he did not come to live with us until he was 14.

Emily was our "first" child—the first of our children to live with us, the first child either of us ever raised, and certainly my firstborn. Twirly, girly, curly Emily. A little girl who loved to dress up and ride horses. A teenager who loved music and iPods and makeup and fashion. She's a young woman living in the New York City area now, with equal passion both for cute dresses and sweaty gym workouts.

Amaya was born in 1998, and in 2000 Travis came to live with us. Emily went from being a *de facto* "only child" to being the "middle child" practically overnight when she was eight. Travis was all boy, a broody and moody teen with a deep voice who wore cool, hand-painted hats. He was into music, DJ-ing, and graffiti art. Always incredibly creative, Travis found his way through tumultuous teen years to be the fine man he is today: a beekeeper, gardener, artist, and wonderful father to our two granddaughters.

It is hard to say how much Amaya began to model himself after Travis, the new man in the house, but it's also hard to ignore the probability. It was not long after Travis moved in that Amaya became attached to wearing a baseball cap, for instance. (What is clear is that Amaya did not model after Emily.) Nowadays when Gabriel, Travis, and Amaya stand next to each other, it is easy to see some of the family patterns in their stances and body language.

Emily and Travis have always been completely accepting and supportive of their little brother Amaya. I'm proud of all my kids, perhaps most of all because they are all proud of each other.

Part 2

THE EARLY YEARS

During the Early Years, a child may begin to exhibit early signs of incongruence relative to gender identity. Perhaps even when they are too young to express it verbally, a child may have an inner sense of who they are, and they may begin to express that self-knowledge outwardly. For example, a boy at age two may insist verbally that "he" is a girl, or a girl may start to refuse to wear dresses. Parents or others may notice at this time that a young person does not behave in gender-typical ways.

Some parents are going to be more comfortable with these differences than others. Those parents are apt to follow their child's lead, perhaps letting their boys play with dolls or allowing their girls to engage in "rough and tumble" physical play when they express a desire to do so at a young age. However, depending on their own beliefs and upbringing, some parents may not easily accept and allow behavior that is non-typical relative to the gender assigned to their children. They may not allow their boys to play with dolls, or their girls to play in the dirt. In response, some children will protest with even bolder expression and behavior. Other children in this situation may suppress their feelings until later in their lives. Some may respond by exhibiting behaviors that are cause for parental and professional concern, and these children may receive diagnoses that include ADD (attention deficit disorder), or SID (sensory integration dysfunction.) And finally, there are those parents who may observe gender non-conforming behaviors during the early years but choose simply to watch and wait, often thinking (and perhaps hoping) that their child will "grow out of it."

For our child, the Early Years were between the ages of three and six, perhaps pushing into age seven. Beginning when he was about three years old, Amaya began making consistent and insistent choices regarding clothing, behavior, and activities that could be labeled as typically *boy* choices. This behavior coincided directly with the child developmental milestone defined by childhood development pioneer Jean Piaget as the "formation of self-identity" stage. Until this stage, a child does not have a clear sense of an individual self relative to other individuals. However, at around three years, a child's brain development leads to the understanding that one is a separate individual. It is often at this stage that a child will begin to express gender differences. As Amaya's inner sense of self developed, he expressed this through his behaviors and choices, and we begin to wonder.

AMAZING

by Gabriel Barkin, Amaya's father

I was putting Amaya to bed one night when he was about two. As I tucked him in and put aside the library book we'd been reading, he said something to me that sounded really smart and insightful, one of those "things kids say" that makes a parent proud and hopeful and happy.

I don't remember what he said exactly, but it doesn't matter now. The best part was his response to my response:

"Amaya," I said, "you are amazing!"

"No," he said, "I'm Amaya."

GIRLS WEAR PINK, BOYS WEAR BLUE (OR NOT)

Amaya expressed himself outwardly as a boy for many years before he transitioned fully from female to male. People who did not know him almost always thought he was a boy until we told them otherwise. It was easiest to say, "She's a tomboy." In our culture, girls who dress like boys and play boy games are often labeled tomboys. Now, however, we have other words available, and we could say instead simply that Amaya's gender expression was male. From the age of three, his clothing choices, activity choices, and behavior were stereotypically male. He appeared to others as "one of the boys."

When some of my closest friends and I were young mothers, we passed on clothes to each other and our babies all wore hand-me-downs. In particular, there were three girls whose names started with the letter "E," so we called them collectively "the E-girls." They all wore each other's clothes in succession (Erika, then our Emily, then Eva), and it was always fun to see how each child would look in each outfit. So, of course, despite the lack of an "E" name, when it came to Amaya's turn, we started out by doing the same thing. But even at a very young age, some of the "E-girl" clothes just didn't look right to me on my toddler. I can't explain why I felt this way, but the frilly dresses were especially awkward on Amaya's body.

Amaya also expressed sensitivity to many of the clothes we gave him to wear. Shirt tags, sock lines, tight sleeves, and leggings were some of the things that were uncomfortable on his body. At first we blamed it all on skin sensitivity, and then we considered he was experiencing sensory integration challenges, but after a while we realized that it was largely the feeling of the "girly" pieces of clothing that Amaya didn't like. The more we went with the "boy" styles and fits, the happier and more comfortable he was. He still wanted the tags cut out of his shirts and shorts, but clearly he liked the boys' cut better than the girls' cut.

We needed a new source for hand-me-downs. We turned to other close friends who had boys. The boys' clothes just seemed to fit Amaya better, and to me they even "looked right." He loved wearing the clothes from these older boys. (After a while, the only "E-girl" clothes he would wear were the ones that came from the girl who, as she got older, dressed in clothes that were in more of a "tomboy" style.) These boys were not only his clothing source; they were his role models. Our circle of friends and families spent a lot of time socializing together in those days, and Amaya clearly identified himself as "one of the boys" early on.

Meanwhile, in his preschool's dress up area, Amaya *only* wore a suit jacket and tie. He never dressed as an animal or a princess. He dressed as a Man: a businessMan, a fireMan, a policeMan, or a dad. And dress-up or no, when the children played role-playing games, he *always* chose to be a boy character, sometimes "the dad" or "the brother."

The last dress Amaya ever wore was when he was three. We were at my brother's wedding on Long Island. Amaya was already dressing as a boy as a matter of course by this time though I do recall that earlier that summer, on a particularly hot day at a music festival near our home in California, he'd seemed happy to take off his jeans and t-shirt and put on a cute tie-dye dress we'd bought from a vendor. It was hot and the dress made him feel cooler.

Even so, it was unusual by this point for him to allow us to put a dress on him.

For my brother's wedding day a month or so later, Amaya had been asked to be a flower girl along with his big sister, Emily. Though he had tried on the flower-girl dress many times, that day he was uncomfortable (to say the least) in it. Well we were all uncomfortable, it was 98 degrees and super-humid, as Long Island can be in the summertime. But really, he was clearly very uncomfortable, and it wasn't just the heat. In photos from the wedding he looks miserable. To this day, any time my mother sees those pictures, she remarks on how easily one can see how much he didn't want to be in that dress. I never made him put on a dress again.

It was about this time that we had to stop buying girls' clothes, as he simply would not wear them. Some people might have said to me, "It's not his choice, you are the parent," but it really wasn't a choice in my mind and heart. My child was having fits and occasional tantrums for up to an hour a day trying to find something to put on. When we finally gave him the choice of boy clothes, he easily got dressed and his daily fits became a thing of the past. (It also helped when I found a brand of socks that had virtually no toe seam.) My child was happy, and there was peace, and that validated my feeling that we were on the right track.

Bathing suits were one of the biggest challenges. For Amaya's comfort and sense of well-being, we went from girl suits at first to a combination of a girl top and board shorts, then to a swim shirt over a girl top with board shorts, and then to a many-layered top situation under a swim shirt and board shorts. Much of the time, a suit solution was not necessary; when our kids were very young, we frequented a clothing-optional beach near our home (we do live in Northern California, after all). Amaya loved this beach because, unlike at a public pool or swim club, he could wear whatever he wanted. And what he wanted to wear, of course, was board shorts with no top, like all the boys and even the grown men he saw at every swimming place. Dressed like this he looked like a boy, and he liked it like that. As we still had the mindset that Amaya was a young "girl," my husband and I felt that "old school" rules still applied to Amaya at the swim club, hotel pools, etc. But here at "the naked beach" (as our kids called it), where everyone was allowed to wear what they wanted or even to wear nothing at all, he felt comfortable to express his true self. We eventually settled on board shorts and a swim shirt for trips to public pools, and he was happy with that compromise for a time.

Amaya's insistent desire to wear boys' underwear proved to be the hardest clothing decision for me. I don't know why it was so difficult for me to allow him this request. It seemed awkward; I just felt that a girl's parts should have girls' underwear, no matter what clothes are on top of them. Looking back, it seems silly now that I felt that way. I think it was because allowing this brought home the reality. I knew in my gut that if I allowed him to wear the boys' underwear he would never go back. I knew it was the start of something long-term, even lifelong. It wasn't that I would love him any less or reject him in any way—rather, my reaction was that of a parent who knows that society is not always kind to people who are different. Wearing boys' underwear as a girl was definitely different. Gabriel had a much easier time with this. For some reason it didn't bother him. He just didn't see what the big deal was. "Just get him the boys' underwear. Who cares?"

I was anxious because my "daughter's" way of expressing gender was becoming more and more consistently "boy." I wanted to support my child and I knew in my heart that it's best to listen to and respect the child. But I wondered, what had happened to my little girl? Where did *that* person go? Still, we could see he was happier and more comfortable with each step we took toward letting him dress entirely like a boy. When I brought home his first Spiderman briefs from Target, Amaya beamed. No longer did we struggle to get him dressed each morning. His comfort level affirmed for us that the decision to let him wear boys' underwear was correct, and we never bought a pair of girls' underwear for him again.

ONE OF THE BOYS

by Tracey Klapow, a very dear friend,
and "Aunt Tracey" to our children

We spent a lot of time with Amaya as a young child. Amaya was one of our son Sam's best friends. From a very young age, we could see that Amaya identified with Sam and copied his every move. Amaya walked around with Sam shoulder to shoulder, mimicking any "boy" sound and movement he made—all those car and airplane sounds, and every other inflection that he thought made him sound more like a boy.

When Sam introduced Amaya to his friends, Sam would say, "This is Amaya. She's a girl, but she looks like a boy, but she's really a girl." He did this over and over. With or without that introduction, many of Sam's friends didn't even realize Amaya was a girl. Amaya was often right in the middle of the wrestling with Sam's friends, and occasionally a parent who didn't know Amaya would discover there was a girl in the mix and get upset that the boys were being so rough.

In recent years, since Amaya told us he identifies as a male, it's been a struggle for me to remember to use the pronoun "he" when referring to Amaya. I always believed Amaya was male-identified long before he articulated it, and I recall that even when they were not yet tweens, I'd call out, "Boys, time for dinner!" without thinking twice. Regardless of my slip, Amaya would follow Sam to the dinner table. Sometimes I would catch myself and apologize to Amaya, and he would say that it was fine. It never bothered him that I called him a boy. But the end result is that I feel like I spent so many years training my brain to say "she" when speaking of Amaya (so I didn't hurt his feelings) that it is now taking a long time for me to retrain my brain to say "he."

I have always been, and continue to be, so proud of Amaya and the person he has become. I know that he is on the right path.

WHEN IS A HAT NOT JUST A HAT?

And then there were the hats.

Well, specifically, there was one hat at first. When Amaya was three, I was the teacher and director of a preschool in our community, and he began to attend my school. This gave me a great vantage point from which I could observe his world. Early on in his first year at the school, he gravitated toward playing with boys, although he did have friends who were girls as well. One boy was his favorite—Amaya talked about him all the time. This boy (I'll call him Chris) was a year older, and he and Amaya played together often. His mother and I became friendly and often traded playdates. Playing baseball was one of their favorite activities, as was riding on scooters. Amaya so wanted to ride a skateboard like Chris. They spent a lot of time together. Amaya started wearing a baseball hat, just like his friend did. It was a greenish-grey cap from the San Francisco Jewish Community Center—just some cap we had lying around the house—and it said "JCC" above the brim. He never wanted to go anywhere without that hat. It was clearly his security item. That was the first hat.

He had to have this hat. Many children have a particular thing that they are attached to. Some call it a "lovey." (I will use this term as applied by T. Berry Brazelton, the well-respected doctor and expert on childhood development.) A lovey is an object that has emotional importance to the child. It comforts them and in some way connects them to home. Some children have one specific item, such as a blanket or stuffed animal, while others are more flexible. For our daughter, Emily, her lovey was a "Raggedy Ann" doll. She had to have a Raggedy with her wherever she went, but it did not have to be a specific doll, it could be *any* Raggedy Ann doll among several that she had.

At first Amaya was flexible too. He had a lovey he called his "mamie." It was a cloth diaper. At some point when he was an infant I had given him a clean diaper for comfort when I left him with his babysitter, and it stuck. Over time, Amaya would welcome any cloth diaper as his "mamie;" he wasn't attached to just one.

When he adopted the hat, "mamie" was left behind. But unlike "mamie," it could not just be any hat, he only wanted *that* hat. The hat became his new lovey; and it gave him comfort. He did not go anywhere without his hat; it was his new security blanket.

As the preschool year progressed, it became more apparent that Amaya was modeling himself after his older friend Chris. He no longer allowed us to dress him in dresses, and he insisted instead on wearing jeans and t-shirts. And *the hat*. ALWAYS that hat. Increasingly picky about the clothes he wore, he often took off whatever clothes we'd picked out and put on him. As I mentioned earlier, he often claimed his clothes were too tight or they just didn't feel good. He would pitch a fit when putting on his socks, the last thing we did before we put on shoes and left the house. It was very challenging getting out the door each day.

He was obviously very uncomfortable, and I attributed it to sensory sensitivity. As a preschool teacher, I had seen similar behavior before: kids who can't stand tags in their clothes, or mud on their hands, to the point where they have very strong emotional reactions. We accommodated Amaya's need for comfort as best we could. We found socks with no seam lines (boys' tube socks), and shirts and pants that fit more loosely. And we made sure we always had *the hat*. We found out what worked through trial and error. Amaya seemed to relax, and so my husband and I did what we could to support the peace and provide for his comfort.

By the time Amaya was four, he was choosing only to wear boys' clothes. He refused any clothing that looked like it came from the girls' section of a store. He continued to play with both boys and girls at home and school, but other parents and our friends often remarked how "she" played just like one of the boys. Indeed, he was a rough and tumble kid, and he was never seen without his hat, *the hat*. He was known for wearing that hat.

His insistence about clothing choices never abated, and as long as we respected his choices, all was fine. When we didn't heed his desires (like that time we left the hat at home on school photograph day!), he could be an emotional wreck, and those days were a struggle for us.

At five, he wanted to sign up for "T-shirt League," the youngest division of Little League in our town. The game was baseball, not softball. Many of the girls his age had chosen to sign up for softball, but he refused to follow their lead, and insisted on baseball or nothing. He was one of just a few girls in the T-shirt League. He was issued his team t-shirt and baseball cap, and thus he released the sacred JCC hat and instead donned his team hat. From that point onward, he was more flexible about which hat he would wear—but regardless of which one, he still always wore a baseball cap.

He continued to do so all the way through ninth grade, when he made his transition "official."

The hat became my child's defining talisman. What seemed a possible explanation to me and Gabriel back then is clear now in light of Amaya's transition; he was expressing his gender identity by wearing that hat. He chose an item for his lovey that was important *not* because it smelled like home, and *not* because it reminded him of his momma—but rather, because it helped him define both the way he was feeling inside (gender identity), and how wanted to be seen by others (gender expression).

He was defining himself by wearing *the hat*. As a BOY.

BEST PRACTICES EVOLVE

by Lisa Treadway, a very dear friend,
and "Aunt Lisa" to our children

I've been an early childhood educator in San Francisco for almost three decades. Throughout that time, I've had the privilege, pleasure, and responsibility of taking care of two-, three-, and four-year-olds in a loving, progressive and supportive environment. The teachers and administrators at our school focus deeply on all aspects of a child's development. We believe that strong, positive relationships, where everyone feels respected and included, are the keys to a successful learning community. The messages and values we consciously impart to our youngest community members include: acceptance of ourselves and others, the celebration of differences, critical and divergent thinking, conflict resolution, and physical and emotional safety. We celebrate each other's strengths and support each other's challenges and journeys. My fellow teachers and I strive to continually grow as educators, which of course means that over the years we have evolved in our thinking—what was a best practice *then* is not always a best practice *now*.

This is perhaps especially true in regards to our thinking about gender. Back in the late 1980s, a child named Andrew [not his real name] came to school each day thrilled to adorn himself with every sparkly necklace in the dress-up corner, and sometimes even the pink ballet tutu. We, the teachers, instinctively knew in our hearts that his right to do so should be supported wholeheartedly. It obviously brought Andrew such joy to gaze at himself and his adornments in the mirror! We reassured his dad that just because Andrew chose to play this way, it did not necessarily mean he might one day be gay. When other children inevitably commented with concern that Andrew was dressing like a girl, we knew how to respond to them: "It's not what you wear that makes you a boy or a girl, it's your *body* that makes you a boy or a girl." We gave the same message to the children who claimed that teacher Tim had "girl's hair" (because he wore it in a ponytail), and to those who teased Sarah for always playing with boys: "It's not how you look, what you do, or who you play with that make you a boy or a girl, it's your body. If you have a penis, you're a boy. If you have a vagina, you're a girl." We also thought it important to help children understand what we called "gender constancy"—"You were born a girl, so you will always be a girl. Girls grow up to be women, boys grow up to be men."

How our thinking has changed! At our school, we now understand that it's not, in fact, your body that makes you a boy or a girl. Gender is not binary, nor is it necessarily constant. We realize that one's biological gender is sometimes different from one's gender identity, and that neither is necessarily tied to gender presentation.

But how do we explain all of this to very young children, especially when their parents don't agree with our perspective? My colleagues and I struggle with this question. We have to do what we know is right for the children in our care, while at the same time respecting the beliefs and values of our students' parents. Although attitudes have clearly shifted in general in our culture, we have not yet reached a point where all parents are comfortable with their three-year-old son wearing nail polish, or with their four-year-old daughter asking to wear boys' *Star Wars* underwear, or saying she wants to marry her best girlfriend. In partnership with parents, we do our best to listen, to acknowledge feelings, and to advocate without judgment for what we understand is best for the child. We explore and share current research. We explain to children that sometimes adults have different ideas. At the same time, we do not compromise those fundamental values that we and our school hold dear, especially when doing so might negatively impact a child's self-image and self-esteem.

So what words do we use currently in the classroom when children ask questions or make comments about gender? "It's not how you look, or what you do, or who you play with that makes you a boy or a girl. Sometimes it's not even your body that makes you a boy or a girl. *It's how you feel inside.*" Might that message evolve over time? I hope so, if it means that we will continue to grow in our understanding of gender.

WALKING THROUGH CEMENT

by Shawn Masia, Amaya's uncle

One day in late 1997, my late father, Aaron, for whom Amaya is named, suffered a severe heart attack. My sister, Janna, was six months pregnant with Amaya. She flew from California to New York the next day to be with my father and the family at a Manhattan hospital. While we wanted to keep vigil as much as we could during his critical illness, there was only so much time any of us could spend in the horrid waiting room outside the hospital's critical care unit. Janna and I took several long walks together, consoling each other and talking about our fear and dread of what was to come. We were told he was the sickest person in the hospital.

On one such walk, we ventured into a side neighborhood while carrying on with our usual, intense conversation. Neither of us seemed to notice an array of carefully placed, low-slung ropes in our path indicating that the section of sidewalk that we were approaching was closed. Instead, we barreled along and stepped *over* the ropes without a conscious thought, and we trudged through the wet cement some workers had just finished laying. Deep in conversation and ignorant of our mistake, we did not stop walking. We continued on our way through the wet cement until a construction foreman called to us and snapped us out of our fugue. We looked down and realized what we had done.

We apologized profusely, and then an amazing thing happened: The foreman merely said, "It's okay—please walk off the wet cement." He said it quickly, and we walked off the wet cement onto the street. We began to apologize and explain our mistake as best we could as we hurried away in embarrassment, expecting to be berated. But not a single one of the many workers who had just finished loading up their truck approached us nor scolded us for making their day longer or harder. It must have been obvious to them that we were going through something very difficult.

Unfortunately, our father passed away later that week. But a ray of hope was born three months and one day later. Now it was my turn to fly across the country as quickly as I could, and when Amaya's big blue eyes greeted me for the first time, we clicked instantly. Our relationship has always been easy, loving, and level. In fact, I think most people have that kind of relationship with Amaya.

Three years later, my fiancée and I asked Amaya to be the flower girl at our wedding. The white flower girl dress Amaya had to wear made him absolutely miserable the second he put it on. For the whole day until he could take it off, Amaya just could not get comfortable in that dress. My bride and I figured it was pretty typical three-year-old behavior to fuss over getting all dressed up, and we knew none of the guests were the wiser when Amaya led us down the aisle with aplomb. In hindsight, I guess things were not that simple—to my knowledge that was the last time Janna ever gave Amaya a dress to wear.

Over the years, I have been so proud watching Amaya grow up into a highly articulate, compassionate, sensible, charismatic, strong person. So much of my father's goodness lives on in Amaya, and it is such a great comfort to our family to see these wonderful and familiar qualities draw people in. The pragmatic approach to life served Amaya well when he walked through the wet concrete of his earlier life, unaware of many of the challenges in his path. And I am so thankful to his parents for responding throughout Amaya's life very much like the cement workers responded to Janna and me on our walk so long ago. Like those workers, Janna and Gabe always knew that wherever Amaya was going on his journey, he needed support and help, not frustrated responses that would make his path harder to navigate. As a result, Amaya has now landed on very firm ground, and I am very proud of the young man he has become.

I WISH TO BE A GRAMPA

Amaya had a vivid imaginary play life when he was very young. When he was in his imaginary world, he would interact with all sorts of characters. He preferred to play alone in his imaginary world, but we could hear him, and what we heard was often fascinating! His best friend in that world was a boy named "Rocco," and Amaya would talk out loud to him and to other "friends" when he thought nobody was listening. He also liked to dress up when he played in this world, but unlike his older sister, Emily (who always chose frilly dresses or tutus), when Amaya played dress-up, he'd don superhero gear or a jacket and tie.

One particular time, when he was about three, I watched unnoticed as Amaya played with "Rocco" in our living room. He had a bunch of his toys scattered around, among them some baby dolls, a few GI Joes, a selection of trucks, and several stuffed animals. And in the midst of it all, he was singing to himself, "I wish to be a grampa, a grampa, I wish to be a grampa."

I thought to myself, "Did I hear that right?" I listened as his singing continued: "I wish to be a grampa."

I didn't understand. He was three. Didn't he know by now that girls grew up to be grammas? Perhaps he doesn't know that yet, I thought, so I decided to talk to him about it. I interrupted his play after a few moments of observation and said something like "Did you know that girls grow up to be grammas? And boys grow up to be grampas?"

He said, "I'm a boy."

I just smiled and said, "Well boys have a penis and girls have a vagina." We talked a bit more, and we acknowledged what parts he had, and so we concluded together that he was a girl.

In my ignorance, I discounted this incident, which was perhaps his very first outward affirmation of his inner knowing. I now know his gender is and always was male. But back then, while I *did* tell him it was perfectly fine to be a girl who likes boy things and pretends to be a boy, I *did not* tell him it was possible he was a boy in a girl body. I didn't yet have the words, nor had I arrived at that insight.

I feel strongly now that this was a pivotal moment for my child. When I discounted his early and perhaps first affirmation, he internalized what I said, and he was not able to talk about being a boy until years later, after much inner turmoil and counseling. I'm not trying to be critical of my parenting—rather, I want to now draw attention to this very early time in my child's life when, even though very young, he was developing an inner sense of gender.

If I were to offer support to someone today who described a similar experience, I might counsel them to listen *without* telling the child who they can or cannot be when they are older. Perhaps I would advise to simply mirror back to the child and repeat what they say. If the child says, "I wish to be a grampa," perhaps the parent can simply repeat affirmatively, "You wish to be a grampa," and leave it at that. This approach would allow the parent to say something truthful without discounting the child's expression. It would also leave the door open for future announcements along the same lines.

My child was telling me exactly who he was, but I didn't quite hear him yet. How different things might have been!

As parents, we often feel it is our job, our role, to tell a child who they are and how they should behave. "You are a boy." "You are a girl." "You are smart." "You are pretty." "You are athletic." Whatever the words, what we say to our children about who we *think* they should be has a great impact on their developing sense of self.

What if, instead of telling my child he could pretend to be a grampa, I had said, "You can be whoever you want to be," and left it at that? Perhaps he would have continued to tell me he was a boy, rather than internalizing the budding sense of knowing. Perhaps he would not have had to go through some of the inner confusion that contributed to his depression during his tween years later on.

I'll never know "what would have been" had I merely affirmed what my child said about being a grandpa instead of using it incorrectly and inappropriately (I now realize) as a teachable moment. I do know I did my best with the information I had at the time. Our children are constantly showing us who they are and who they are not. If we pay attention, listen closely, and resist jumping to conclusions, all will be revealed.

SPIKE!

When Amaya started kindergarten he begged us to cut his hair short. He got a spiked-top haircut, and he was so happy. He gave himself the nickname "Spike" (though he didn't try much to make it stick). The "Spike" haircut was a turning point—from that time on he was seen as a boy by almost everyone who didn't already know him. In a way, the outside world at large now began to "read" Amaya as male, though he would not come to affirm his gender as male until years later.

For our family and those who knew him, however, we just figured him to be a tomboy, and we were perfectly fine with that. We supported him, or so we thought, by correcting people who referred to our "daughter" with male pronouns, ostensibly to avoid embarrassment on Amaya's part. I know now that we didn't actually avoid his embarrassment; rather, our verbal defense was often the *cause* of embarrassment. We thought we were protecting him, but actually we were drawing attention to him, and he didn't like that. From time to time as he grew older, my husband and I noticed in his eyes and his body language that he seemed to like it when people saw him as a boy.

While we may have ignored clues or missed opportunities to support him appropriately, certainly Gabe and I thought it was cool that Amaya was expressing different ways to be a girl. We thought Amaya was a teacher for our entire community with much to share regarding gender roles and stereotypes. Our belief was, and still is, that it's okay to be different. In light of this, we rose to the occasion to challenge people, and we spoke up to reinforce the notion that a girl can be anything she wants, starting with her haircut and clothing choices. Although we have a very different perspective now in hindsight, we were compelled then by good intentions to correct those who called Amaya a boy or used male pronouns.

The people we corrected (like the restaurant waiters who asked what our son wanted to order) often felt embarrassed and sometimes made a scene by over-apologizing, which prolonged the span of attention on Amaya. I reflexively tried to downplay these situations, assuring people that we and Amaya were used to it, and telling them not to feel badly. But as I've said, while we thought correcting others would help him avoid embarrassment, rather it would often lead to greater embarrassment for Amaya. There were even times when someone would argue with me in front of Amaya, incredulous that what I was saying was true, that this little person, so boyish looking, could actually be a girl. They assumed I must have misheard them and was talking of some not-present girl. "No, I mean your son." I often wondered why it was so difficult for people to accept what I told them, and why they felt they had to argue right in front of the child we were talking about! How insensitive!

Gabriel and I felt that as parents it was important to be supportive of our children in every way we could. We thought we were doing so when we corrected people who mistook Amaya for a boy. For the first year or two of elementary school, we thought he wanted us to jump in and make sure people did not think he was a boy so he could avoid the embarrassment of having to correct them himself. When occasionally we'd ask what he wanted us to do in such situations, he'd say, "I don't care," or "It doesn't matter." I should have paid more attention to his response; as a mom, I should have known that as often as not, when any of my children said those words, it *did* matter and they *did* care. They just didn't want to talk about it or didn't have the words to express their feelings. (It's also just like Amaya, the young adult I know today, to want to avoid conflict and be agreeable to what others want to do.)

As he got older, Amaya showed increasing levels of discomfort with our corrections. At around age six or seven, I asked him how he would feel if we only disclosed that he was a girl on a need-to-know basis. That way, those people we thought should know would know, but we would avoid the scenes that would often emerge when we told strangers. Gabriel and I felt this would make for the safest, most comfortable environment for our child. We didn't want him to be judged or embarrassed because of his style of dress, behavior, or activity choices. Isn't that what most parents want?

He liked this idea, so we moved forward by making sure those who would be interacting with Amaya regularly knew he was a girl. When we were out and about, strangers we met addressed my child as they would a boy, with words like "Hey little dude," and "What can I get for you, little man?" It was clear Amaya liked this treatment. He looked people in the eye more often, stood taller, and he responded to male pronouns people used when they talked to him.

Looking back, I can see that with his new haircut and identity as "Spike," he was making what is called a social transition. While many people were acquainted with him as a girl, the haircut enabled him to "try on" living as a boy and to interact with strangers in that manner. He was not necessarily able to articulate why this was important for him, but it was more and more clear to us as time went on that he was happy to be seen as male. Clearly, he was experiencing incongruence between his gender assigned at birth (female) and his gender identity (male). His chosen outer expression was male, but at the same time he'd been taught via the usual channels (parents, peers, preschool, TV programs) that people who are born with vaginas are girls. This was understandably very confusing to him, as I am sure now that he really did know even at an early age who he was on the inside. He showed us repeatedly, but we were slow to follow his lead.

ONE IN 200

Although we did not identify Amaya as transgender until he was in his teens, we did know of someone else who had a transgender child during our early parenting years. According to a 2016 survey conducted by the Williams Institute,[6] one in 200 people in the United States identifies as transgender, so it shouldn't be a surprise that our family (or yours) would have a family with a transgender child in our orbit. Indeed, as our society advances and trans people find more support in their communities and families, we are all likely to know more and more people who identify as transgender. But that was not the case even just a few years ago.

When Amaya was about five years old, in the earliest stages of expressing himself with male preferences for dress and hair, we found that we had a connection to another child who did not express gender in a typical way. That child was the granddaughter of one of my mother's close friends. Though the child's mother and I were friends as kids, we had lost touch with each other over the years. Yet I was comforted to know that someone I knew, however distantly, also had a child who was gender non-conforming. I felt it was fortuitous that our mothers, the grandmas, shared this commonality and could support each other (and commiserate).

The child, a natal boy, had insisted from 18 months of age that she was a girl. By five years old, after much research and counseling, her family decided to enroll her in kindergarten as a girl (her affirmed gender). Their daughter, Jazz Jennings, was the first transgender child in the United States to attend a public school with enrollment records reflecting her affirmed gender. In 2007, the family decided to go public and recorded an interview with Barbara Walters for the TV show *20/20*. Jazz and her family welcomed ABC's cameras—and the world— into their lives, and she has since then assumed the mantle of being a spokesperson and leader for her generation of trans youth. Her book *I am Jazz*, co-authored with Jessica Herthel, was a best-seller. The book is about a transgender child, based on Jazz's real life experiences, and was the first of its kind to find its way into the public eye. Gabriel and I were, and continue to be, inspired by the bold steps taken by Jazz's family in supporting and affirming their transgender child's true self.

When we heard about Jazz, I asked Amaya if he wanted me to call him a boy. I told him it was okay with his dad and me if that's what he wanted, and that we loved him no matter what. But he said he didn't want that. Whatever was happening on the inside, and however he appeared on the outside, he had not yet reached a stage in which he could affirm he felt he was male, certainly not verbally. In some ways I just wanted him to declare a preference. It was hard to wait, to be in the unknown. And he was too young for me to think everything was settled. No matter what I *thought* I knew, and no matter how much I wanted my child to affirm what was becoming clear in *my* mind, I had to let him experience his own process.

Even in those early years it felt like we were living in the in-between. People would ask if I thought Amaya's extreme version of tomboyish expression meant he would be a "butch" lesbian. Or they would ask, "Do you think Amaya wants to be a boy?" I remember my mother once saying something like, "It seems pretty clear that Amaya wants to be seen as a boy, so maybe he does just want to be a boy."

I did not know in those early years that one in 200 Americans identify as transgender. That figure alone might have pushed me sooner to a conclusion about Amaya, or set us down a different path in our quest to support him. At the time, my suspicions about my child's gender were hardening into a strong theory—but it would be quite some time before I reached out for resources.

I FOUND A FRIEND IN YOU

Amaya was never without pals. One of my closest friends had a boy, Sam, the same age as Amaya, and he and Sam were very close. At preschool, Amaya had boys and girls as friends, but his favorite playmates were always boys. He had a couple of friends who were girls in kindergarten, but the ones he continually asked to play with after school were boys.

And then came first grade, where he met his first real "bestie," a girl whom I will call "K."

To be clear, I met K before Amaya did. The first day of school is often emotionally charged with a mix of excitement and anxiety. Knowing that the first day can be easier for a child who has a friend in the classroom, I was looking for someone to pair up with Amaya before I left. While I lingered in the classroom and mingled with parents and students, I noticed a girl who was wearing boy-cut jeans, a "Sponge Bob" t-shirt, and the same shoes Amaya was wearing (complete with a red light-up stripe). She had no frills or flowers on her clothes; on the contrary, I picked up a "tomboyish" vibe. I introduced the kids to each other and pointed out their similar taste in shoes. They hit it off instantly, launching a friendship that lasted until K and her family moved away after middle school.

Those kids themselves were like two little peas in a pod. They wore the same type of clothing, liked the same activities, and often were mistaken for little boys. There were, however, differences we observed in how each kid's parents responded to their child's expression. While we were of the "follow the child" style of parenting when it came to clothing and the like, K's parents were quicker to draw the line when it came to testing gender norms. But to be fair, though they were not at the same comfort level as us regarding clothing and haircuts for their child, they nonetheless seemed to be tolerant of our permissions relative to Amaya's appearance, and they welcomed our child into their lives.

One day, Amaya told me K had said she was jealous of Amaya because we let him wear boys' underwear, which her parents did not allow for her. K said her parents told her that girls wear girls' underwear, period. She also said she was jealous because Amaya was allowed to have a "boy" haircut, but her parents didn't want her to cut hers so short. It was then that I realized that by allowing our child to express himself and be himself, *we* were making a particular statement about parenting. We were taking a stand. We were choosing to honor our child's wishes even though they ran against the mainstream gender norms of the day.

Though I cannot say for sure, I believe a large part of K's parents' discomfort stemmed from religious beliefs. As Catholics who regularly attended church, I can imagine it may have been difficult for them to accept differences that are often cited as "sinful." Again, not knowing them very well, I cannot say for certain that religious dogma impacted their thought process, but I note that it's one possible explanation for how strict they were and how strongly they felt about clothing and hairstyles for their child.

Both kids were very sad when K's family moved away shortly before eighth-grade graduation. Amaya visited K once at her new home that summer, and then they lost touch. It's been years now since we heard anything about K. But certainly, some people come into our lives and remain forever a part of our story. Like most people, young Amaya needed a friend who shared his likes and dislikes, who understood his idiosyncrasies and differences, who wanted to push at the same boundaries and explore similar territories. Amaya found in K a compadre and confidante, someone who admired and reflected his emerging expression of maleness. They were role models and supporters for each other; and who doesn't want their kid to have that?

TOMBOY

When Amaya was in the second grade, his teacher brought something very interesting to our attention. At the time, Amaya was considered a tomboy by many of the other students and was often mistaken for a boy because of the way "she" dressed and behaved.

When we met that year with Amaya's teacher, Ms. G, for a routine parent–teacher conference, she told us that another child's parents had raised Amaya as a topic during their conference. These parents told Ms. G they were very concerned about our child's well-being, and they asked the teacher, "Why do Amaya's parents make her dress that way?"

Ms. G told us she was taken aback by this question, as she knew we were *allowing*, not *forcing*, Amaya to dress the way he did. Ms. G said she'd tried to explain to these other parents that we, the parents, were following Amaya's lead, and that we were not making Amaya do anything against his will. The parents, according to Ms. G, just couldn't understand or accept this.

My husband, Gabriel, and I were shocked. We had no idea that other parents could or would ever think we were forcing Amaya to appear as a boy, nor could we imagine doing anything of the kind to our child. All this time, we had been listening to Amaya and doing our best to allow him to be who he was—and then we heard that some other people thought we were forcing him to be that way! *Wow!*

This brought up so much for me about being a parent, and about the expectations we impose on our children. From the moment they are born, and even way before a child is conceived, we develop an image of who our children will be. We may even daydream about our future children right down to their names, their gender, the things they will do, the adventures they will have, even the hand-me-downs they will wear. But of course there are many variations of being human that challenge our notion of who our children will be. We are all asked as parents to adjust and adapt. Some of these adjustments are easier to make than others.

Certainly, parents of transgender children need to make many adjustments to our preconceived expectations. Does any parent imagine their child will say he or she was born in the wrong body? How many mothers and fathers predict that their child will want to remove a part of their body, or add another part on, or become so depressed they don't want to live? Who presupposes a time when they will no longer be allowed to utter their child's given name or have old photos of the child around the house in order to support their child's health and well-being? It can be heartbreaking when our children do not become who we think they will be—it's a lot to take in and a lot to let go of. But we must adjust. We must love our children and support them.

Why make a special case for loving and supporting transgender children in particular? I referred to these statistics earlier, and they bear repeating here:

- LGBTQ youth have among the highest suicide rates in the nation. While more studies are needed, currently it is believed that at least 25 percent of transgender people have attempted suicide, and rates as high as 41 percent have been cited. Compare that to the general population in which 4.6 percent attempt (or complete) suicide and one can see that there is an acute need for action.[7]

- In 2012 the Human Rights Campaign conducted a groundbreaking study in which 10,000 LGBTQ identified youth ages 13–17 were surveyed. Forty two percent said that the community in which they live is not accepting of LGBT people. Twenty six percent say their biggest problems are not feeling accepted by their family/trouble at school/ bullying, and fear to be out/open.[8]

- The social climate of today is shifting, but there is a long way to go toward acceptance and equal rights. Violence against transgender people happens all too often. The Human Rights Campaign states there were at least 22 reported deaths of transgender people due to violence in 2016 alone; one more than the 21 tracked in 2015.[9]

Being transgender is not a "lifestyle choice"; rather, it is just one more beautiful, normal variation of being human.

Having the support of family is the number one way to prevent depression and suicide among transgender youth. Every child deserves to be loved and supported unconditionally.

There is support for parents who need help when struggling with the possibility or reality that their child is transgender. Our family found support through Gender Spectrum in the years before Amaya transitioned. In addition to Gender Spectrum there are many national support organizations with local contacts across the United States for parents of gender-expansive, transgender, and questioning children. Among these organizations are PFLAG (Parents, Families, Friends, and Allies of LGBTQ People), Stand with Trans, Ally Moms, and TransKids Purple Rainbow Foundation. (See the "Resource" section at the end of this book for contact information.)

I received a very special gift when Amaya was 17. He wrote a Mother's Day card to me that read: "I really don't know where I would be without you." So many feelings came to me when I read that card! His words rang heavy in my heart as I remembered earlier days when my child, before his transition, was often sad-eyed and suffered feelings of dysphoria. But at the same time, my heart overflowed with joy. Rereading those words today, I remain ever grateful for the knowledge, spirit, and love that guided me to support and stand for my child when he needed me.

— *Part 3* —

THE TWEEN YEARS

The "tween years" are so named because they are the years one lives in the *in-between*. No longer a child, but not quite a teenager, it is common for tweens to feel awkward in their changing bodies. Puberty is, of course, a main catalyst for that change, and most people experience some discomfort and confusion during this time of life. (My husband points out that it is no accident that we isolate tweens from older and younger school age-groups by sending them to middle schools during this time of emergent hormonal change.)

For transgender youth, feelings of discomfort, confusion, and disconnection to one's body that typically accompany the onset of puberty can be so profound that they manifest as gender dysphoria. Regardless of any "foreshadowing" expression of gender variance during early childhood, hormonal changes during puberty often force feelings of disconnection to the surface, where they may fester or explode (sort of like a pubescent zit!). When external changes do not line up with one's inner sense of gender identity, tweens can experience persistent and consistent depression, disassociation, withdrawal, anxiety, or any combination of these symptoms. Untreated, gender dysphoria can lead to suicidal ideation, self-harming, drug abuse, or suicide.

The Tween Years we discuss relative to a trans person's gender affirmation and transition may not actually coincide with tween years identified by behaviorists (broadly defined as the period spanning ages 8–13). Some trans children announce their gender differences early in life. I wrote earlier about Jazz Jennings, who transitioned socially at age five, when she went to kindergarten. There was only a brief "in-between" for her; once she and her parents affirmed her gender as female, she never turned back. Now 16 years old at the time of writing, she has said that she is still on her journey. She is currently preparing for sex reassignment surgery and does not consider her transition complete.

These Tween Years can be tough on parents too. My advice for parents is to always support the child, ideally with age-appropriate behavioral and medical responses to a young person's explorations and expressions. Be proactive: parents who recognize during the early childhood years that their child is questioning their gender, or expressing in gender non-conforming ways, can take time to inform themselves and perhaps seek out medical support. If appropriate, parents may support their child on a path toward social transition, giving the child time to explore and reflect outwardly the gender they feel on the inside.

Puberty often brings unwanted changes for trans youth, the result of which can cause severe distress, depression, and anxiety, and sometimes leads to suicide attempts. Today's transgender people do not have to suffer these unwelcome changes. Pubescent changes can be delayed under close medical supervision by the use of hormones known as puberty blockers. This approach gives a child time to explore and understand their gender identity and allows them to undergo puberty in a manner that best aligns with their gender identity. Children supported by their parents in this way do not ever have to experience going through the "wrong" puberty, and thus may avoid some of the gender dysphoria that so often burdens transgender and gender non-conforming people, particularly tweens and teens. (Hormonal intervention of this sort has only been in use for about ten years, and has only become more common in the last seven years. More on this subject can be found in Part 4 of this book under "The lay of the land: current medical practices for transgender youth.")

For many reasons, some trans individuals do not exhibit outward signs that they are grappling with their own understanding of gender identity, and many trans people may not transition until well into adulthood (if ever). Such was the case regarding Caitlyn Jenner. Caitlyn was assigned male at birth, and lived as "Bruce" Jenner for decades. Caitlyn (then known as Bruce) became world-famous as an Olympic gold medalist in the 1970s, embodying the very picture of masculinity for many Americans at the time, and more recently re-emerged as a reality TV star. But she had been suffering inside for many years. At some point during her life Caitlyn began to realize on the inside that she was transgender, she was a woman and not a man. She did not present this part of herself to the outside world. Caitlyn was "Bruce" and lived as "Bruce." Some reports say that "Bruce's" wife at the time, Kris Kardashian, knew her spouse liked to wear women's clothing in private at home. Caitlyn was "Bruce" and lived as "Bruce." Caitlyn's trans status was not affirmed nor was it public. We can say that she was living through the Tween Years of her transition.

Fascinatingly, much of Caitlyn's Tween Years were captured on camera and shared with the public. As a cast member of the hit Kardashian family reality TV show, viewers followed Caitlyn as she "tried out" letting her hair grow long, painting her nails, and wearing increasingly feminine styles of clothing more frequently. Before Caitlyn Jenner actually made her gender status as transgender public, she clearly made some changes in her life. (Later, after transition, Caitlyn starred for a time in her own reality show, documenting her new life as a woman and dealing with some of the challenges associated with transitioning in public and private life.)

When a parent first notes that a child is expressing a non-traditional gender variation, it is common to think, "Perhaps they will grow out of it." And for some this is true, the child might indeed grow out of it. Some don't. When these behaviors are accompanied by evidence of a child's mental/emotional stress, anxiety, depression, or other discomfiting symptoms, parents would be wise to consider exploring a likely connection to gender identity.

It is increasingly common for parents today to explore resources and seek support when they notice their child expressing in non-typical ways relative to gender. Most parents of trans kids whom I have talked to report having some knowledge during early childhood that their kid was expressing gender preferences and behaviors in some way opposed to the gender they were assigned at birth. "She was a tomboy." "He liked to wear dresses and makeup." "He sang about how he wished to be a grandpa." These behaviors were not just a fad or phase, but rather were *persistent, consistent,* and *insistent.*

These are the characteristics that specialists look for when evaluating the possibility that someone is transgender. Youth who are insistent, consistent, and persistent in regard to their gender expression should not be ignored.

The Tween Years were not easy for my son Amaya, and it was often heart-wrenching for me to witness his experience. As a younger child, he'd been able to live in the world in a way that was comfortable for him, free from judgment from the outside world. Though he was known in our community as a girl, he could express himself openly back then in ways that were true to his inner sense of gender identity. He could participate in activities he enjoyed, such as baseball and soccer, both of which were co-ed. As one of only two girls in the entire local Little League, he was often mistaken for a boy by new teammates, and he seemed to like it like that. He could dress the way he wanted, in stereotypical male clothing. He told us at one point to call him "T-ball" (another brief-lived nickname, in addition to the short-lived "Spike" moniker recounted earlier). He'd been friends with both boys and girls, but most of his close friends during those years had been boys—and although his best friend at the time was a girl, she was a full-on tomboy.

These "Early Years" only lasted until about the time Amaya was seven or eight, a time when children are expected to adhere more rigidly to social norms regarding gender. In the fourth grade, as he and his classmates came into their tween years, Amaya's social world shifted. As is so often the case around that age, the boys and girls he'd been used to playing with began to self-separate into new social circles aligned by gender. At lunchtime on the schoolyard now, boys sat with boys and girls sat with girls. He didn't quite fit within either circle. Although his female "bestie" remained his friend, I could tell Amaya missed his male friends. It was at this time that I noticed he had begun to withdraw socially, and he was spending a lot of time alone in his room. He moved his dramatic play behind closed doors. Still, and as ever, I would hear him enacting scenes in which he was the hero, the dad, the dude.

CHICK DUDE

One day, when Amaya was about eight, I took him to our local swim club. While I checked us in at the front desk, Amaya walked down the hall, passing a few boys from his school as he headed to the locker room. I passed by these boys myself moments after Amaya had disappeared down the hall, and I heard one say something to the other that caught my attention: he said, "Hey, there's that chick dude!"

At the time I was sure I heard it correctly, like this: "Hey there's that *chickdude*." I immediately assumed the words were combined as one, "chickdude," and they were using the words to describe my child. I felt both concern and amusement. I was concerned because I thought the kids were talking about my child's gender, and I wasn't sure if it was meant as a nice comment or not. Perhaps they were making fun of my kid! I was also amused—what a perfect word to describe my child! Most of all, I wondered how Amaya would feel if he knew kids used a made-up word, chickdude, to describe him. He might pass it off as nothing, or he might be deeply wounded; I wasn't sure. I wanted to ask those boys what they meant, but I decided not to bother them, and Amaya and I went swimming.

Upon speaking to Gabriel and some friends later on, another way of interpreting the comment was suggested: Perhaps the boy was not calling my kid a chickdude, but perhaps he merely was saying "There's that *chick*" to his friend, a.k.a. "*dude*," with no reference to gender variance implied or intended. That is a reasonable interpretation, and perhaps my response was a biased reflection of my overt sensitivity at the time to what others might be thinking or saying about my child's gender expression. Or maybe I was right, maybe that kid did call my child *chickdude*, and perhaps it *was* meant as an insult! There's no way to know the truth now, but this incident rattled me at the time. Back then, it was certainly awkward for me to hear comments or notice reactions to Amaya's gender expression, real or imagined.

Regardless of the original intent of the boy's comment, this anecdote illustrates a moment when I became keenly aware that our family and close friends weren't the only people taking notice of Amaya's gender differences. I began to wonder and worry about kids—and adults—making fun of my child. I worried that maybe Amaya would hear words like chickdude used to describe or disparage him at school or on the playground, and I worried that such words would upset him. As far as I know to this day, he was never the target of any direct or even indirect bullying, other than perhaps this one perhaps-misconstrued and certainly minor incident. But always I'd been full of worry. Isn't every parent?

"FAGGOTS" AND "TRANNIES"

by Gabriel Barkin, Amaya's father

I did not meet any LGBTQ folks (as far as I knew) when I grew up in the 60s and 70s. I'm not even sure when I first became conscious that there was any such thing as being gay, or lesbian, or transgender, or bisexual—and "queer" was a word used in children's alphabet books to avoid a cliché, "queen" (ironic, now that I think of it). I can recall Anita Bryant being in the news for hating gays or something; I knew her only as the spokesperson for Florida-produced orange juice, and here she was leading marches and yelling stuff. I was not impressed. I was raised to live and let live.

Like many people who grew up in that era, my perception of gay men was all mixed up with notions of transgender people and transvestites alike, and I suspect I also lumped "them" all in with pedophiles too. To me, these were all dress-wearing, men-kissing, young-boy-liking queers, no variation among them. When I was about 12, while riding my bike around a park in slow circles on a day of lonely boredom, a young man approached me and asked if I wanted to come to his house and see pictures of naked women. I rode off quickly, the word "fag!" echoing in my young, scared mind as an apt description for my stalker. (Good on me for skedaddling at least. Creepy stuff.)

And yes, my young friends and I called each other "fag" and "faggot" as both innocent taunts and venomous insults. I don't think I even knew what a "faggot" was when I first heard and then started using the term, other than perhaps it referred to a weakling or a scaredy-cat, interchangeable (ironically?) with "pussy." Once I found out what it meant, it just underscored the impact of the insult.

One day in sixth grade, I was hanging with friends on the playground yard, and we were teasing each other as boys do. Someone must have called me "faggot," because one of the schoolyard monitors pulled me aside and kindly lectured me on how to suffer insults: "If they call you a fag or a pussy, just own it and say, 'Yeah, I am a fag, so what?!' They'll stop calling you names because they'll realize they can't hurt you." Essentially, it was good "sticks-and-stones" advice. I took it to heart as a lifelong lesson, even though I clearly recall feeling that I hadn't been the brunt of any cruelty that day and was wondering why this fellow had singled me out and pulled me aside for some coaching and support. It was many years later that I realized, upon reflection, that perhaps he was a gay man who saw Little Gabe as a budding gay person in need of help. Maybe not, but that's my lasting impression today. I'm pretty sure that's when I stopped calling friends a "faggot."

During high school, I worked briefly at a bookshop on Hollywood Boulevard, which has long been one of those urban places that attracts all types and holds onto the most bizarre and flamboyant among them. Often I would see "trannies" (as I called them then) order a slice of pizza or a cup of coffee—tall and skinny dudes with flowing dresses and a taste for big wigs and heavy makeup. I didn't cross the street to avoid them, but they were otherworldly to me, and I'm sure I also assumed they were on smack, generally to be shunned. I also thought they were all just gay men and that dressing like women was part of being gay. I had no notion that there was anything other than gay or straight—gay was weird enough.

And then came *Soap*. Billy Crystal's "Jody" was the first recurring gay character on television. Jody was smart, the funniest person on the show, and his flamboyance was often checked and always counterbalanced by his humanity. He lived a fairly normal life within a manic and comedic family setting, eventually fighting for and winning the right to raise his child as a single parent who happens to be gay. My brother and friends who watched the show, we all knew he was the moral center of a show about people, most of them straight, who were as immoral as hell. I'm sure I was not the only young man whose perception of gay people was shaped largely by Crystal's sensitive and human portrayal. We rooted for him.

Still, I had a long way to go. For instance, I thought it was bizarre that a woman college professor who taught a class I took in Santa Cruz had a beard; I couldn't stop thinking in class each day, "Why doesn't she shave?!" I deeply disrespected a lesbian relationship and slept with a workmate who was the girlfriend of a very close female friend of mine—a complete ethical failure on my part. I'm sure I did not consider their relationship to be equal in any way to, say, a boyfriend–girlfriend thing. My friend discovered our affair, and she chewed me out royally and deservedly, our relationship spoiled forever by my actions.

In my early twenties, I finally started to grow up and recognize the equal and respectful value of gay relationships and commitments. I met some gay and lesbian people, and I found out someone I knew already was gay. I allowed myself to feel a bit of pride (oh, youthful hubris!) that the revelation this guy was gay didn't change my feelings about him one bit.

Certainly something clicked. Kids can be dumb, kids can be cruel, and some of us take a long time to grow up. I can remember the way I used to think about LGBTQ people. Even now, I can tap into the soft bigotry of my youthful ignorance and lack of exposure, and the memory of those impressions helps me understand the fear that people feel when confronted with things that are new, things that have been portrayed with negative and pervasive stereotypes for so long. I know we live in a bit of a progressive bubble here in the San Francisco Bay Area, but it gives me great joy that my elementary schoolteacher friends report use of the word "faggot" as a slur has nearly disappeared in their young classrooms.

TWO MOMS

During the elementary school years, Amaya had a friend who had two mothers. He often went to their house for playdates, and I became friendly with the girl's moms. One of the mothers wore suits and worked full time, the other was a stay-at-home spouse who took on carpool duty and often signed up to be "room mom" for her kid's classes.

One day, when Amaya was a young tween, I started a conversation with him about the future and what it might hold. At the time, I had no clue which gender my child might be attracted to, or even whether he yet felt any prepubescent glimpses of attraction. Still, I thought to help him understand that it was normal for two women to be in a relationship and have a family, in part thinking at the time that he might grow up to be a lesbian (based on my very limited understanding of gender at the time). I wanted to make sure he knew he had his parents' love and full support if indeed that was his path. I said to him, "When you are older, maybe you will be in a family that has two moms, like your friend."

He looked at me with his well-practiced, matter-of-fact expression, and said, "That's just not *me*, Mom."

That was it. He did not know yet how to articulate what he was feeling, but even then he knew in his heart that he was not going to be in a relationship where he was one of two moms. Although it wasn't until a few years later that he affirmed his attraction to girls, as a young child he'd never seen himself as someone who would become a mom. In hindsight, I realize now how silly my statement must have seemed to him—he'd always envisioned himself (as I'd observed in his role-playing games) becoming a dad!

This was one of the most telling things he'd relayed to me about his gender identification up to that time. It was perhaps the biggest eye-opener for me since he'd been little and said he was a boy who wished to be a grandpa. I filed his response away in my mind with a burgeoning collection of clues about my child's identity. I began to feel deep in my heart that my child was transgender.

It would still be years before he could understand and articulate it for himself.

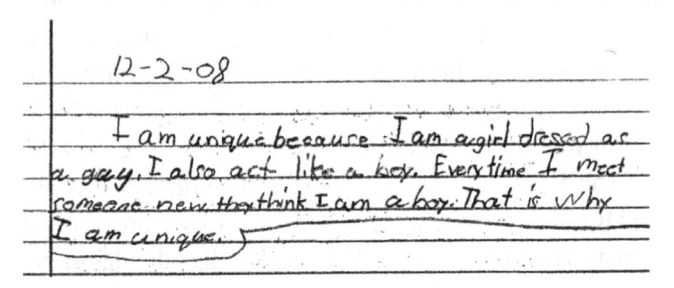

"I am unique because..." (written by Amaya when he was ten)

I am unique because I am a girl dressed as a guy. I also act like a boy. Every time I meet someone new, they think I am a boy. That is why I am unique.

HEROES

by Gabriel Barkin, Amaya's father

Those who frequently traverse along the northish–southish vertical bias of California invariably find themselves on Interstate Highway 5 (a.k.a. "the I-5," or just "the 5"). Like a Titan's tape measure laid across a dusty garden, the I-5 rests mere inches above the topsoil, a concrete ribbon that divides and conquers the irrigated desert, feeds the cities and suburbs, hums and keeps warm 24/7 with the friction of 18 truck wheels driving driving driving, ceaseless but not deathless, obscenely persistent, constant, and insistent. It beckons all, gives us a few inches of pavement, spits us out when it thinks we're done with it, lies in wait for our return.

The 5. Gas stations, aqueduct crossings, grapes of wrath and Riesling, cotton dust balls and truck-tossed tire-crushed tomato sauce for the roadkill, hours to kill and miles to fill. Bring a bunch of CDs, it's a long-ass way to the Valley. Iron Skillet, Anderson's Pea Soup, that place in Kettleman City with the pedal cars, was it Mike's? How long 'til we get there, are we there yet, what are we going to do when we get there, when are we going home? Daddy, I need to pee. Rest stop in six miles, can you make it?

Indeed, everyone in our immediate family has made the crossing from the Bay Area to LA (where my parents live) too many times to count. Personally, I'm sure I've peed at every rest stop between Sacramento and San Fernando. They're all pretty much the same, those I-5 rest stops, a wide strip of parking lot pavement with trucks over here and cars over there and RVs (motorhomes) everywhere, a pair or three brick or adobe restroom and maintenance buildings painted to match the golds and browns of the summertime hillsides flanking the Central Valley. A kiosk with tales of days gone by or fun facts about wildlife soon to be gone. A few junk food and soda and "coffee" vending machines, a place to let your dog poop over by some picnic tables.

You get the picture.

Amaya and I were traveling on the 5 heading south to see my mom and dad one summer—just the two of us this time for some forgotten reason. We needed a pee break. We pulled into a rest stop somewhere on the 5. Like I said above, they all sort of look the same. I can see this one clearly in my mind's eye but I can't for the life of me tell you which one it was. Let's just go with "Somewhere on the 5."

I can't recall my kid's age exactly, but Amaya was probably about nine and "she" had not yet begun transitioning and was using female pronouns. I will use the female pronoun for this tale, because my child was still a "girl" at the time, at least in my mind if not in Amaya's.

From about age three or four Amaya had insisted on keeping her hair cut short like a boy. She wore boys' board shorts and t-shirts with video game or superhero pictures on them, and she even walked with a bit of a lanky boy's gait. By the time of this story, waiters in restaurants were asking us, "And what would he like for lunch?" One of only two "girls" in the local Little League, I was pretty sure a lot of parents and kids who didn't know Amaya thought she was a boy. I imagine some of them were quite confused to hear us parents and the team's coaches use female pronouns "her" and "she" when talking about Amaya. She was a slugger, too, and bigger than many of her teammates.

For a while prior to this I-5 journey, Amaya had been leery of using public restrooms. At school, as well as in restaurants, at public events, and other places with assigned-gender restrooms, some girls and grownups had started giving Amaya curious glances and even the "Hey boy, don't be an idiot, this is the women's room" stink-eye. I'm pretty sure there had even been one or two instances where people actually said something to her. So Amaya was not fond of using any busy, multi-stall public restroom, and she would "hold it in" rather than risk embarrassment and harassment.

Let me just pause here and point out that Amaya's experience is exactly why we need to allow trans people to use the bathroom they feel is the most appropriate. Amaya was a pre-teen at this time, and both my child's discomfort as well as the discomfort of others in public bathrooms was only likely to grow if this boyish "girl" continued to use the women's room. At any time, this situation might come to a head, perhaps a confrontation with a violent or abusive person, or the enforcement of a bigoted law. Laws like the one passed in North Carolina in 2015 (and proposed in several other states as of this writing) to prevent trans people from using the bathroom in which they feel most comfortable and appropriate—and, especially, safe—are a public menace. They resolve nothing and only serve to make trans people despondent and unsafe. I only have to reflect on my child's life to know how wrongheaded, ignorant, and dangerous these laws are.

At this time, I was only beginning to truly understand what my child was going through regarding the bathroom thing. Not too long before this road trip, I'd taken my Little Leaguer to see a big league Giants game. Unlike my two older kids, both camels who could make it across a desert, there was no way Amaya could make it through the game without peeing—especially after a big soda and all the junk food a dad buys his kid at a special "daddy–daughter" outing like that. So when the expected "Daddy, I need to pee" finally came, we hiked off for the nearest restroom.

Unfortunately, the lines were snaking out the door of the women's rooms everywhere. Amaya really did not want to spend that much time out in the open, so to speak, exposing herself to myriad stares and hushed comments whispered between others in line ("Do you think he knows he's in the wrong line? Should we tell him?"). It was one thing if mom was there with her, or her big sister at least; a family female being in the women's room with Amaya seemed to comfort curious strangers and reassure them, or at least give them pause to reassess the situation and conclude that Amaya must be a girl. But this was a worst-case scenario—while a near-empty bathroom gave Amaya the opportunity to get into and out of a stall and the girl's room quickly without notice, a long line was unacceptable.

Amaya asked me to bring her into the men's room. The men's rooms had lines too, not as bad. But Amaya was of the age that I thought too old to bring into a men's room. It's just one of those things, or so I thought, that at a certain age, the male parent isn't really supposed to be bringing the nine-year-old girl into the boys' room with him—nor vice versa with any mom and a nine-year-old son. Notwithstanding a disability of some sort requiring assistance, I figured it'd be weird for guys peeing in urinals to have a lanky girl standing in the stall queue just over their shoulder. (In retrospect, I have never had any issue with women waiting in line for boys' room stalls when the women's room line is insanely long—say at a rock concert or something like that—but those considerations are always different when it's one's own daughter.)

So we set off for the upper deck of Pac Bell Park, hoping for a lack of lines at the ladies' room in the boondocks. But alas, they drink a lot of beer in the 300 sections too, and there was no respite. I tried to cajole Amaya, who had to pee now more than ever, but she was adamant: something must be done! And I did not want to be the dad who could not figure this out.

Finally, we sort of stumbled upon one of the ballpark's "family" bathrooms—single-stall bathrooms designed for parents with kids, disabled folks with assistants, etc. There were only about four people in line, it moved fast, we got in, we got out. A crisis narrowly averted—I had already begun wondering if they sold board shorts at the concession booth (you know, just in case of an accident).

So now, fast-forward, here we were at the rest stop on I-5, and Amaya had to pee. The rest stop was alive with automotive comings and goings and dog-walking and picnicking, and there was a steady stream of travelers moving briskly along the sidewalks toward the restrooms with focus and resolve.

Amaya balked right away at the sight of all the road-weary queen bees who were buzzing toward the honeycombs of the women's restroom to join a slow-walking queue that stretched beyond the doorway. Again she asked me, "Can I just go in with you?" I thought about it, but only briefly. The men's room was equally frantic, a line almost as long. My "daughter" was barely younger than puberty. My concerns about a girl Amaya's age in the men's room had not abated. I had a realization that my kid needed to learn how to deal with this. I whipped out my mental thesaurus, trying to cajole, wheedle, beg, advise, consult, threaten, inspire, force, help, and/or bribe my kid to go stand in that line. And as I did so, I had a second realization: I was helpless here. It was me who needed help.

Deus ex machina. When you least expect it but need it most…

Lo and behold, as I was emotionally throwing my hands up and wondering if anyone would notice my kid squatting in a far-off corner of the dog-run area, along came a pair of ladies ambling toward the restrooms. Something about them made me think they were going to be my heroes. I don't even recall if I asked Amaya if this was okay, but on the spur of the moment, I stopped them with an "Excuse me…" and humbly asked, "Would you mind chaperoning my kid into the bathroom? She's shy and there's a long line and…" I don't think I even knew what to say.

The women quickly looked Amaya up and down and smiled at me. Only now did I notice that these women, both perhaps in their 40s or young 50s, were dressed in jeans and t-shirts and sneakers, and neither had any makeup on. One had fairly short hair, the other a bit of a mullet. Both could answer to the description of a grownup "tomboy." Somewhere in the back of my mind I said to myself, I think I picked exactly the right people.

The one with short hair looked me right in the eye with a friendly grin and then turned to Amaya and said, "I know exactly what it's like. I've always dressed like a boy and had short hair. No problem." Yup, indeed she knew exactly what was going on. "C'mon," they said to Amaya, and to my delight and surprise, my kid walked right off with them to stand in line.

Five minutes later, Amaya and I had both done our duties, and we reconvened on the sidewalk. Our saviors had vanished, two angels flown back over the great road, our sidewalks likely never to cross again. Beautiful strangers, even I-5 rest stops are full of them. The unsung soldiers who mow the dog-run lawns, who scrub the steel urinals and polish the metal mirrors, who restock the candy machines, they're all part of the vital infrastructure, part of the structural mechanical mumbo-jumbo that keeps and cares for truckers and travelers, part of the I-5 community, heroes all. And the same with strangers and stragglers and drivers and passengers pulling in for a moment's respite from the accelerated motion of a journey spent in the passing lane, they too can be heroes.

POSTSCRIPT

Several years later, Janna and I took Amaya and Emily to see *Avenue Q* on Broadway. Amaya, age 14, had not yet transitioned, but he had dressed up for the occasion in a nice shirt and jeans, boy clothing as ever, and he looked very handsome.

At intermission, I had to pee really bad, so I jumped up from my seat as the house lights rose—but despite my inspired intention, I did not beat the throng of men to the lone bathroom in the theater lobby. Waiting in queue just outside the men's room door, I smiled as my wife and daughter Emily got in a longer line just a few feet away for the women's room. But where was Amaya? I turned and scanned the room, and there was my kid a few spaces behind me in my line. He stood nonchalantly with arms folded like a lot of the other guys in line, an unobvious member of a gaggle only aligned by common anatomy, an anatomy he lacked, but who gives a shit? Just another guy in the crowd.

PERIOD STOP

Amaya started puberty early. At age nine his puberty hair had begun to grow, and his period started around the time he turned ten. I taught both of my "girls" about female puberty before it hit them, and they both knew what to expect. When Emily started menstruating, we celebrated with a women's circle that included our closest friends, Emily's grandmothers, and her great-grandmother, Essie. Amaya, on the other hand, absolutely did not want to celebrate this onset of womanhood in any outward way. Still, he also did not seem to dread that milestone as I thought he would. He took it in his stride and he was very matter-of-fact about it.

For several years, Amaya took the necessary precautions each month and cared for his menstrual needs. He occasionally complained about cramps and asked to stay home from school, as many teens do. As a tween and young teen, menstruation seemingly was not a major contributor to Amaya's gender dysphoria. Rather, he was upset primarily about his growing chest and the way people perceived his gender as a result. It was true—his breasts *were* difficult to hide. It was only after his top surgery that Amaya told us he felt the effects of the dysphoria were now being triggered by his monthly menses. Once he began hormone therapy and the effects of testosterone took hold, his menses stopped, and he felt released from the dysphoria that caused his suffering. He was greatly relieved to not have to experience this monthly reminder of who he is *not*.

I had my concerns and fears about hormone therapy, just as I had concerns and fears at each stage of my son's

transition. (I'll share more about hormone therapy later on
in this book in the part about Transition.) In most cases,
hormone therapy participants will become sterile. Some
people choose to save their sperm or eggs for future use.
A medical practitioner offered the latter option to Amaya
when he started hormone therapy, but he declined it. He
did not want to go through the process of harvesting his
eggs. He knows he does not want to be pregnant or birth
a child: "That's just not me," he said. He does want to be a
dad someday, and he is aware of, and open to, the different
ways this could become possible.

From my understanding, it is a common experience
among transgender and gender-questioning people to
experience different levels or degrees of gender dysphoria
over time. As each person resolves one layer of their
dysphoria, others may be revealed. The journey of
discovery and healing is not unique to transgender people;
it is a common experience among those who undergo
any process of self-discovery and healing. Humans are
multilayered beings. There is the surface layer: the part of
us we show to the world, the part the world sees. There
is our inner world: our layers of thoughts and feelings.
There is our subconscious layer: our dream world. There
is our DNA: layers and layers of genes passed down from
generation to generation. There are layers of ourselves
created by our personal perceptions: layers of experiences
we hold in our memory cells, experiences that influence
our physical forms, our thoughts, our emotions and our
responses to our experiences. Behind all these other layers
are unknown parts, secret even to ourselves. And at our
deepest core, we find the unwavering truth of who we are.
If we choose to do the work, we can peel back these many
layers and uncover our deep truths. Who *are* we?

Most humans never embark on this oftentimes arduous (and only sometimes joyful) journey of self-discovery. For some, such as my transgender son, the need to peel back the layers and fully reveal and affirm their truth is overpowering and compelling. In Amaya's case, peeling back yet another layer and looking deeply at the variance between his body functions and his inward identity led him to yet another truth, one that freed him from his period and his dysphoria.

HOLDING TOGETHER WHILE
─────── FALLING APART ───────

The middle school years are not easy for any child. Puberty rears its head and hormones go wild. Changing bodies, erratic emotions, and daily melodrama serve as the vanguard for most kids' middle school experience, and parents often find themselves on the battlefield as well.

We enrolled Amaya in the local middle school, the same school our daughter, Emily, had attended before him. We were already well-connected to the school's academic and administrative community because Emily had required some support and resources during her middle school years. The school had helped us find suitable tutors and implement a plan to keep her on track. We were glad that many of the same administrators were still on staff when Amaya enrolled for his first year, and we were happy to learn that that the newly installed principal was the same person who'd been the principal at Amaya's elementary school. Amaya was "known."

I felt it was important to write a letter to the staff and teachers to introduce my child, and to give them a sense of who I thought he was at the time. (That being, more or less, "a girl who acts and looks like a boy.") I wanted to ensure there would be no embarrassing "discussion" among students about his gender status. I wanted the teachers to be on the lookout for bullying or ostracizing regarding Amaya's gender expression and tomboy style. My husband and I had not heard reports from Amaya about being bullied, but still I wanted to be a protective and proactive parent.

By all accounts, Amaya was happy in middle school. A good student in general, he adjusted well to the increased homework load assigned by middle school teachers. He rode his bike to school with his best friend every day (when it wasn't raining). He played in organized sport leagues after school and on the weekends, and he played with the kids on the block at home all the time. But as the school year progressed, he seemed to withdraw from the things he loved to do and spent more and more time in his room lying in bed or watching TV.

The summer after sixth grade was one of the most difficult times to witness. Where was our happy child? Gabriel and I were beside ourselves with what to do. Thankfully, Amaya was hired on as a volunteer at a weekday science camp he'd attended for a few prior summers. He was an assistant counselor, his first erstwhile "job," and the assignment gave him something to do out of the house each day. But in the afternoons after camp he'd come home, go into his room, and close the door, and he generally wouldn't leave the house unless we took him out somewhere. It was so hard to witness and heart-wrenching not knowing how to make it better.

I struck up a conversation during this time with a woman I'd met in one of my yoga classes. She introduced me to her partner, a woman who some might describe as a "tomboy" or "butch." I felt safe telling these new friends my feelings about and concerns for Amaya, thinking they might have perspectives and experiences that would be helpful in my quest to understand and support my child during this trying time. I told them about Amaya's self-seclusion and his dark mood, and they shared their own unique stories with me (adding that they wished they'd had parents who were open and supportive like I was trying to be). They encouraged me to read a book called *The Transgender Child*, by Stephanie Brill and Rachel Pepper. I got a copy as soon as I could, and I have to say, reading that book was a life-changer! I saw my child and my parenting experience reflected in every page of that book.

These women also encouraged me to reach out to Gender Spectrum, a non-profit group based across the Bay in Oakland. I gave them a call, and I talked to Joel Baum, who was Executive Director at the time (he is currently the organization's Senior Director of Professional Development and Family Services). Joel was warm and reassuring when I shared our family's story. He encouraged Gabriel and me to come to a monthly parent support group he facilitated. I found some comfort in attending these sessions, and I went to meetings for a few months. Gabriel attended a few times with me as well. It was good for us to connect with other parents and share experiences, but there were hardly any parents in that group whose children had already gone through puberty, as Amaya had. At one point, I weakly attempted to cobble together a group of parents and trans tweens who could meet nearer to our Marin County home. I had a few conversations and email exchanges with other moms whom Joel put me in touch with, but we did not ever meet in person.

Meanwhile, Amaya's social world shrank as seventh grade progressed. There were only a few boys left in his orbit. One of the few boys still in that small world lived on our street. Amaya liked going to this boy's house after school, and they often walked to the store or hung out on the block together. On the weekends, Amaya often spent time with Sam, the younger son of our dear friends Adam and Tracey. As Tracey recounted earlier in this book, Sam and Amaya were close when they were little kids. Sam had always been quick to explain to his own friends, whenever they were meeting my child for the first time, that Amaya was a girl who dresses like a boy, adding that they should just treat him like a dude. And off they would go. But by this time they'd grown older, and with *older* sometimes comes *apart.* They were happy to see each other when our families got together, as we did often, but outside of those encounters, they didn't ask for playdates with each other anymore.

Seventh grade is a blur in my recollection. I remember Amaya and his best friend K were in class together, and their homeroom teacher was just not a very good teacher. (She was new to the school, and parents and children agreed in short order that she was very dull.) Amaya had a small group of friends, all girls. He had ups and downs and did his best to keep his chin up, but his discomfort with his changing body was clear, and he had no hobbies or passions to divert his focus. He spent a lot of time on the weekends with us, his boring parents, doing whatever we did and going where we went. While we loved our time together, we also wondered why he didn't want to hang out with his friends.

After seventh grade, Amaya again spent the summer helping out at the science camp in town. He was comfortable working there—it was easy—and he was also unwilling to try anything new. Just as he had the summer before, he spent a lot of time when he wasn't at camp alone in his room. Gabriel found a few odd jobs for him to do at his office workplace from time to time just so Amaya wouldn't sit at home alone all the time between camp weeks.

At the start of eighth grade, Amaya was happy to get back to school and reconnect with his friends. As the school year progressed, he made some new connections. A few of the kids had known each other since they were very little and their families were accustomed by now to the co-ed group sleepovers that were all the rage in this set that year. Some parents elsewhere might be alarmed that boys and girls at that age were sleeping over at each other's houses, but I felt relieved that we were not the only parents in this circle comfortable with this arrangement, knowing our kids were relatively responsible and smart young people. In this group Amaya did not stick out as the girl who looked like a boy. He just got to be one of the group, and he was able to be himself.

It was during this autumn of change that Amaya stopped playing baseball. Before that year's "Fall Ball" season, Amaya had spent three seasons playing on teams in our town's so-called "Minor League." He had loved being part of those teams, and he'd always had at least one coach on each team who would take Amaya under their wing and make sure "she" was fully supported by the other coaches and teammates. (There was only one other girl in the league, and never on the same team. Most of the girls who were athletic at that age were choosing to play softball in the springtime.) Amaya had proven himself to be a good hitter and a great base-stealer. He was often the tallest kid on his team and was usually the calmest. Coaches would often point out his calm behavior and ask the "wildest" and loudest boys why they couldn't be more like Amaya.

That fall, however, things were different. In previous seasons, the coaches' focus had been to identify and harness the strengths of each kid. The Minor League had a rule that everyone played in every game, in rotation, no benchwarmers. Now that Amaya was over 12, he had to step up an age group to the Major League. Suddenly he was one of the youngest kids—and one of only two girls in the league. He was the lone girl on his team. Amaya was going through female puberty while all the other players were experiencing the male version. The differences between boys and girls were becoming more pronounced. Competitiveness amongst the boys was reaching a fever pitch, and I am sure that Amaya was more reserved and less engaged in athletic endeavors than most of the boys in the league due at least in part to the different changes his body was going through.

Amaya found himself on the bench a lot that season, often not playing for an inning or two in a row. It was upsetting for him, and for us as parents too. He lost his love of being part of the team. When we spoke to the coach, we were told that this was the "big leagues" and he was just not as strong a player as the other kids. To be fair, Amaya was not putting in extra effort outside of practice like most of his team mates. I understand that the Major League is where the competition heats up and the less capable athletes are weeded out. But while this may have been the case, I couldn't help but feel that this new coach really didn't understand how to connect with Amaya and make him feel more like a part of the team. He didn't spend time with Amaya trying to motivate him or explore his strengths, as earlier coaches had. Though I can't say for sure, I think the coach was confused and uncomfortable to be presented with a girl on his team who looked and acted like a boy.

Amaya quit mid-season and that was that.

In general, my kid was a good student throughout middle school, and he had a close group of friends. At the same time, as already mentioned, he also spent many afternoons and weekends at home, alone and often (I am sure) lonely. When he wasn't doing something with our family, he spent most of his time in his room, either watching TV or interacting on social media. Occasionally, as we had so often in past years, we would hear him play-acting in his room—always in male character of course.

He seemed increasingly depressed. As his female puberty progressed and his chest began to develop, we noticed his posture became ever more hunched and closed. Photos of my child from that time show him with sad eyes and a heavy heart.

At this point, Gabriel and I turned to Amaya's school for help. We hoped they could provide some insight and work with us to help Amaya. I had been reading more about transgender children and learning a lot from Joel and other Gender Spectrum resources by this time, and Gabriel and I had many discussions about how to support our child's needs. I looked forward to sharing my growing body of knowledge with Amaya's teachers and the school administrators. I wanted to start a conversation at the school about gender, and specifically about Amaya's gender. I also wanted to encourage the staff to educate themselves about gender-questioning children. Finally, I intended to urge the school to engage with Gender Spectrum to offer training on this topic—at no cost—to staff, parents, and students. I felt that an increased understanding among the school community would support not only my child, but also others like him.

The school administrators, including the principal, were very happy to talk to me, but they told me they had not noticed any of the behaviors symptomatic of depression that Gabriel and I had reported seeing at home. Teachers had reported that they saw him as someone who was happy and connected. He was always with friends, and he could be seen smiling and laughing with his friends on a daily basis. His grades were good and he was engaged in classes. Any parent would be glad to hear these things about their child, of course, and I was. Still, Gabriel and I had concerns.

I told the administrators that we didn't always see that same person at home. I told them he was spending more and more time alone and that lately Amaya often told us that he was tired. We were concerned.

The administrators agreed to keep an eye on him at school, and they also encouraged me to let Amaya know their office doors were always open for him to come see them for *any* reason. They did not have anything to say about Amaya and the possibility that his confusion surrounding gender might be the cause of his distress. They didn't have any other suggestions. And I was not done.

I broached the subject of Gender Spectrum training, but the response was disappointing. The administrators told me the entire school district staff had just been through training with Gender Spectrum. (One of them mentioned that Amaya had even come to mind as she went through the training.) Still, they did not want to offer the training to the school's parents and children. They said they felt they'd already implemented a great anti-bullying program, and they thought that program had provided sufficient training regarding this topic as well as others. I said that I disagreed, and I asked them to consider that this was not just about bullying, it was even bigger than that. I said it was important to focus specifically on educating parents and children about gender differences. Standing on my soapbox now, I spoke to them of the school district's responsibility, as I saw it, to help foster each student's understanding about their own gender identity and expression, and its responsibility as well to create more open communication, understanding, and acceptance regarding gender and gender expression in the community at large.

I said that I not only wanted the training to be available for the school community as a whole, but also I particularly wanted my child to go through the training with his peers. I wanted him to hear from experts and share in a learning experience about gender that was not targeted at him alone, but rather at his entire class. Perhaps the Gender Spectrum training would demystify what he was going through and open a doorway for communication. Perhaps this type of training could erase some of the shame many LGBTQ youth feel before they come to understand and accept themselves for who they are.

Unfortunately, even after attending a Gender Spectrum training, the school administrators were adamant about not offering Gender Spectrum training to parents or students. They were of the mind it would just "open a can of worms" and "put the spotlight directly on Amaya." One said, "Since he isn't having problems with bullying, why put that kind of focus on it?"

I left downhearted. I felt they were missing the point. I felt my child, others like him, and a lot of parents would benefit from the training. So few people really understand what it means to be transgender, and I wanted my community to learn more. I knew the school administrators were right, that a strong and possibly detrimental reaction to the subject from some parents was a distinct possibility even in our Marin County community. Yes, I realized, we might be opening a proverbial can of worms in bringing this subject up. But I didn't see that as a bad thing. Don't you catch fish with worms? The heck with worms, I wanted to have a sumptuous feast of understanding and acceptance! But the school wasn't ready, and I just didn't have the confidence (yet) to be the mom who was going to fight harder and push the school forward. I did provide them with some books I thought they should read, and I more or less gave up.

In retrospect, I know the administrators who met with me were still processing all that they had learned at the Gender Spectrum training they had attended. The subject of transgender children was still *very* new to most educators. The topic was not yet hot in the mainstream media, only a very small handful of people were by then widely known to be transgender, and only one child ever—Jazz Jennings—had made her story public. Many people were not at all familiar with the word "transgender," never mind terms like *gender creative* or *gender expansive* or *non-binary*. In our school district, the idea of sex education was still somewhat controversial when Amaya was in eighth grade, and to this day, the parents of quite a few students in our area opt to deny their kids access to those classes. If I'd pressed the school to support the radical (at the time) idea that there could be something called a "gender spectrum," and that everyone isn't all male or all female, most likely that would have caused some uproar in the community. Still, while I didn't want my child to be the center of attention (and I assure you he has never wanted that!), I did want to find some way to open up the conversation in our town. It was no secret that my child's gender expression was not typical for a girl, and this was confusing for him, for us, and for others.

Despite answers being available to help ease our communal confusion, it clearly wasn't yet time for this conversation to emerge.

Recently, many years after my fruitless meeting with the middle school administrators, that very same principal stopped me in a supermarket aisle. Now retired, she said she wanted to thank me personally for pressing the school staff all those years ago to educate themselves, parents, and students regarding the subject of transgender children. She told me that the books I'd provided at the time, which I imagined had gotten dusty on dark shelves in forgotten rooms, were well read and continue to be used as a resource for teachers and staff. And she remarked on the flood of attention currently being given to transgender people in the media, noting that the school has recently had quite a few parents come to the office to talk and ask questions about their children's gender. As we parted ways in the supermarket, she thanked me for being proactive so long ago, and for encouraging her and the other administrators to grow and learn how best to support *all* students.

Wow! The seeds I'd planted and forgotten in despair had taken root.

HALLOWEEN SCREAM

Halloween gives us the chance to try on different archetypes. Anyone can be the superhero, the princess, the animal, the clown, the zombie king. Since he was old enough to choose, Amaya consistently opted for stereotypical male costumes. There was Spiderman, Hulk, the skater dude, and my favorite, the nerd who had just been beaten up.

One year during middle school, Amaya dressed as the masked character from the movie *Scream*. A group photo captured my child ghoul with a bunch of his friends. I am looking at that picture now: The friends, all girls, are in pre-adolescently "sexy" versions of stereotypical female costumes: the nurse, the cheerleader, the doll. As middle school girls often do at Halloween, they're showing off their burgeoning sexuality by wearing excessive makeup and costumes that show lots of skin. Amaya, in the midst of seven or eight girls, is trying to look scary, a masked and robed apparition in stark contrast to his costumed peers. While his female friends are showing off the young curves they've sprouted during puberty, Amaya's costume hides his bodily form completely.

When I pulled up this picture recently and saw what all those girls wore that Halloween, I was reminded that our daughter, Emily, was admonished at school one year for her costume choice. She'd left the house that morning wearing a short skirt with ripped fishnet stockings, and I remember pointing out that I wasn't sure the outfit was in compliance with the dress code. (I'll table any discussion about dress codes and gender bias for another time.) She refused to change her clothes, and off she went to school. Upon arrival, the principal told her she had to put pants on under her skirt. Apparently, I was correct.

Left with only the sweatpants in her PE locker as a choice, she was devastated; her costume *ruined*. My "I told you so" ringing in her ears was no comfort.

If the girls pictured with Amaya had worn the costumes they donned that night to school the next day, they probably have been admonished as well. But not my kid. My kid was sure to cover every bit of skin, and then some. There was no telling who was under those robes. I imagine it must have been comforting and perhaps empowering to be anonymous—as well as androgynous—in that costume.

WATCHING AND WAITING

While we followed Amaya's lead and waited for him to figure things out, I gathered information and learned all I could. I read the books *The Transgender Child* by Rachel Pepper and Stephanie Brill,[10] and *Gender Born, Gender Made* by Diane Ehrensaft.[11] I reached out to his school for help (to little avail). I engaged with Gender Spectrum but found few parents with children the same age as Amaya. My husband and I soldiered on.

When Amaya was young, there was not much distress in evidence. Even without knowing what we now know, we gave Amaya a lot of room to be who he felt he was inside, bending without much resistance to his demands for boys' clothes, haircuts, toys, or activities. So, to a great extent, we did the right thing. It was only when we interacted with new people that the subject of Amaya's gender even came up—that is, when we corrected people who thought "she" was a boy.

However, as his discomfort and distress heightened during his tween years, we had to step up our efforts to support and understand him. As I've mentioned, Gabriel and I found some support for ourselves when we attended Gender Spectrum's support group meetings, but Amaya had no interest in meeting other kids "like" him. In fact, the more I learned about gender identity, gender expression, and what it meant to be transgender, the more I understood that there was nothing really that we *could* do to help. At least, nothing to do until Amaya gave us clear signs regarding his gender identity. So we watched and we waited. I remember people asking me about what I thought the future held for Amaya, did we think he would be a lesbian, or what? I would say, "I don't know but I can't wait to see!"

We did our best to follow Amaya's lead and provide a supportive, accepting, safe environment for him to be himself. But it *was* hard to wait.

Cristin Brew is a marriage and family therapist (MFT) with 15 years' experience working with trans and gender-expansive youth in northern California. She has been one of our family's greatest supporters and an invaluable source of comfort and information as we've walked down our path with Amaya. Cristin says:

Oftentimes parents and caregivers feel that their child/ teen has begun to identify as transgender, gender fluid, agender, gender queer (etc.) out of the blue. Sometimes the realization is fairly recent, other times the young person has been grappling with and exploring their gender for quite some time, and only now feels ready to share it. The issue of suddenness often leads parents to wonder if this is a passing phase, an impulsive but fleeting experiment with a new identity. The disparity between the certainty a young person may feel and the uncertainty a parent may feel generally leads to competing needs and frustration for all parties. This "hurry up and wait" phase calls for the creation of a supportive environment in which the young person can unfold, and also requires attending to parental concerns about permanent medical interventions that may accompany gender transition. (Cristin Brew, personal communication, October 16, 2016)

It's very painful for a parent to watch one's child struggle and not know how to make it better. As Cristin says, it is a "hurry up and wait" kind of process. It is important for us parents to educate ourselves, to arm ourselves with as much information as we can so we are ready when our child is ready. It is also important for us to get the support we need so that we can be present for our children.

Parents must develop patience.

Patience can be hard to come by. *All* children will test the boundaries set up around them. Testing boundaries is in fact a key component of how humans develop and learn. Learning happens not when we keep doing what we always do, but rather when we push at the edges. As parents, we learn (we hope) how to set boundaries while remaining open to the shifting needs of our children. So how does one know that one's child is not just "testing boundaries" when they express gender differences or question their gender?

The answer is that we look for behavior that is *consistent*, *persistent*, and *insistent*. As we observe a child, we note this pattern when it emerges relative to gender expression, and we follow the lead of the child.

Patience grows out of understanding. Just as all children develop a sense of self on their own, unique timeline, the development of a sense of self for a child who is gender expansive or gender questioning follows its own timeline. As parents, we cannot force our children to be someone they are not (though many will try, often with tragic results). We also do not want to squelch self-expression. We must be careful not to label our children before they have a sense of themselves. Parents of transgender, gender-questioning, and gender-creative children must at once be actively seeking information while still remaining patient with their child's process.

Individual gender identity can only be understood fully from an inner place, and the development of this inner understanding can take time. Each person will undergo their own process. Even when our children do tell us about their gender identity, it may take time for them to allow others to know this very personal information. A child may ask the parents to use a new name when among family members only, or may ask for different pronouns to be used in the home—but in any case, the child may at the same time want to use their "old" pronouns or name outside the house. Some children may say they feel like a boy one day and like a girl the next day. As a parent, it can be challenging to know how to respond in a supportive way when things change from day to day.

A 2012 survey of transgender youth, conducted by Ontario Canada's Trans Pulse, revealed that the number one factor trans kids feel leads to their happiness and self-acceptance is *parental support*. Sadly, to the contrary, trans and gender-expansive youth without family support have been shown to be in the highest risk pools for depression, anxiety, and suicide.[12] These are sobering statistics. Children who do not express gender in stereotypical ways *need* parents who are knowledgeable, flexible, and patient.

It is up to us as parents to be the adults, to take charge of our own process so we can be there for our children. It may take a radical move on our part, and it may require us to let go of deeply held beliefs regarding both gender identity and our expectations for our children. Often, it can be helpful for us parents to seek counseling for ourselves, in addition to any therapy we may seek for our children.

Yes, parenting is hard—*and* we can do this. As parents, we must have patience with our youth, and, most of all, have patience with ourselves. It may give us comfort to remember that we are never alone, there are always countless parents who feel the same and have experienced things similar to our experiences. Among those parents is Julie Adams, one of Amaya's high school teachers (one of Julie's twin children is transgender). She says:

It's a wild ride, to be sure, but that's true of parenting in general. It's also interesting to see how different family members react (generational differences, regional differences, religious differences, etc.), as well as to observe my personal growth.

[My son] Cayden has reminded me of some things I've said that were (unintentionally) hurtful, for which I have apologized, and we have discussed the fact that for parents there is almost a mourning process. Even though you never stop loving your kid (or at least you SHOULDN'T), the visions that flash through your mind when they lay that baby in your arms for the first time shift and suddenly, even though it's still the same little spirit you've always known, you have to re-frame some things. As I told Cayden, "You're not the only one undergoing a transition." (Julie Adams, personal communication, January 13, 2017)

WHY CAN'T MY CHILD JUST
—— MAKE UP THEIR MIND? ——

In 2015, when Amaya was nearing the end of his high school years, I co-founded a local, monthly support group for parents of transgender and gender-expansive youth. My son had transitioned, I had learned a lot, and I wanted to help other parents who had non-binary or gender-fluid kids, parents who felt the challenges of "keeping up" with their child. I wanted to share my family's experience and provide both support and resources to other parents in our community. I partnered with Cammie Duvall, a marriage and family counselor who specializes in working with transgender and gender-questioning youth and their families, and who is herself (as she describes it), "an out, queer, transgender woman in the community." By working together, I believe Cammie and I have been able to help many other parents on journeys similar to mine. I am grateful for Cammie's knowledge as well as her candor as I continue to learn and grow in my understanding about the complex subject that is gender. I am always inspired when meeting with the parents in our group upon hearing about their own experiences. In some ways, we are all on the same journey, but in other ways, each of us has a unique path to tread.

Most parents, I am sure, truly want to understand. They want to "do the right thing" but they don't know how to respond to a child who does not behave or define as the gender assigned to them at birth. Feelings can vary among parents too, in part because there is no one way to be transgender or gender expansive. Parents whose children do not define clearly as either male or female sometimes say they are envious of those of us whose trans children simply "switched sides" in the male/female binary system. I can see that for some parents it might seem easier to just be able to say, "Okay, you say you are a boy, so we can go with that."

It can be surprising or shocking to parents when they discover their child is not behaving in accordance with typical gender norms. Yes, we know the visibility of trans people has been increasing in our society, and we see that many people today have become familiar with what it means to be transgender. Understanding and acceptance is on an upward trend. However, this acceptance is more of a reality for transgender people who fit into the male/female paradigm. People are still most comfortable thinking in terms of the gender binary. Those who transition and present clearly as either male or female have the highest likelihood of being accepted by family and community. Many gender-questioning or gender-expansive people, on the other hand, do not fit into this binary paradigm. These people typically have a much more difficult time being understood, supported, and accepted.[13]

Parents may feel anxiety or loss when they learn their child is transgender. Those feelings may be compounded for parents whose child defines not merely as transgender, but as gender expansive, or gender fluid, or non-binary, or agender, or anything else that does not fall cleanly into "male" or "female" buckets. There are people who describe themselves as "gender fluid"; they may feel they are male at certain times or in certain situations, and then later (in a minute, an hour, a day), or in a different environment, they feel as though a switch has flipped and they are female. Some people describe themselves as both male and female. In any case, the way one expresses oneself on the outside may not even match the way one feels on the inside. The variety is seemingly endless, and parents are rarely well equipped to understand it all.

I have heard Diane Ehrensaft, PhD, tell the story of a child who described herself as a hybrid "gender Prius"— male on top and female on the bottom, as she put it. Imagine the confusion for a parent of a child who says one day, "I am a boy, please use male pronouns," and the next day says, "Today I feel I am a girl, please use female pronouns."

It is often said that the *T* in "LGBT" is about 30 years behind *LGB* in terms of acceptance. As recently as three decades ago, parents were likely to be distraught if their child came out as gay. Currently there is a much wider level of acceptance in the United States for gay or lesbian people *vis-à-vis* transgender people. Research by the Pew Research Center (2013) shows that acceptance of lesbian, gay, bisexual, or transgender people increases with specific familiarity[14]—for instance, the more gay men a person knows, the more likely that person will be accepting of gay men in their community. As acceptance of gays and lesbians has outpaced acceptance of gender-variant people over the past few decades, parents who have learned they have a transgender child have occasionally reported saying to their children, "*Transgender?* If only you were *gay*, it would be so much easier to understand and accept." This disparity is in big part due to the fact that 90 percent of the US population as of 2016 reports knowing someone who is gay, while only 10 percent report knowing someone who is transgender.[15]

By nature, we are creatures who fear the unknown. So naturally, now that people in the United States are becoming more familiar with, and increasingly more accepting of, transgender people who "cross over" from one gender to another (in popular culture, for instance, we have Jazz Jennings, Caitlyn Jenner, and Laverne Cox), we find parents saying, "Non-binary? If only you would choose a side. If you're trans fine, then just be a boy or a girl, but this *in-between* is just too much!"

Our culture is even now leaping and bounding regarding our understanding of gender identity. The latest research shows us that gender is not a binary "black or white" paradigm constructed along rigid male or female lines; rather, gender is a *spectrum* of possibilities ranging from male to female along several strata and even extending outside the spectrum itself. One's identity can exist anywhere on this spectrum, or not at all.

To illustrate this dynamic, consider the "Gender Abacus" pictured below. Individuals can use a visual tool like this to describe their identity relative to gender and sexual preference. For many people, their gender identity, expression, and sex have characteristics that are male, female, both, neither, or any unique combination of gender—and these characteristics may be fixed or fluid. Hence, for any given person, the "beads" may not be placed all on one side of the Gender and Sexuality Abacus or the other. Likewise, sexual preferences do not always fall neatly along either/or lines. Using an "abacus" like this to define oneself along multiple spectra (however limited and imperfect this depiction may be) allows for introspective insight and gives people an alternative way to express the subtle nuances and variations that shape us all.

Again, patience comes out of understanding. Cristin Brew offers a good starting point:

Non-binary expressions and identities may be more difficult to assimilate into our binary society, but they tend to be deeply authentic. Slowly but surely, we seem to be recognizing that the gender binary system is antiquated and does not work for many of us. The impact is not limited just to those who identify as non-binary or transgender. I have observed that the past couple of generations are notably less brainwashed regarding gender roles, rules, and expectations.

Generally speaking, youth have less difficulty accepting and understanding transgender and gender-expansive identities than older generations. Having said that, it still sucks to feel different. Young people need supportive environments in which to discover their authentic gender while still feeling like they belong. Maintaining a connection to peers and family members substantially increases their feeling of well-being. (Cristin Brew, personal communication, October 16, 2016)

Gender & Sexuality Abacus

Male/Masculine — Female/Feminine

Gender Identity (how you feel inside)

Gender Expression (how you want to be seen)

Biological Sex (genitalia, DNA, etc.)

Men & Masculinity — Women & Femininity

Sexually Attracted to... (could be "nobody")

Romantically Attracted to... (could be "nobody")

The "Gender Abacus" (graphic by Gabriel Barkin)

— Part 4 —

THE TRANSITION YEARS

Transition is defined in the *Oxford English Dictionary* as follows:

- *noun:* "the process or period of changing from one state or condition to another"

- *verb:* "to undergo or cause to undergo a process or period of transition"

- *synonyms:* "change, passage, transformation, metamorphosis."[16]

When a person is in the process of actively affirming their gender as anything other than their natal or assigned sex, we say that they are *making their transition*. Each person will experience their own unique process of transition, and only that person can say if their process is ever complete or not. Some people may even complete their transition at one point in life, only to initiate a new transition later on to comport more fully with a growing sense of self. My son Amaya has told me, for instance, that his transition is complete, for now.

A brief pause about privacy before I continue: All people have a right to privacy regarding any affirmations they express or choices they make on their path toward transition. Certainly, it is never appropriate for anyone to ask if a person has had surgery to change their genitalia! (Would you be comfortable if someone asked you about your surgical history?) That being said, let me be clear: my son has given me permission to share some private information in this book regarding his transition in order to demystify the subject and support those who may be in need of guidance. (Thanks Amaya!)

During transition it is common for an individual (whether a child or an adult) to first explore their gender identity and changes in their gender expression in private, often outside their circle of their family and friends. My son, for instance, started exploring gender identity online when he was about 13 or 14. It wasn't until several months into his explorations that Gabriel and I found out about his internet research. We now know that he learned a lot by watching YouTube videos made by transgender boys describing their transitions. From these videos, he learned methods he could use to change his physical appearance, including how to bind his breasts and layer his clothing to hide his burgeoning bosom. He followed links and read suggestions in comments sections and chat rooms, and he discovered there were medical and surgical interventions available for...well, people like him. (Let me underscore that key factor: he learned that there were other people *like him*!) He now knew there was a way to surgically remove breasts and sculpt a male chest, a medical intervention known colloquially as *top surgery*. He began to present himself as male in online interactions with strangers. He made friends online as a boy, and even "went out" for a time with an online girlfriend who lived in Texas. (More about the Texas girlfriend and about how we found out about Amaya's online explorations, later.) He was beginning to transition.

At some point, in order for a person to transition, they have to begin to disclose themselves to others. Some people will opt to start new lives in new towns explicitly to avoid disclosing this very personal information to those who already know them. Some parents will decide to change the schools their kids attend. However, it is increasingly common for people starting their transition to stay in place and begin to come out to people in their lives. And yet, all too often this is not an easy task, and in some cases public transition can be devastating, perhaps with tragic consequences. It takes great courage for people in transition to share their very personal information. Sadly, many people at this stage are spurned by family, friends, workmates, or others in their community. Unfathomably to me, some parents kick their trans teens out of their household. Perhaps worst of all, some people experience physical violence, sometimes from family members and close friends, when they disclose that they are transgender.

Even when a person is blessed with acceptance from their family and community, transition is fraught with challenges. Transition is a process, and it can be daunting. Possible steps a person may take toward social transition may encompass the following: changes to clothing and hair styles; name changes; flipping personal pronouns to an opposite or neutral gender; changes to legal identity documents; using the bathroom or locker room of one's affirmed gender; and a myriad of other possibilities. There's a lot to consider—at best it's a very complex project to manage!

For Amaya, transition lasted from age 14 to 17.

FACEBOOK TOLD ME MY
———— DAUGHTER WAS MY SON ————

Oh, the things we learn online.

When he was 14, I discovered that the gender shown for Amaya's Facebook profile had been changed from an "F" to an "M." The gender switch had triggered an email notification to let me know that Amaya had updated his profile; he had been my "daughter" on Facebook, but now an email told me he was identifying himself as my "son." "Hmm," I thought, "Why did he change his gender marker? Is this Amaya's way of telling us he wants to transition to male?" I was intrigued. Amaya's sister, Emily, my husband, and my mother also got similar notifications. (I guess Facebook doesn't want people to have profiles saying they are related to people they are not in fact related to.) Though it did not come as a shock to any of us that Amaya would define himself as male, we were surprised to hear of this shift through Facebook. We wondered why he did not want to tell us, or if he felt afraid for some reason.

Gabriel recalls that he was driving somewhere with Amaya around that time, and at one point he said to our kid, "So I see on Facebook that you're my son now." Amaya replied that he and some friends were just fooling around—to which Gabriel responded tersely and somewhat disbelievingly, "Uh huh." He left it at that, perhaps wisely and patiently aware that there would be more someday, when Amaya was ready.

For me, it was time to reach out to our allies again. Here is my correspondence with Joel Baum, the Director of Gender Spectrum, during Amaya's eighth grade year (note that this correspondence has not been edited, and that we used female pronouns to refer to Amaya at the time).

EMAIL FROM ME TO JOEL, 4/27/12

Hi Joel,

It has been awhile. I hope all is well. I hope you remember me, and also my husband Gabriel. Our child is Amaya. Now in 8th grade. 14. We stopped coming to the group as Amaya seemed to be adjusted happy living and defining as the girl she was born. She has a big group of friends. Mostly girls with a few guys. While we were in NY recently she chose to use the men's bathroom as the women's had a huge line. I was okay with it, but was not sure it was appropriate. And now today I noticed her Facebook profile has her listed as male...she shows up as my son. This is new. Hmmmm...any thoughts? Do I ask her about it? Ask if this is what she wants to be, he? Do I let it be and wait for her to come to me? Maybe she wants to be girl here and boy out there? Any thoughts would be most welcome. We are meeting with HS [high school] staff in June. We want to be prepared so we can support Amaya. Thanks!

EMAIL FROM JOEL TO ME, 4/27/12

Hi Janna,

Of course I remember Amaya ("she's not amazing; she's Amaya!"). I'd be happy to talk in more detail if you'd like, but my initial thought is you don't ignore it, but instead set up a chance to check in about it. With you getting set for the HS mtg, it is a perfect opportunity to say, "So we're getting ready to meet with folks at the HS, and we realized we haven't checked in in a while about how things are going for you...when we meet with them, we want to be sure to send them a clear message about how best they can support you in a variety of ways, including around your gender identity and expression. If you could wave a wand and have things exactly as you'd like, what would it look like next year?"

Not knowing the exact purpose of the meeting, or who you are meeting with, this may be off course. The other piece to consider is that even if it is NOT off course, it is important that she (and you!) don't assume what is or is not impossible about how she goes about navigating this landscape next year. Start from the ideal and work from there.

With this wise guidance I decided it was time to take action in some way.

First I approached Amaya to ask about the Facebook gender switch, making sure he knew he could tell me anything and that Gabriel and I would support him. He said, "I don't know how that happened." He said, "Maybe a friend did it," but he also said he just didn't feel like changing his gender back to female was important. I asked if he wanted us to use male pronouns at home; his answer was no. I asked if he wanted to go to school as a *he* and he said no. When I asked him what he would like to see happen in an ideal world, if anything, he said, "I don't know."

We learned several months later that the Facebook change was just one web profile among many where he had made a pronoun switch, or was now presenting himself as male. (I'll tell some stories about these explorations later on.) At the time, unbeknownst to us, his closest friends were already using male pronouns to refer to Amaya, particularly online. A year or so later, Gabriel and I met counselor Cristin Brew, who provided invaluable support and advice to our family throughout Amaya's transition. We asked Cristin about Amaya's early online activity, his first steps toward affirming as male in a public sphere. She assured us it was normal behavior, and she affirmed that many tweens and teens follow a similar path to begin their transition. She explained that making the switch online or in small groups can feel much safer and less overwhelming for many kids.

But to be honest, at the time I felt left out. I wondered if I had done something to make Amaya feel like he couldn't tell me or trust me. I so very much wanted my child to live fully as his authentic self, and I was utterly compelled to support him in any way that I could. So why didn't he ask me to make the switch too? Did my child not have confidence in my support?!

With hindsight, of course, I understand. Although Amaya had already started his social transition online and amongst a small group of friends (by using male gender markers in particular), he was not yet ready to make this shift within his home/school life. It can be overwhelming to think of all the implications that may arise when coming out to people who have known a person for years, or for a lifetime. Even though Amaya knew he would have our support, and that we would love him just the same no matter what, he knew there would be other people who would question, perhaps judge, perhaps ridicule him. As he was never one to enjoy making a big deal out of *anything*, particularly in public places, I can understand how conflicted Amaya must have been regarding a topic as big and daunting as his own gender identity. "Coming out," as my friend and colleague Cammie Duvall describes, "is actually *letting people in* on very personal and intimate information." She says, "It can be less overwhelming to think of disclosure as an *invitation in* rather than a *coming out*. Each person gets to decide who they let in and when they let them in." Amaya was being very careful and slow to let people in, just a few at a time. Gabriel and I had not yet been let past that velvet rope.

As Cammie also tells me, "Coming out can be a very lonely process. No matter how much support one has, letting people in to one's most inner world is a vulnerable and courageous act."

Many transgender and gender non-conforming people take a gradual approach to transitioning and coming out. People who have shared their own stories with me concur that this is common. It is noteworthy that in the stories I have heard and read, many trans people report that they felt deep concern about the impact of their transition on *other* people in their lives. The following is a collection of some of the thoughts that might add to one's challenges during transition:

- "I don't want to make things hard for them."

- "I don't want her to worry if she makes a mistake."

- "I don't want to draw attention to myself."

- "How will they react?"

- "Will she still love me?"

- "Will I be safe?"

Exposing our innermost thoughts and experiences to others calls for bravery and vulnerability. Coming out is risky! Some people face unaccepting friends or families. Some trans and gender non-conforming youth are kicked out of their homes before they are even 18. Trans people may experience violent reactions to their transition, perhaps becoming victims of "hate crimes" (crimes committed against people based specifically on animosity toward their identity or ancestry), including assault, rape, and murder. Many will suffer discrimination or bullying at school or in their workplace. It can be challenging or impossible in some states and communities for trans people to get necessary medical care or insurance coverage. These risks will remain significant until our society is more understanding and accepting of gender differences— but sadly, we have a long way to go. So it's no surprise that many people choose to take baby steps and move slowly through their transition with a reluctance to reveal themselves to some audiences.

Not coming out has risks as well. For many trans people, the many secrets they have to keep may at some point become a bigger burden than the risk of coming out. It can be very stressful, painful, and isolating to live a life *other than* that which is authentic and true to one's inner sense of self, and doing so can have devastating consequences. We know that transgender youth are at risk of depression, anxiety, suicide, and self-harm, as these concerns are disproportionally high among that cohort. As I mentioned previously, we also know trans people who report the highest rates of success and happiness in their lives are those who say they were able to transition and live as their authentic selves with the support of their families and communities.

I asked Amaya recently about his gender change on Facebook when he was 14. He laughed when I reminded him he'd told me then, "I don't know how that happened." Now fully transitioned, he said on reflection that he didn't talk to us about it back then because he was not ready yet to make the change on such a broad scale. He said even though he knew we would be supportive, he didn't want to draw attention to himself or be the cause of a commotion if someone misgendered him in public. He also said he didn't want to make things hard for other people, as he knew it would take effort to make the change. (Allow me a "Momma Moment": My son always was and continues to be a considerate and thoughtful person who considered the feelings of others, and of that I am certainly a proud parent!)

Despite those concerns and worries, Amaya at age 14 continued making his transition in his own gradual way. Like many teens, trans or not, he gave his parents access to understanding him on a "need to know" basis. Even though it seemed clear to us by then that he wanted to be seen as male, he was not ready to affirm this out loud. It was not until the end of his freshman high school year, in 2013, that he asked us to start using male pronouns at home. As his inner understanding and confidence grew, he invited us in.

BOUND IN SO MANY WAYS

Gender dysphoria is defined by *Merriam-Webster* as follows:

- *noun:* a distressed state arising from conflict between a person's gender identity and the sex the person has or was identified as having at birth

- *also:* a psychological disorder marked by such distress.[17]

As puberty set in during his early teen years, Amaya experienced increasing levels of distress. His body had begun to change. He felt less and less comfortable in his clothes and more stressed regarding his outer presentation as he matured. His bodily changes—the growth of his breasts in particular—made it more difficult for Amaya to imagine others would see him as he wanted to be seen. It was becoming clear to him at that age, even though he hadn't expressed it yet to us, that he wanted to be seen as male.

Bra shopping with Amaya was always a truly awful and drawn-out experience that taxed and stressed both of us. Amaya's chest started developing early, when he was ten, and when we tried at first to find bras that fit, they never looked right in my eyes; a bra looked so odd and out of place on his body, even then. To Amaya, no bras felt comfortable, and many times a shopping trip would end in frustration and tears. Often we would buy something that seemed to fit in the store, only to have him throw it across the room in uncomfortable frustration when he tried to put it on again at home. In contrast to his matter-of-fact acceptance of a menstrual cycle at the onset of puberty, this was developing into a crisis.

I realized the best approach was for me to do the shopping and bring home bras for Amaya to try on. We finally found some sports bras that worked well enough (he could tolerate them, at least). But as he grew, we had to increase his bra size from time to time. We would try to find something new that would fit, but we never found anything that really resolved his comfort issues.

Amaya tried wearing layers. He sometimes wore two bras together. Nothing felt right.

One day, not too long after I'd noticed Amaya (or someone) had changed his Facebook gender to male, I received the following email from my young teen. (This method of communication was a bit unusual; we talked together all the time and rarely sent emails to each other.) I knew we were entering a new phase of our journey when I read this:

EMAIL FROM AMAYA TO ME, 4/28/12

I have been thinking of getting one of these for a few weeks but didn't know how to talk about it. But anyways, I've done a little bit of research and this seems to be one of the best...[here was a link to a chest binder he'd found online]

EMAIL FROM ME TO AMAYA, 4/28/12

I am very proud of you for letting me know. Looks like a useful product if that is what you want. I would like to find one on a site that would take returns for size. This one does not. Let's research and explore. I am here to support you! And this binder will support you big time! Let me know if you find one that takes returns for size. Talk later...or email about it anytime. xxoo Mom

So we began to talk about binders, and binding, and what that would mean for Amaya.

Once again, Amaya had found what he was looking for on YouTube and other sites on the Internet. Now it was my turn to learn from Amaya, as well as from my own research, and I found that binding is a common practice among trans guys (and also for some women who are not comfortable with their breasts or want a more masculine-looking chest). I learned that binding can greatly reduce the level of dysphoria one feels due to one's breasts. In theory, a binder sounded like a good solution for Amaya.

To constrict his growing breasts (unfortunately, his maternal DNA gave him a strong potential for D-cup breasts), Amaya first tried Ace bandages, then a combination of sports bras and binder tops, and at some point he experimented with an "under-" type of shirt that was made specifically to pair with a binder. Meanwhile, his body began to compensate, his posture and shoulders slumping forward to hide his chest. His breathing was definitely compromised by the tightness of the various binders, and it seemed he had a lot of stomach aches (probably induced as much by stress as by the physical restrictions of his binders). He had to check and recheck his appearance before leaving the house each day to be sure he was concealing the parts that were the cause of his distress.

He really was bound, in so many ways.

Finally, one day he came to me, again via email (so now I knew it was important), and told me that he wanted to talk to someone because he didn't want to have breasts anymore. He said they didn't feel like they belonged to his body. He wanted them gone.

EMAIL FROM AMAYA TO ME, 9/8/12

So it's been a while since we've talked about this but I wanna bring it up again. Using the bandages to bind works but hurts my back and is uncomfortable. I've tried using duct tape but it restrains me from being able to breathe in deeply. Right now I wish I just didn't have my boobs. I don't know what I want to do or what I can do. *I just don't really want them anymore.*

EMAIL FROM ME TO AMAYA, 9/8/12

Hi love. Thank you for sharing this with me. Let's spend time together tomorrow and talk ok? I will support you on your path whatever that is, but it is not an easy decision to make. Let's talk and explore options together ok? Love you, Mom

EMAIL FROM AMAYA TO ME, 9/8/12

Alright that sounds good to me.

Binders can be very useful and often reduce the level of dysphoria that a trans person with breasts may experience on an ongoing basis. However, this solution can also be harmful. Binding can be very uncomfortable, and regular use may cause a host of medical issues. Binders can cause shortness of breath and digestive issues. Wearing one daily can affect one's posture and bone growth, and can even lead to fractured or broken ribs. For Amaya, binding was not a long-term solution. I shared this latest round of emails with Gabriel immediately, and we realized we needed to follow Amaya where he was leading us.

THE DOCTOR DILEMMA

When Amaya was 14 and he told us he wanted top surgery, Gabriel and I weren't sure where to turn. We weren't exactly shocked by his request—we were well aware that Amaya was consistently and significantly discomfited by his post-pubescent female chest. His discomfort distressed him to the point where he'd taken to binding his breasts daily with a combination of Ace bandages topped by layers of several sports bras. He would not even walk to the mailbox without this setup under his clothes. So, while we were not shocked that he wanted his "boobs" gone, we didn't know anything about the surgery, or if the cost would be covered by our health insurance, or if any surgeon would perform the procedure on someone under 18.

I asked Amaya if he would talk to a counselor or therapist, but he said he didn't want to talk to someone new. I thought perhaps he would be willing to speak with our family doctor. We had been patients of doctors within a particular medical group for many years, but we were new to this particular doctor, as our previous physician had passed away recently and her patients had been distributed randomly to other members of the staff. When we first met Dr. D, Amaya was still living as a girl "on paper" so to speak, but presented as a boy. I proactively made sure Dr. D knew Amaya was a girl who looked like a boy, and she'd responded professionally and seemed supportive. Faced now with his willfulness to remove his breasts, and with a reminder from me that

Dr. D had invited Amaya to talk to her if "she" ever had *any* questions, he agreed to talk to her.

I strategized. I wanted to talk to the doctor by myself before we had our appointment. I didn't want to blindside her with the idea of top surgery before we had a chance to talk as adults, without Amaya in the room. Amaya clearly was insecure about sharing this information and asking questions. It was hard for him to talk about the subject. I felt the discussion would go better if Dr. D had a "heads up" and was given a chance to formulate a thoughtful response.

When I called the medical group to ask if I could make an appointment for a phone consult, I was told that the doctor didn't have phone consultation hours. I was surprised—I'd never had an issue getting in touch with my old doctor in the past. I was told it was a group policy, no phone consultations, and that I could discuss whatever I needed with my doctor at the scheduled appointment. I wasn't comfortable with this response and lack of access, so I asked if Dr. D had an email address. I was told the medical group did not have an email system for doctors to use to communicate with the patients. I was really frustrated at this as it was 2012, and email wasn't exactly a new thing.

My final resort was to ask if I could fax something to the doctor for her to read in advance of our appointment, and I finally got an affirmative response from the person on the phone. At the time, I was not ready to share my child's sensitive and personal information with many people, so I asked if my communication would be kept confidential between the doctor and me. I was assured that indeed my fax would be treated as confidential. With that assurance, I sent a letter to Dr. D via fax. I have included it here because it captures a moment when

Amaya was clearly already in transition, taking steps that, in some cases, were hidden to my husband and me. He'd learned all about top surgery and other medical options online. Perhaps he chose to tell us he wanted surgery only because he'd realized it was something he could not do without our help. He'd gone as far as he could on his own. (Note that this letter has not been edited, and that we used female pronouns to refer to Amaya at the time).

FAX CONFIDENTIAL

415-xxx-xxxx

To: Dr. D
From: Janna Barkin
Date: September 13. 2012

Dear Dr. D,

My daughter Amaya and I have met you a few times. Last time I saw you was for a puncture wound to my foot, right after Amaya had seen you for a twisted ankle! We are both better now.

As you might remember Amaya is not just a tomboy, but she is someone who can be considered on the gender spectrum. You had mentioned to her on a previous visit that if she ever wanted to talk she could talk to you. You planted a seed and now she has asked to do that. Amaya has been coming to me to talk about some things, which has been great, and I told her I would connect with you next.

She has been exploring ways to bind her breasts all summer, and tells me she has been frustrated about having breasts for a while now, but does not know what to do about it.

She said she does not want to make a full change to being a boy right now, but I can tell she is thinking about it. She even said something about college being an easier time if she were going to do that. She also said she wanted to work it out soon as she really does not want to keep going on feeling bad about her breasts as she thinks she will just feel worse over time.

Her Facebook page says she is a boy, though she says she is not sure how it got that way, and to me seems totally honest about that. However, she has not changed it back either. She still does not want us to correct others in public when they think she is a boy, which is always, but she does want people who will know her over time to know. She would be quite happy though if there was a pronoun for people like her too, more androgynous. When asked if she wants us to call her a boy she says no, but seems unsure really.

She has asked to get her ears pierced this weekend and we are going to do that. Interesting, as pierced ears used to be a way to distinguish male/female, as it used to be that women had both ears pierced and men only one, but that is not the case anymore as most young men who have earrings have one in each now too!

I have been in touch with Joel Baum at Gender Spectrum. He is very helpful. If you do not know about this group, I highly recommend you check them out. Here is their website: www.genderspectrum.org. A few years ago Gabe and I went to a few Gender Spectrum parent support group meetings. I have not been in touch with them much lately. Amaya is resistant to any peer group meetings but I really think that would be great, and I believe there is a teen group in Marin. I will try to reconnect with them through Joel.

Another great resource is the book The Transgender Child by Stephanie Brill. I have been in touch with a woman mentioned in the book who works with trans children in the East Bay and said she would see us, but also rec. a counselor in Marin to us. I think I will reach out to them as well to see what resources are available.

I look forward to hearing from you, and then I will set up and appointment to come in.

Is there any way we can communicate by email? It would be so much easier that way. My email is [...].

Our wish is for Amaya to be happy, and we are here to support her on her journey, whatever that may be. We hope we can count on you as part of our team.

Thank you for your time and help in this matter.

Janna Barkin

A few days after Gabriel faxed this letter for me from his office, I received a call from the medical group. The call was from a medical assistant, not from Dr. D, and I was taken aback, as I had specifically inquired to ensure confidentiality between the doctor and me. Now I was hearing that another person had been brought into the mix without my knowledge or approval. I told the medical assistant that I didn't want to speak to her. I needed to have a conversation directly with Dr. D as I'd requested. The medical assistant told me that was not possible and said, impatiently, that Dr. D "was just going to refer you anyway"—implying that she wasn't even going to give me the time of day regarding my child's needs.

I thought, "A referral? Without even talking to me?!"

I was really upset. I felt I was wasting so much time and energy when all I wanted to do was talk to someone I could trust to help me regarding the health and well-being of my child.

Since I was getting nowhere with the medical assistant, I asked to speak to the manager of the medical group. After some verbal pushback on her part regarding the office's policies, she agreed finally that it was time I spoke to Dr. D, and she made arrangements for me to do so. Finally, one day I got to speak to Dr. D. Why was that so hard?!

Our conversation resolved nothing. Rather than talking about my child and his medical needs, the doctor steered the conversation repeatedly to focus on the medical group's doctor–patient communication guidelines. Dr. D explained to me that the group did not provide its doctors with time to make phone calls or respond to email requests for consults. I countered with my concerns about the lack of access to my doctor, and more critically about the lack of confidentiality I'd experienced. Feeling heated by her defensiveness about the office's processes and policies, I told her it felt to me like she'd purposely avoided an important conversation I'd requested, having her medical assistant contact me rather than doing it herself. I also told her I thought it was unprofessional for her medical assistant to blurt out the words, "She was just going to refer you anyway," which felt like a buck-passing blow-off. She claimed that the medical assistant was part of the chain of confidentiality in her office. We had words, many words.

I cannot remember how the conversation ended, but I am sure it was not on a positive note. I may have become unprofessional myself—but in my defense, I'd felt completely abandoned and shunted off by my physician, a professional to whom I'd turned to in a time of great need. We never did get past that intense conversation about policy, access, and confidentiality in order to talk about Amaya and the actual reason I wanted to talk to the doctor in the first place.

Coincidentally, Gabriel had an appointment with Dr. D later in the same week that I'd had my conversation with her. He'd never met her before, and in his eyes she was cold and impersonal, seemingly unconcerned about his health history and current complaints. A few days later, we received a certified letter in the mail from Dr. D. She wrote that due to the uncomfortable discourse between us, and because she valued good, clear communication in the patient–doctor relationship, she no longer felt comfortable being our family doctor. Further, the letter clarified that while she could no longer see us, we were not being asked to leave the medical group, and we were told we were welcome to see other doctors in the group. Ironically however, there were no openings for new patients with any of the other doctors at the time. So there we were, abandoned by our primary medical resource.

Looking back, I can see how the medical group's doctor–patient communication policies were only partly to blame. Perhaps if Dr. D had contacted me personally, we would have had a fine conversation about Amaya. Perhaps if the medical assistant had not said so casually that the doctor was "just going to refer us anyway," I might not have felt abandoned by my doctor. I can imagine that Dr. D may have thought she was being helpful by telling us she would refer Amaya with no questions asked. But because of our dysfunctional communication, my feeling at the time, right or wrong, was that Dr. D either was ill-equipped with knowledge of transgender medical interventions to counsel us, or she harbored personal feelings of animosity toward trans people, or both. On my end, I really wanted Amaya to get to talk to an adult who could help him (and us) with his transition, but surely I was also overly-protective of his "secret" this time. He may have gotten to have that promised conversation with Dr. D if I'd been more accepting and understanding regarding the limitations of the medical practice's communication polices.

Regardless of any blame, motivation, or policy limitations, I am certain we are not the only family who has been met with confusion, challenges, a lack of knowledge, or a lack of compassion and understanding when approaching their primary doctor with concerns regarding gender.

In hindsight, I am glad we were sent on our way by Dr. D. We ended up as patients of a fantastic practice in our area that is well informed and welcoming of diversity. It was important to Gabriel and me to find a medical group that put patient–doctor communication first. Indeed, we are now patients of a group of doctors who are available for email, phone, and in-person consultations within 48 hours of any request. We also specifically prioritized finding a group staffed with progressive doctors who stayed informed regarding gender-questioning youth. When we made his new doctor aware that Amaya was gender questioning and experiencing dysphoria centered around his female chest, she was attentive but also appropriately blasé. She recommended we find a good therapist (which was already and active item on our to-do list), and we felt we finally had found the right medical support!

At this new practice, Amaya was treated with dignity and respect from Day 1. When the time came, Amaya's doctor was glad to write the necessary letter, required for insurance coverage, in support of our child's decision to have top surgery. When the surgery was scheduled, the medical staff at the new practice were instrumental in Amaya's successful pre-op preparation and post-op recovery. After surgery, when Amaya was ready to start hormone therapy, he was referred to an in-house nurse practitioner who specializes in transgender care for adults. Although the policy of the medical practice typically provides transgender care (such as hormone therapy) only to adults, the administration evaluated our case and granted Amaya an exception to the policy. Amaya and his nurse practitioner have a wonderful rapport to this day, and my husband and I have great faith and trust in his expertise and his services. Because we did the research and found a place that caters to our needs for communication and for expertise regarding transgender health concerns, I trust that my son is in good hands when it comes to his medical needs as a person who is transgender. We also know that we are lucky, and that not all transgender people have the medical support they need.

FINDING CRISTIN

Finding Cristin Brew was a gift.

There had been many times in Amaya's life when I'd thought I should bring him to see a therapist. For instance, there was the summer before seventh grade, when he didn't do much of anything with any friends and hid in his room every day. Later on, there was our struggle to find bras that fit Amaya comfortably, as all attempts to try something new were met with anger, frustration, and tears. At various points during his tween years there were unexplainable stomach aches and headaches, and Amaya at times complained of overall exhaustion which had no obvious cause. But whenever I asked if he wanted to see a therapist, the idea was met with a firm "no," and I would let it go for a time. The catalyst that ultimately motivated me to press him hard to go talk to a professional counselor was the email he sent me in which he wrote that he couldn't live with his breasts any longer and didn't know what to do about it. I knew in my gut there was no other way but forward, and that meant it was time, finally, to find a good therapist. This time, Amaya finally said "yes."

I can recognize now that that just as it was difficult for Amaya to understand and accept what was really going on in his brain and body, it was also difficult for me. I wanted to help my child, but I did not want to put a label on what was happening. Gabriel and I never wanted to force Amaya (or any of our kids) to go to therapy. We didn't want him to think we thought there was anything wrong with him. Perhaps I was not ready to admit in my head what I knew in my heart—not because I think it is wrong to be transgender, but rather because of the challenges one can face being a transgender person in today's world. It is perhaps getting easier, but even today there are those in our society who are unkind to those who differ from expected norms. In hindsight, I would encourage myself to seek out a therapist for Amaya sooner, and somehow get him to agree to engage. It might have helped him to avoid some of the pain and anguish that he experienced.

When I find myself thinking this way, I try to remind myself that Gabriel and I were doing the best we could to support Amaya at the time, and that our kids (all three of them) seem to have grown up to be happy, healthy, and pretty cool adults. But I'm getting ahead of myself.

At the same time as we were struggling to find support from our child's primary doctor, we were also on the hunt for a therapist who was skilled with transgender youth. I contacted Gender Spectrum, as they had been helpful in the past, but they did not have any information on resources that might be available in Marin County at that time. Based on their recommendation, we considered traveling to Oakland so we could meet with Diane Ehrensaft. As I mentioned earlier, Diane is the author of two important books about gender and children: *Gender Born, Gender Made* and *The Gender Creative Child*.[18] Today she is the mental health director of the Child and Adolescent Gender Clinic at the University of California, San Francisco. I spoke with Diane over the phone, and indeed she offered to meet with us, but Gabriel and I felt it would be a struggle to get Amaya to and from appointments that would require well over an hour's drive each way in rush-hour traffic.

Diane gave us the name of someone in our county whom she thought might be able to help. (At that time the network of practitioners skilled with trans youth was not as connected as it is today.) When we met that person, she confessed she didn't have much experience with trans youth. We were looking specifically for expertise, and also we just didn't see her as someone Amaya would easily connect with. A "no-go."

After trying a few more leads, I stumbled upon the local LGBT center, Spectrum of Marin (now the Spahr Center of Marin). I wondered why I had not discovered this place up until that point. The administrator I talked to at Spectrum referred us to Cristin Brew, an MFT associated with the center. After just a brief phone consult, I could tell already that she was "the one," and we made an appointment right away. Thankfully, Amaya clicked with her instantly! We all agreed to bi-monthly sessions for Amaya to meet with Cristin, starting immediately.

The change in Amaya was almost instant. He actually looked forward to these sessions, and I could tell the experience was helping him. In my eyes, Cristin has a special gift, an ability to connect with young people. She's cool, witty, and smart. She was just what he needed. Amaya beamed when she said one day she was his "#1 fan," and she called him a "rock star." Their meetings together helped Amaya immensely as he navigated his inner process, and his interactions with her allowed his true gender identity to emerge and fly.

Among the various techniques Cristin employed, some of the most effective were the cognitive exercises she offered to Amaya. Working through these exercises with a skillful counselor helped Amaya understand who he *was* and who he *was not*. As he underwent this self-inquiry, Cristin reassured him that he was not alone, but rather was merely one of many people in the world who feel incongruence between their assigned sex at birth and their inner sense of their gender identity. As his understanding and acceptance grew, in great part due to Cristin's support and guidance, Amaya affirmed that he is male, and that he is transgender.

On Cristin's recommendation (certainly, *we* were never able to convince him to do anything like this!), Amaya agreed to participate in a support group for LGBT youth that met weekly at the Spectrum of Marin office. He agreed to attend only because it was run by Cristin. Here he met quite a few young people who were questioning, or in the process of affirming, their gender. In fact, most of the kids in that group were there because of their gender identity, not their sexual preferences. So Amaya indeed found support in that group, and he also developed empathy for others experiencing challenges related to their gender identity.

After some time, Cristin passed the facilitation baton to her intern, Cammie Duvall. A few years have passed now, and Cammie has become a licensed MFT who specializes in working with trans youth. She still leads, and has expanded, the same youth support groups at the Spahr Center of Marin. As a group facilitator who is also a queer trans woman, Cammie is able to share her own experiences and wisdom with group members, and often she is the first trans adult a kid has ever met or interacted with. (Me too; as far as I recall, she was the first adult I met whom I knew to be transgender.) Today, Cammie continues to be a role model for kids and adults in our community, and I am proud to partner with her as co-facilitators of the parent support group we host at the Spahr Center of Marin.

So yes, finding Cristin was a godsend. It was such a relief to know we now had an experienced, caring ally (and soon, several allies) in our child's corner. We had already learned that it can be very difficult for parents to live in the unknown while their children are finding themselves. Now we were learning that we had help.

And now, some wise and appropriate words from Cristin Brew:

> The unfolding of authentic gender identity and expression can be trusted. For some it may seem counterintuitive to implicitly trust children and adolescents to plot their own gender course. Indeed, this population does need support and adult advocacy to successfully interface with society. However, my work with gender expansive and transgender youth has taught me that, with adequate time and safe spaces to unfold, kids and teens come to find identities and expression that fit for them. (Cristin Brew, personal communication, October 16, 2016)

Amaya met with Cristin regularly for 18 months, tapering down after a while to just one monthly meeting. He still checks in with her from time to time, not for counseling, but because he has warm regard for her and they are very close. Gabriel and I will always be grateful for Cristin's incredible skill and intelligence. We hope more counselors will educate themselves about gender identity and youth, as so many need help navigating these challenging waters. We know that we are lucky, and that not all transgender people find the counseling support they need.

I'LL GO WITH YOU

How do you know which bathroom to use?

For cisgender people this is a simple question to answer: You use the men's room if you're a man, and you use the women's room if you're a woman. (A reminder: "cisgender" refers to people who identify with their birth sex.) But for transgender and other gender non-conforming individuals, just going into a public bathroom can be a challenging and even dangerous experience.

There are many people who want to legislate which bathrooms people get to use. These bathroom police want laws that say a person's gender as recorded on their original birth certificate is the only basis for determining whether a person uses the men's room or the women's room. Such laws are discriminatory against transgender and gender non-conforming people. They also are a violation of privacy—who's going to be checking?! And what exactly are they checking for?

As a mom to a transgender child, I can say that public bathrooms posed some of the biggest challenges and were the cause of so much anxiety for my kid. When he was very young, bathroom trips with our little tomboy were easy. Either my husband or I could go into any bathroom with him. But as he got older, he began to look out of place in the women's room.

In our culture it is acceptable for a parent to take a child of opposite gender into the restroom when they are very young. Tolerances shift around age five or six, and certainly by age nine children are expected to use the facilities that match their birth gender. Things can get tricky for children whose outward appearance or inner gender identity differs from the gender they were assigned at birth, and for their parents as well.

Very early on, our "girl" looked out of place in the women's room. When I took Amaya to a restroom, it was clear many people were concerned. Some stared and whispered. I often noticed surprise and even shock on people's faces. I know they were thinking: there's a boy in the girls' room. I would even call out to my child, "Hey girl, you can wash your hands over here," to subtly assure these people that everything was okay. I felt uncomfortable, to say the least. My child was well aware of the commotion and would hold my hand very tightly.

My husband and I discussed our problem: Amaya looked like he belonged in the men's room, but it is not acceptable in our society to take one's daughter into a men's room after a certain age. We were confused, and so was our child.

Using the restroom at school caused Amaya to suffer from anxiety that only increased as the years went by. He would frequently have stomach aches. We discovered that he was not using the bathroom at school. When we spoke to the school counselor and principal about it, he was offered use of the office bathroom as an option (we did feel they were trying their best to be supportive). He didn't like doing that, as he felt it made him "different." When he got older, he figured out that going to pee during class made it less likely that there would be others in the bathroom.

I remember the day Amaya took matters into his own hands. He was about 14, just beginning his transition, and we were on a family trip to New York. We were at a Broadway show and the bathroom lines at intermission were incredibly long. While standing in the line for the women's room, I looked over at the men's line and saw my husband—and to my surprise, Amaya was in line just a few people ahead of him. Gabriel and I looked at each other in acknowledgment of what we were witnessing. This was our child affirming his gender as male. Amaya was looking forward, resolute, and didn't notice us noticing him.

No one else seemed to notice either.

He had made a conscious decision to stand in that line. It was clear he felt more comfortable in the men's line. It was also clear by the utter lack of attention he received that everybody else was also comfortable with him being in the men's line. Had my child been waiting in the women's line with me, he would have received only confused looks and stares. Not one person in the men's line that day batted an eye.

Most individuals know instinctively which bathroom they feel is right for them, and they will choose the one that most closely corresponds to their gender identity. Since that day, my son has used the men's room in all circumstances; thankfully he has never had an issue. He is a trans man with a very masculine presentation. Not all people have that same privilege. Not all people fit into the male/female gender binary. It is not up to the general public to decide for a person which bathroom they should choose.

Denying a trans person the right to use the bathroom that matches their gender identity is an act of discrimination, one that can have devastating consequences. Social media movements in recent years, including conversations grouped by trending hashtags such as #wejustneedtopee and #Illgowithyou, have brought internet attention to the absurdity of laws that would force trans men into the women's room and trans women into the men's room. They just want to be left alone to pee and poop in peace.

To understand the effect these laws have when enacted, just imagine a brawny-looking person with a full beard and bulging muscles. Masculine right? Next, imagine the reaction this person might engender when going into a woman's restroom—which he would have to do to comply with any law mandating which restroom trans people can use. He doesn't want to make anyone uncomfortable. He just needs to pee. And yet, it is certainly likely that someone who sees this apparent male enter the women's room will respond with alarm, possibly even calling security guards or police. Or imagine a tall, average-size person wearing heels, a skirt, and long hair walking into the men's room. Though she identifies as a woman, lives as a woman, and is known to all who interact with her as a woman, a law that says she has to pee in the men's room exposes her to unnecessary and degrading humiliation, and possibly even to assault. Who is this situation unsafe for?! Certainly not the men who are in the men's room with a trans man. Certainly not the women in the women's room with a trans woman. Trans people are not there to alarm anyone. They just need to pee. Yet, in both the scenarios above, the potential for confrontation, embarrassment, harm, and harassment often drives transgender people to withhold their pee for unhealthy periods in order to avoid using public restrooms. As with my son, the fear of being called out in public restrooms can result in depression, and in some cases can contribute to thoughts of loneliness and suicide.

Everyone goes. Everyone should feel safe when they do.

HIGH HOPES FOR HIGH SCHOOL

Amaya, Gabriel, and I took proactive steps to make our son's transition to high school go as smoothly as possible. We asked to meet with the school's administrators before the start of the first semester. After experiencing less-than-ideal support from middle school administrators who were just beginning to understand challenges unique to gender-alternative kids, we wanted to start Amaya's high school years by opening some lines of communication and making sure Amaya would be treated respectfully by faculty and students.

As it turns out, the high school's principal and guidance counselor were very welcoming and supportive. We told them we wanted to write a letter to his new teachers introducing Amaya, saying that although he may look and carry himself as a boy, he was indeed a girl (or at least living as a girl), and so should be referred to and treated as such. The principal and counselor were happy to help distribute such a letter to the teachers. We also talked about how Amaya would use girls' bathrooms and lockers, and they said he was welcome to use the school's office bathrooms as well. We asked if teachers and administrators could be on the lookout for any bullying or teasing or confusion around our child's gender, and we underscored that we did not want Amaya to have a teacher use the wrong pronouns. His woodshop teacher in middle school, for instance, never seemed to get it right, could not grasp that Amaya was (at the time) a girl. We did not want a repeat of any misgendering. The principal and counselor were agreeable and promised to be watchful, proactive, and responsive in the event of any bullying or misgendering.

And so Amaya entered high school in his freshman year as a female. Here is the letter we wrote on 8/20/12.

Dear Teachers,

We are writing to introduce our child Amaya Barkin to you. In our communication with Mr. L—and

Ms. B—we were assured they would communicate with you about her and we hope this has happened. We asked for this to be sure there was no confusion about Amaya on the first day of school.

Amaya is a person who is gender non-conforming. She is a girl who looks and sometimes acts "like a boy." This is in quotes because while there is no one way a boy or a girl acts, there are norms and stereotypes. Amaya is one who is often outside the norm, especially when it comes to appearance. Many people think Amaya is a boy when they meet her. She says she does not mind this and does not really mind what pronoun people use to refer to her. When we meet people we will not see again, for example a server or clerk, we usually do not correct them if they call her a boy. If we are going to have an ongoing relationship with someone, at some point we will inform the individual. We often do this for her, though she has told us she does tell people sometimes. Mostly, she does not want to make a big deal or a fuss so we tell on a need-to-know basis.

She currently defines herself as a girl in that she uses girl bathrooms at school, changes with the girls for PE, and will align with girls whenever there is a split of the group for activities and such. She is known as a girl to her friends, but we know there are children at school she does not really know or hang out with who think she is a boy, and some parents too!

Our main concern is that adults at the school are aware that she is indeed a girl. There is often confusion when people first meet her. There is sometimes discussion and even disbelief or debate. Please watch out for this and be proactive if you ever hear debate or even discussion, or especially teasing.

There are many ways a classroom teacher can support those like Amaya who are outside the norm with regard to gender expression. One way to support Amaya and others like her is to be mindful, when dividing up groups, to use ways other than gender as the separating factor. Another idea is to use words other than pronouns "he"/"she" to refer to individuals. Of course, there are many other ways, and we hope her teachers will explore ideas and share them with each other, and with us.

To support the San Marin staff in regards to this subject, we have donated a copy of the book The Transgender Child by Stephanie Brill. This is a great reference book. While Amaya does not consider herself transgender as such, she does fall on the spectrum of gender expression that is described so well in the book. We highly recommend this book and hope you will take a look at it. If you need another copy to share amongst yourselves, you can borrow ours. Another great book is Gender Born, Gender Made by Diane Ehrensaft.

Thank you so much for your time and consideration in this matter. After school gets underway, we will get in touch again to see if you have any questions, concerns, etc. Hope the school year gets off to a great start!

With regards,
Janna and Gabriel Barkin

The letter was well received, and we were assured the teachers and administrators would keep a good eye on our child. Freshman year is often challenging enough, as those kids become the youngest ones in school again after living high-on-the-hog as eighth graders. Amaya blended in for the most part because anyone who didn't know him just saw him as a boy. But because he looked like a boy, it was challenging for him to use the female bathroom or locker rooms without being noticed. Though he had been using male restrooms outside of school for a few months now, he was not ready to make that shift at school. I think it was very overwhelming and scary to him. He had known many of the kids in his school for *so* long, and he just didn't want to be judged, or made fun of, or to have to deal with whatever other reactions people might have in response to him using the male facilities.

Grades and keeping up in school had never been a problem for Amaya, and that didn't change in high school. Even so, he told us he felt anxious in classes; he felt he just couldn't sit still. (It didn't help that a few of his teachers did not seem to have control of their classes, by all reports, and there was not much teaching or learning going on in those classrooms. But Amaya was never reported as the cause of any of those issues; rather, the impact was that he felt those classes were an inefficient waste of time.) As the school year progressed, his anxiety increased. It was common for Amaya to have stomach aches on Sunday evenings, and more than a few times he called me or Gabe from school to say that he didn't feel well and asked if he could go home. We even took him to the doctor to check out his stomach aches. He was sent him home with a prescription for antacids. They helped a little, but did not root out the source of the problem. I knew in my heart that the issue did not have a physical cause.

Thankfully, Amaya had a steady group of friends during freshman year whom he'd known throughout (and in some cases before) middle school. This group was Amaya's "safe place"; when he was with those friends, some of them lifelong "besties" to this day, he could be himself and his anxieties abated. The group were mostly girls with just a few boys in the mix. By this time a few of the kids in the group had come out, within the circle and sometimes within their own family, as gay or bisexual. Amaya easily blended with these kids. Their parents were also accepting of Amaya, and he felt welcome in their homes. Amaya later said he once had a realization that many of his friends were "part of the community." ("Community" here means the LGBTQ community and their allies.) He hadn't consciously sought such company, but it's not surprising to any of us in retrospect that he felt comfortable with those kids.

As it turned out, Amaya made it through freshman year without any significant incident, and he received his usual As and Bs. Gabriel and I were proud of his studies as always, and we were equally glad he was socially active with kids who were also good students and responsible young adults. (Well, they were good for the most part, but of course they were kids, and we're not naïve.) But as I will tell you next, the summer after freshman year brought its own excitement. That tale is captured here in a story titled *Texas*, in which a mother and her son take a trip to a distant land and encounter...well, some Texans.

TEXAS

Yes, Texas. Mind you, I have nothing against Texas *per se*. I certainly know there are good people everywhere, and Gabe and I have friends in Texas. I mean no insult to any reader who hails from the state. Still, Amaya and I did have quite a time in Texas, and the story is worth sharing here.

As his freshman high school year wore on, Amaya continued to struggle with the way his body had changed as a result of puberty. As I've recounted, by this point he no longer inhabited an androgynous child's body, and he'd begun binding his growing breasts and wearing several layers of shirts and sweatshirts in order to hide his chest. He already knew he wanted top surgery (removal of the breasts and creation of a male chest) immediately, if not sooner. He was meeting regularly with counselor Cristin Brew.

He was also active online, and he had begun chatting with other teens he'd met in social chat rooms—identifying himself now as a guy! As I mentioned earlier, I did not know this was happening at the time, as he spent a lot of time surfing the web on his phone while alone in his room and usually behind a closed door. My husband and I believe in giving our kids space and privacy (within certain limits, of course), and while we often discussed with him how to be safe online in general, we did not snoop into his online affairs.

One day Amaya came to me and asked if he could visit his friends in Texas.

The request came completely out of the blue. Friends in Texas? What friends? Do we know *anyone* in Texas?!

Amaya began to tell me what was up. Apparently, he'd established online friendships with three girls his age who lived in Texas. The kids had been meeting in video chat rooms, so each of them was able to see what the other kids looked like. He'd met one of the moms online as well. These friends, and the mom too, all knew Amaya to be a boy. One of the girls even became Amaya's "girlfriend." (How do people "date" online?! Apparently this has been a "thing" with teens for some time. To me this was like having a pen pal.) Remember, in our family and at school, Amaya was still identifying as a girl who looked like a boy, so Amaya's report was full of all sorts of new facts for me to parse and digest.

Amaya went on to explain his newfound relationships to me, including his choice to come out as his birth sex, female, with these strangers to whom he had first presented himself as male. He told me that as the relationship with the girlfriend had blossomed, he'd told her that he was born as a girl and is transgender. She didn't take it well at first, and told him she felt betrayed. She said she was breaking up with him and that she needed to "think about it" before resuming any relationship at all. (For ease of storytelling, I will continue to refer to this young lady as "the girlfriend.")

Although he said he understood her feelings, the truth is that Amaya was crushed. (No wonder I'd sensed he was depressed in the weeks prior to him coming to me!) But he remained in contact with the two other girls from Texas, and they continued to use his newly preferred male pronouns. Eventually, the girlfriend wrote a handwritten letter to Amaya and sent it through the US Mail. (Yes, you read that correctly: a 14-year-old sent something through the US Mail!) The letter told how she'd come to accept and embrace Amaya for who he is, and that she wanted to be friends.

He hung the letter on his wall and decided he *must* go visit the former girlfriend and the other friends. Once again he came to me. He showed me the letter. He told me about his online presence as a male. My mind was reeling, I'd had no idea any of this was happening. The former girlfriend had written, "I love you for who you are not your parts." *Wow!* There I was in the kitchen, standing next to Amaya when he showed me that letter, my heart blown wide open and tears flowing down my face.

And that is when he said, "So I want to go to visit them in Texas this summer."

This request shocked me and I did not know what to say. My gut reaction was to say NO! I also wanted to say, "Have you seen *Boys Don't Cry*?!" That's the movie that tells the true story of Brandon Teena, an FTM man who was murdered in 1993 in Nebraska. "Do you know about the South and Texas?!" (I know I was making assumptions and throwing around stereotypes about Texas and its reputation of non-acceptance toward LGBT people, but I was a bit shell-shocked, and fear was my first reaction.) But my son pleaded. With tears in his eyes (very, *very* rare), he said, "I want to see them and meet them in person, they are my best friends."

Best friends. Those words hung in the air. Here he was telling me that there are people who know him as a boy, and that he is transgender. And they accept him for who he is, even after he shared his secret, his truth.

My husband, Gabriel, and I were so conflicted. Visit strangers in a far-away place (Texas, no less) whom our child had met online? Even in light of the obvious warning flags, we felt we needed to consider the request carefully. When your child, who in recent years had spent a lot of time holed up in his room instead of going out with friends, says, "They are my best friends," a NO can shift into a *maybe*. It did not feel good to make a decision based on fear. We called Amaya's counselor, Cristin, for advice, and she agreed we should all come in together to discuss this emergent request.

(To be clear, even at this point, we knew we would only acquiesce to letting Amaya anywhere near these kids after much verification of these friends' identities, and their respective parents' approval of such a visit; and certainly one of us would be accompanying Amaya. I mean, we're not *that* crazy. More on the parental approvals later.)

It was at this meeting that Gabriel and I really began to understand how important these online relationships were to our child and his development. As Cristin pointed out, he'd found a way to explore his gender identity. He'd found friends who accepted him as male. In fact, Cristin acknowledged to me and Gabe that she'd been aware of Amaya's online social activities, and in some way that comforted us. She said online experimentation like this is a common way for teens to explore their gender without any outward change in daily life—a way to "try it on." We opened our minds to the idea that this was a healthy way for Amaya to come around to understanding himself.

With encouragement and advice from Cristin, I decided it was time to meet over the phone with the mother of the erstwhile girlfriend. As it turns out, this mom already knew all about their online relationship, Amaya's revelation, the breakup, and the subsequent friendship. She told me that she was proud her daughter was able to be so accepting of Amaya. She was quite forthcoming, and told me she and the girlfriend's dad were divorced. He was a minister and more conservative than her. She also mentioned that when she found out Amaya was assigned female at birth, she'd started using female pronouns in reference to Amaya, out of respect. (We were just beginning our pronoun switch at home and Amaya didn't want to push it too fast, so I said nothing about that.) The mom assured me that we were welcome to visit.

After I got off the phone with her, I felt good. I felt like we were about to take off on an adventure, my kid and me. We would spend time together and connect with people from a different part of the country. I also felt excited to be going with him to friends who knew him as a boy. With Gabriel's hesitant blessing and after he and I had much discussion, we made our plans.

I made plans for us to stay at a hotel near the girlfriend's house, which was an hour from Dallas airport. I had planned at first to rent a car, but the mom insisted she pick us up from the airport, and bring us back as well at the end of our stay. The other two friends would meet us over the weekend, so Amaya would get to see all his Texan friends. The mom said she had some ideas about things we could do together. She spoke of a town with a street fair and a community that was very accepting and had all sorts of folks; she felt it would be a good environment for us to explore. It sounded like we were going to have a fun time.

Then things started to go south. The night before we flew, the mom texted me to say she wasn't feeling well and might not be able to pick us up. Still, she assured us we should come; she was positive she'd feel better. We were all ready to go, and we'd lose a lot of money spent on plane tickets if we had to cancel, but Gabe and I thought it was probably a bad idea to go if our host was ill. However, faced with that prospect, Amaya was completely heartbroken, and the mom kept saying she was sure she would feel fine the next day, and that we should come. So in the end, we decided to go. I switched our hotel reservation so we could stay near the airport (and not have to drive all the way to the hotel near the girlfriend's house when we landed, just in case the mom was still ill), and the mom agreed to bring her daughter to meet us at our new hotel the next day.

It turned out the mom continued to feel unwell that night, even after we'd landed in Dallas. Amaya and the friend communicated back and forth online, and it became apparent from the girlfriend's messages that what her mom was experiencing was not a physical illness; rather, she was feeling a lot of emotional distress about our visit. Still, the kids texted each other all evening and into the morning, and the plan remained that mom and friends were coming to meet us at the hotel for lunch.

Amaya was clearly excited and nervous to meet his new friends. I was nervous and anxious about the way things were going.

I could tell something was not right as soon as the mom arrived with her daughter and one of the other friends. I took the mom aside while the kids were greeting each other in the flesh (at long last!). She said her older daughters had seen their sibling's comments, on Facebook, about the visit. They knew about the online relationship and why the kids broke up, and they knew about Amaya—and they did not approve. They had been threatening to tell the dad what was going on—

that a transgender kid was visiting. The mom was clearly afraid of that possibility. She said the older girls believed allowing the girlfriend and Amaya to see each other would turn their sister into a lesbian. The mom said she was afraid the older siblings were going to come find us and "make trouble," so she was not sure where to take us.

We found a place near the hotel for lunch but no one really ate. The mom kept stepping out to talk on her phone or smoke a cigarette. I found it very odd that she had invited us to come—and in fact had *insisted* we come—but then did not have a clue as to where we could go or what we could do. I asked if we could just go to a mall or a park. She could not make a decision. Finally, we ended up going to a nearby park, but it was really too hot. She wouldn't let the kids out of our sight, so the teens were bored. The situation got more and more uncomfortable, and finally I suggested we go back to our hotel. At least it was a place where the kids could interact in a safe public space (and also it wouldn't be so hot).

We sat for a while in the hotel lobby and tried to make the best of the situation, but the mom was more and more on edge. She couldn't sit still and, as at lunch, kept stepping outside to smoke cigarettes, and to text and talk on her phone. Her fear of being "caught" by her other daughter or her ex was palpable. I think she wanted to make it work in her heart, but she wasn't able to stand up to this part of her family.

When she pulled the two Texas girls outside with her at some point to check in with them, I told Amaya that it was time to be done, the situation was just too uncomfortable. We walked outside and I told the mom that I felt we needed to end today's get-together, and she agreed. She then proceeded to make all sorts of excuses for her edgy behavior, including an admission that she'd been raised by a Grand Master of the Ku Klux Klan. Yep, the Klan. Shocked, I responded with something incomplete like, "Well our family is Jewish so..." Both she and I were crying as the kids said their goodbyes, and that was that.

I was quite shell-shocked and wanted to call off the meet-up we had planned for the next day with the third Texan friend and her mom. I felt protective and remorseful and tired and frustrated. Amaya felt differently, and he was begging me to go forward with our plan for the next day. At dinner we had a very deep conversation about our challenging meet-up. It was apparent my son was learning that we did indeed live in a San Francisco Bay Area bubble, and not everyone everywhere was open and understanding toward people who were different from them, especially toward LGBT people. My son, ever persistent and logical, insisted the third friend's mom would be completely different, and after much cajoling he convinced me to meet them for lunch before we flew home. I think I was just looking for any way to salvage the effort we had made in travelling so far from home.

I was really glad we did meet this other friend and her mom, as they were very welcoming and helpful. This mom also offered to come pick us up, take us to lunch, and then back to the airport, and she did not worry herself sick trying to welcome us Californians. It was comforting to receive her hospitality after our trying day. We had a lovely lunch together and I was grateful to end on a positive note. Amaya of course was so glad we didn't blow off this last friend.

Oh Texas! Our trip wasn't pretty, but it was a big reality check and growth experience for both of us. Travelling out of our comfort zone made both me and Amaya even more appreciative for the unwavering support our family and friends have offered throughout our son's life. It was heartbreaking that my son had to learn this reality: that not everyone is open and accepting; that not everyone has the tools to be welcoming to those different than themselves; that not everyone is given the support they need to be who they are, nor a safe environment in which to explore themselves. It was also scary to be told that there were people who wanted to "make trouble." Eyes opened.

Sadly, my fears are reinforced by statistics. The high rates of hate crimes (including assault and murder) perpetrated against transgender and other gender non-conforming people are alarming.[19] Transgender youth are the most at risk for suicide attempts.[20] Many end up on the streets because they do not have support from their families. Often they have been kicked out of their own homes by unaccepting parents.[21] The current push in some states to regulate which bathrooms transgender people should use is evidence that there are many more hurdles for transgender people to jump over before they can live safely and comfortably as their authentic selves.

As of this writing, it has been over four years since our trip to Texas. At this time, I don't think my son has much contact (other than perhaps the occasional Facebook "Like") with any of the Texan friends. Kids grow older, friendships move on, especially those that are not cemented by proximity. I can only hope that our journey to Texas somehow led to an opening in the hearts of the people we met in the Lone Star State.

———— COMING OUT IS A PROCESS ————

EMAIL TO AMAYA'S THERAPIST, CRISTIN BREW, 9/3/13

Hi Cristin,

Hope all is well with you. I wanted to catch you up on a few things.

First is that we have been asked by Amaya to try using the male pronoun at home and we have been trying, practice, practice. I will practice here.

Amaya has asked to move out of regular school and into independent study with NOVA [the name of independent study school]. He is uncomfortable and unhappy at school, feels disconnected, and has admitted to overall feeling of depression.

(I am so sad right now.)

While we are open to the change in school we are worried about the overall feeling he has and if it is the right move as he is already isolated, save for school.

We are really concerned about the lack of peer interaction there will be if he starts independent study, and at the same time we can see how being out of a stressful environment would really help. He told us that none of her friends have been reaching out to him for a long time, and that while they can hang out at school he has grown away from his friends and does not feel he can make new ones. No one shares his interests, but he cannot say really what his interests are.

Maybe the support group will offer what he needs from peers right now.

He is willing to go to the support group now. We said that has to happen if we are to go ahead with the idea of NOVA (which we have not agreed to yet but we are researching it).

So much more to say but better maybe to just talk. Maybe a phone chat would be good before you see him Thursday?

As his sophomore year approached, the end of summer was an anxious time for Amaya, as it is for most kids anticipating the start of a new school year. But for my son it was different. Each school year brought the challenge of meeting new teachers. Each year now, Gabe and I would reach out to inform his new teachers about Amaya. We remained worried that a teacher would be confused when they met Amaya, setting the stage for embarrassing or awkward moments of misgendering. Although Amaya had already asked us to start using male pronouns at home, he was still using female pronouns at school. In his teachers' roll books, his name would be marked with an "F" for female, but the teachers would see a boy answer to the name. This was a challenging place to be, living in the in-between.

We again sent off our introductory letter to Amaya's new teachers, the same letter we'd sent the previous year. Since he had not yet asked to transition pronouns or anything else at school, Amaya would start the school year identified as a "girl," would use the bathrooms and lockers designated for girls, and the teachers would be asked to be mindful to use the correct pronouns and watch for any signs of bullying or distress.

The stomach aches persisted. His anxiety increased. He didn't want to do much with friends or family. Although he'd found support in his social group during his freshman year, Amaya was not hanging out with the local gang very much, spending less and less time with the kids in that crowd as the freshman year wound down and the summer wore on. The trip to Texas may have contributed to Amaya's funk too; he'd been focused on those new, online friendships, but now the bloom was off the rose and he wasn't so excited about his Texas "besties." As he had before high school, he was holing up in his room frequently.

A few weeks into the school year, Amaya asked to talk with me and Gabe. He told us he wanted to start using male pronouns at home. "Finally!" was my reaction. We had been waiting for this definitive shift. It was time. It did take some practice to change the pronouns from *she* to *he*, from *his* to *hers*. We had been using female pronouns for so long it took a lot of practice to use male pronouns. We had always called our two daughters "*the girls*." *The girls* became *the kids*.

We quickly agreed to his request. We knew this was a big moment in our child's transition and certainly we wanted to show him our support as we knew how important it would be to his health and well-being. Statistics show that the number one factor in a transgender or gender non-conforming teen's overall mental, emotional, physical, and social well-being is the support of parents and family members.[22]

The idea of changing his pronouns at school was intimidating and overwhelming for Amaya. It was more and more stressful for him to be referred to with female pronouns as he grew older. Gabriel and I told him we were fully supportive, and that we would do all the work to make sure the teachers, administrators, and other students at school would start using male pronouns in reference to him. It was a lot for Amaya to think of making such a big statement at his school. He had known many of the kids in our school district for all of his school days, and he did not want to make a big deal and call attention to himself. The idea of "coming out" freaked him out. He just wanted to *be*.

In true Amaya style, he told us he'd found a way. As mentioned in my email to Cristin above, he said he wanted to leave his current high school and enroll in NOVA, an independent study program run by our school district. He told us he'd already talked to his school guidance counselor to get information about the program. At NOVA, he would be responsible for his own school work, and he'd be meeting with a teacher weekly. He'd be able to structure his days as he wanted and work at his own pace. (In addition to his other concerns, Amaya was not at all a "morning person"; Gabe and I were aware that natural rhythms make early morning classes challenging for some students who perform better later in the day, so we had some sympathy for him setting his own schedule.)

Amaya reminded us how anxious he had been feeling in his classes, and how exhausted he felt from having to get up so early every day for school. When he told us it was getting harder and harder for him to be living as "he" at home but as "she" at school, tears came to his eyes. Mine too.

As with all the big changes Amaya wanted to make, Gabriel and I were hesitant at first. It seemed like a lot of responsibility for him to do all his work independently, and we did not want to be in a watchdog position all the time. He assured us he would willingly meet with a teacher once per week and be held accountable for keeping up with his work. We were also concerned about the idea of him being alone so much. It seemed like a way of withdrawing, and very isolating. I was concerned about what might happen to his social connections.

Amaya had done his research and had his answers prepared. He explained that NOVA did not offer the higher-level math classes and so he would have to continue to attend his high school for these classes, and for foreign language (he studied Spanish). He would co-enroll in both schools, the one he'd attended the previous year as well as the new independent study program. He would see his friends when he attended classes on campus, and would eat lunch with them.

We felt we wanted a bit more commitment; we wanted to be sure he wasn't just getting a "get out of school" pass. So he agreed to attend a support group facilitated by his counselor, Cristin Brew—he had resisted this until now. He was even willing to do yoga with me to earn his PE credit! Yoga! (That one was the real kicker as he had not been willing to do any yoga with me for many years. I teach yoga—it's a passion of mine, and I love having my family practice with me! So I say, well played, Amaya, well played.) Gabriel and I could see Amaya had thought this out. We could feel his distress, his desperation. We could also feel his excitement about this new possibility. We agreed to meet the principal at NOVA.

Upon meeting NOVA's principal, Kessa Early, we knew Amaya had made a good choice. Warm and welcoming, Ms. Early set a tone right off the bat that told us, "We can do this." Her job as the principal of NOVA, as well as Marin Oaks Academy (the district's school for underperforming but promising students) is challenging but rewarding. The two schools are designed to meet the needs of students who, for different reasons, are not a good fit for the traditional school model. Some are travelling athletes, or dancers, or musicians. Some have full-time jobs and need a more flexible school schedule. Others are physically ill and cannot attend school daily. Many kids in these categories end up at NOVA. Other kids may have mental or emotional challenges that make it difficult for them to find their way at the traditional school, and Marin Oaks provides an appropriate environment for those kids to excel. Some students are mandated to attend Marin Oaks because they have broken the law. The reasons for attending either of these two schools are unique for each student.

Ms. Early assured us of her strong feeling that NOVA would be a good fit for Amaya. In her words:

It is my responsibility to ensure that each and every student feels safe is this learning environment. I use the word "safe" in the broad sense of physical, emotional, and academic protection. In order for students to learn and function successfully, they must feel completely safe and supported in their environment.

The school environment is comprised of both staff members and students. Therefore, part of my responsibility as principal is to ensure that our entire community has access to a wide range of informative experiences—classroom speakers, appropriate seminars, and counseling services.

Prior to accepting the job as principal, I taught a health science class at Novato High School. I first learned about the experience of transgender people from one of the classroom speakers associated with a group called

Spectrum of Marin. When we speak of "diversity," we often refer only to ethnicity or religion. By definition however, "diversity" also means the inclusion of such characteristics as socioeconomic level and sexual orientation. And so it is with transgender students.

I consider our public school system to be the great "equalizer" in this country. Our backgrounds, families, and experiences are as diverse as our population. But well-run schools can level that playing field, offering all students equal access within a safe, supportive learning environment. Former President Obama is a perfect example. In spite of his ethnicity and nontraditional upbringing, he persevered, succeeded, and achieved—ultimately rising to the highest elected position possible. I believe that the educational opportunities granted him had everything to do with his success. If we can address all student needs—academic, emotional, and psychological—the sky is the limit for our students! (Kessa Early, personal communication, November 17, 2016)

After our discussion with Ms. Early, Gabriel and I felt much better about Amaya attending NOVA. We quickly came to realize that attending this school would provide an opportunity for him to start over, as *him*self. All of the teachers, and most of the students, were people he would be meeting for the first time. As far as the academic component, Amaya had always been a good student, and we didn't have any cause to think that would change. We decided to let him go for it.

Amaya enrolled in NOVA at the start of his sophomore year. True to expectations, we found it was a great match. He got along well with his teacher, who told us she found Amaya to be bright, mature, and self-motivated.

He continued to attend his math and Spanish classes at his old high school, and he saw his school friends at lunch, after school, and on the weekends. Gabriel was telecommuting from home a few days each week at the time, and for the first month or two, my guys sat at our kitchen table together for a few hours each day, working side by side in a silence punctuated only rarely by a request for help from Amaya. And yes, he even practiced his yoga with me in the mornings.

Attending NOVA provided the space Amaya needed to transition. We proceeded to request that the gender marker be changed from female to male on his school documents, and the school district agreed without hesitation. We sent another letter to his new teachers at the old school—certainly a different letter than the one we'd sent the prior year, now affirming his male identity and asking for the use of male pronouns when referring to Amaya. A while later, when he had his top surgery, both schools were very understanding and supportive. He was able to make up his work in his own time. He kept up his good work throughout his first two semesters at NOVA, and finished his sophomore year with high marks: one B+ and the rest all As.

A LETTER TO OUR FAMILY

Within a week or two after Amaya asked us to start using male pronouns at home, Gabriel and I sent email messages to our parents, siblings, and closest friends so we could tell them the news and ask for support. The following version of our letter was sent specifically to my mother and brothers, as we were going to be seeing them shortly at Thanksgiving.

EMAIL FROM ME AND GABE TO FAMILY AND FRIENDS, FALL 2013

Hi Family!

We are so excited to come for Thanksgiving! I want to share some important information regarding Amaya so you can be prepared when we see you.

As we all know, Amaya is who Amaya is, an awesome person! Also, Amaya is a person born as a girl who has always presented outwardly as a boy, but has always been called a girl.

In the last year Amaya has been exploring his gender identity, and has now asked us to use male pronouns at home. We are fully behind Amaya as we support him and feel it is important to follow Amaya's lead, which is what we have always done. We use "he and him" as much as we can now, and it feels right, but "she and her" still come out. It is a stretch for our brains, which are very used to using "she or her." We are practicing and it is getting smoother all the time.

One way Amaya has taken the lead has been to move into NOVA, the independent study school in our district. He can attend fewer classes in person at the high school and do the rest of his schooling independently. He meets with a teacher to guide him once a week, and has a science lab once a week. At this school he is known as a boy and treated as such. He has been very focused and is doing really well in school now.

Amaya has not changed his gender pronouns at the original high school where he goes for math and creative writing. This idea is very intimidating to Amaya. All the kids and parents that have known Amaya since kindergarten would have to adjust. Most would be good with it, as many have known Amaya to be the way he is all this time. But, I am sure some would be not so cool about it, and the last thing Amaya wants is to make a big deal anywhere.

When we are out in public Amaya is always, and has always been, seen as male. It is easy for him to pass in public and he has been doing so. We stopped correcting people many years ago, but informed people on an as-needed basis. Now we are not informing unless Amaya wants to. This has made life much easier in many ways as we used to get attitude and even arguments about Amaya's gender from strangers!

Amaya feels happy with the way it is going so far. When we visit, we will be using "he" and "him," but you may hear the opposite too, as we are still re-patterning our brains. Amaya would like us all to use male pronouns, but most of all does not want to make anyone uncomfortable. So, if "she" comes out but you meant to say "he," don't worry, Amaya says there is no reason to apologize. He really wants us all to do what is comfortable, but I know "he" is the preferred pronoun. Amaya also likes "dude" or "man" and whatever else goes with being male. If you are still getting used to the idea and want to still use "she" that is fine too.

As far as the kids go, we imagine that the younger cousins already see Amaya as male, and the very youngest will be meeting Amaya for the first time. Of course, the older cousins will each process in his or her unique way. We will leave it up to you as parents to communicate with them, and trust you will, but if you need any words or ideas on how to do this, please let me know. There are great resources out there and we can share them with you.

Please do not hesitate to ask us any questions or share any concerns. Please also feel comfortable talking to Amaya about this, but privately rather than in a group. Knowing all of you, we know you will do your best to support Amaya because you love Amaya.

See you soon.

Love, Janna and Gabriel

THE GIRLS

by Gabriel Barkin, Amaya's father

In retrospect, it wasn't too difficult to transition from using "she" to using "he." After Amaya asked us to switch pronouns at home, I think I was getting it right about half the time within a few weeks, and I probably hit 90 percent accuracy within a few months. Remarkably, I believe that just changing the words I was using from "she," and "her," and "girl" to their masculine counterparts was very powerful relative to how I actually *thought* about my child; the conscious shift from one gender to the other produced a mental shift that accelerated my conceptualization of my child as male. Now, several years later, words like "son," "dude," and "my boy" come out of my mouth without filter or stumble; they are simply the right words.

Well, mostly. The female pronouns slip out frequently when I speak of times gone by, the days of our children's youth, when Amaya was still a "girl" (albeit a very tomboyish one). The hardest change for me to overcome verbally has been my use of the collective phrase "the girls." This was the phrase we used to refer to our two younger children for, oh, about 14 years. You know, "What are the girls doing?" "I'm taking the girls to a movie." "The girls want ice cream." Always "the girls."

Even now, when I tell a family story about a trip or a birthday party or pretty much anything that happened before Amaya was about ten or 12, "the girls" slips out. Sometimes I notice it and correct myself. But sometimes the memory is drenched in the *then* and not the *now*, the imagery in my head inseparably intertwined with my thoughts and feelings of the era. I'm telling a story and

I am there, transported nostalgically (after all, isn't that what nostalgia is all about?), remembering and watching and holding and loving my children.

But really, they were never "the girls." Amaya was always my son.

"IS HE CHANGING HIS NAME?"

Amaya was named for the two most important men in my life when I was growing up: my father, Aaron, and my grandfather, Joseph. My son's name means a lot to me, and I am grateful that Amaya chose to keep his name when he transitioned. I know it can add to the difficulties for parents when their children change their names during transition. For many parents, the names we chose for our children hold special meaning, hence a name change is often one of the most difficult adjustments. I can understand the grief that often emerges for parents who hold those newly abandoned names dear. Because we love and support our children, we often do have to let go of many of our dreams, our expectations, and even our *perceptions*, of who are children are.

Here is an email exchange between my mother and me shortly after our family's first visit following Amaya's pronoun change:

EMAIL FROM MY MOTHER TO ME, 12/2/13

Hi Janna,

Here's something interesting...was talking with someone about Amaya. He said his name is really feminine and can cause confusion. I told him I'd suggested to you that he use Jael, but that Amaya doesn't like that name. He said, "Why not just AJ?" Well, funny thing, but all day yesterday and today when I think of Amaya, I think "AJ" and then it becomes so easy to use male pronouns. What might Amaya think of that? I think he doesn't want to change his name but it might be something to ponder.

Love you, Mom

EMAIL TO MY MOTHER, 12/3/13

I think it is interesting that people still want to put Amaya into a binary system, as in "if he is male he should use a male name." I will say the same thing here that I say to people when they bring up the same thing to me: Amaya likes his name and for now he is keeping it. He does not like the nickname AJ (never has), and he is most likely not going to change his name in the near future. There is no reason why he should have to. That may make it easier for others, but Amaya needs to stay true to Amaya. (And frankly, everyone who does not know Amaya sees Amaya as male and often, they even comment at what a cool and interesting name he has.)

If we look at a person as more of an open slate rather than having to fit everyone into a binary system, then we can have boys who wear skirts and girls who have penises and boys who have feminine names and girls who have masculine names.

Having a "masculine" name might make it easier for others to adjust, but right now that doesn't feel necessary for Amaya in Amaya's mind and heart.

Feel free to share that. And also to share thoughts with me.

Love, Janna

Many people who transition do change their name. On the other hand, some say that their old name does not fit their gender identity. Some call their old name their "dead" name—and some say it is an act of violence to refer to someone by their "dead" name, as it can trigger an episode of dysphoria. For some parents of transgender children, it can be very difficult to let go of the name they chose for their child. Some may grieve the loss of this name as they process all the changes that gender transition brings.

Amaya says he kept his name because he likes it and feels connected to it. When he first transitioned, there were those (usually adults, not kids his age) who asked, "Why doesn't he want to change his name?" They'd say, "Wouldn't it make it easier?" Or they'd challenge his decision: "Isn't he changing his name? It seems so feminine." My response was always, "Easier for whom?!"

Amaya said to me a few years ago, "Thanks for giving me a gender neutral name."

I said "I'm glad you feel that way." And that was that.

TOP SURGERY

When I began my research about top surgery, I found that there were *many* people who had been documenting their transition process on YouTube. (I will note that none were as young as my teen.) It was from these video testimonials that I learned many people hired one physician in particular, a surgeon named Dr. Michael Brownstein, to perform their procedures. Dr. Brownstein was highly recommended in this circle. At the time, he had been caring for transgender people for 30 years. Even better, he was located in nearby San Francisco.

I did not contact the surgeon's office right away when I first heard of his expertise and success. I just wasn't ready yet. I wanted to buy some time. Top surgery is *major* surgery, and it's permanent. I knew in my heart Amaya would want to have this surgery one day, but I wasn't sure yet that it was appropriate for him at age 14. I also wasn't sure how we would pay for a $10,000 procedure if our medical insurance wouldn't cover it. While Amaya continued his counseling with Cristin, Gabriel and I got to work exploring our options as parents and also as financiers for such a venture.

It took me many months to come around to and support Amaya's surgery. This was a difficult decision. I was nervous. How do I know this is the right decision? Is my child old enough to make this life-changing choice? I talked to doctors, family members, friends, and even friends of friends. One close friend's perspective was to the point: "Sure, why not lop 'em off?!" This was a refreshing perspective. It helped me let go of attachment and open my heart to what needed to be done.

Another key conversation was with a friend of a friend. This woman's child, Eli, was the first person under 18 years old in California to be approved by her insurance company for sex reassignment surgery (SRS). Eli's family's journey was not easy. The mother had to fight in court to have the insurance agency cover her daughter's medically necessary SRS surgery. She won that right and set a precedent for all trans youth in California. Eli Erlick is now a trans rights activist who, along with Alex Sennello, started the vital resource Trans Student Educational Resource (TSER) in 2011.[23] She is a leader of her generation; surely, Eli is making an impact in the fight for the rights of trans students.

When I spoke with Eli's mom, who happens to be a physician, she told me that at first she was not on board with the notion that her child was transgender. She said she had considered herself very open-minded, and she had no qualms to think her child might be gay. But *transgender*? That was a different story. When Eli first came out to her as transgender, she said she was not open to, nor accepting of, the news at all. At the time there were no transgender youth role models in our culture. Eli's mom told me she had a change of heart when she realized just how seriously her child was suffering. Eli, just like Amaya, had been diagnosed with gender dysphoria; she was depressed, and things were just getting worse as she grew older. Eli's mom knew she needed to take action. Her child's life depended on it.

One piece of advice Eli's mom offered was exactly what I needed at that time to spur me into action. I shared with her my struggle over making this permanent decision. Since Amaya was under 18, a parent's signature would be needed to approve the surgery. I knew Amaya felt very strongly that surgery was necessary—and in my heart of hearts, I did too. Still, I thought I would have felt better if he was already 18 and could just make the decision on his own as an adult. Then I wouldn't have the responsibility of signing off on the choice. But Eli's mom told me there was no better time to do the surgery other than *right now*. She pointed out that by doing it *now*, before he went off to college, I would be able to be involved, to help prepare him for the process beforehand and take care of him after, both physically and emotionally. She said it was the perfect opportunity to support his affirmation of his authentic self before he went off to college. She said, "You are preparing to launch your transgender child.

What could be more important than helping him realize his true self?" Yes, I thought, I was preparing to do just that, and knew I needed to get in gear.

I contacted the office of Dr. Brownstein in September of 2013, only to find out that Dr. Brownstein was retiring and passing on his practice to Dr. Curtis Crane. Dr. Crane had recently joined Dr. Brownstein's practice. I was assured by an office person on the phone that Dr. Crane was highly qualified, and that he was accustomed to working with youth. I still wasn't sure if I felt right about making this permanent decision regarding my child at this point. But we knew we needed to do something. We made an appointment with Dr. Crane for December 9.

Dr. Crane is a friendly man with a big head of curly, on-its-way-to-gray hair. In his office for that first meeting, he immediately put us at ease. He was dressed in blue-gray scrubs and at first he spoke directly to Amaya. He asked Amaya why he wanted top surgery. Amaya told him it was because he was very uncomfortable with his chest. He said he felt like "they" (his breasts) didn't belong there, and he explained that he had been binding his chest for some time.

Dr. Crane told us about his experience and expertise. An innovator in his field, Dr. Crane is both a plastic surgeon and a urologist. In addition to these specialties, he had completed several fellowships in transgender care by the time we met him. When I asked him recently what he found compelling about working with trans youth in particular, Dr. Crane told me he is "drawn to the excitement of giving this young person, the next generation, a healthy start on their life." He described hearing the same story from parents time and time again, the story of children who were happy during their early years, but who suffered from deep, profound depression and disconnection with their bodies when puberty hit. He said surgical procedures are "normalizing for a person so they can be comfortable in their body. They can go out and be who they are."

At our first meeting, Dr. Crane told us he was happy to hear that Amaya was in counseling, as a therapist's approval would be necessary in order to proceed with the surgery. He said he would not proceed with any gender-related surgery unless a mental health practitioner had seen the patient regularly for at least a year. He also said he has to feel confident the patient, no matter their age, was physically, mentally, and emotionally stable and resilient enough to handle the surgery and recovery.

Because Amaya was under 18, we also needed approval from our insurance company's medical board. Dr. Crane advised us that people who want to undergo SRS typically must live and be identified as their affirmed gender for a year *and* they must begin hormone therapy before they undergo surgery. Even though Amaya had not yet changed his pronouns in every sphere of his life, Dr. Crane agreed to do Amaya's surgery because he had the full support of his parents—and because we, along with his primary doctor and his therapist, agreed that this was a necessary step for Amaya to free himself from gender dysphoria. Dr. Crane said his office would do the appeal to the insurance company's medical board on our behalf.

I felt encouraged, yet still I was hesitant. At our first meeting, I told Dr. Crane my concerns and said, "I am nervous about the surgery itself." He replied reassuringly: "That's okay, I'm not."

Although some might interpret his response as cocky or overconfident, I was comforted. On the way home from our meeting with Dr. Crane, Amaya said he was ready "yesterday," and he asked when we could have the surgery scheduled. Gabriel was very matter-of-fact about the situation (Amaya gets his cool head from his father), and he said he felt we were in good hands with Dr. Crane.

After much research and counseling over the next few days, we agreed with Amaya that for the benefit of his emotional health and well-being, it was best he have top surgery to remove his breasts and create a male chest. We all agreed Dr. Crane was the surgeon we wanted to work with. The next day I made the call to get our child the chest he was meant to have.

A reflection: I can see now, as I write our story, that there were times when I went into a bit of a "denial and delay" mode. This mode would arise whenever Amaya brought a new phase of his transition to our attention. So true to form, my first response to his request for top surgery was to deny and delay. Despite all the times we'd struggled to find bras that were comfortable, those trips to Macy's or Target always ending in tears or fits, I was still resistant. It was hard for me to wrap my mind around the fact that my child wanted surgery, permanent surgery. I was scared. While I knew in my heart it was inevitable for Amaya to make some major changes at *some point*, still I hesitated when the point came to a head. I had never had any type of surgery myself at that time, and neither had any of my children.

Yes, I was nervous about the whole idea of surgery. And I felt an impending loss when I thought of his breasts. I felt a hole in my heart knowing he would never breastfeed a child as I had. I felt the value of my own breasts, and I imagined the pain and suffering I'd feel to lose them. True, I did not feel like I was losing my child, I knew

Amaya would always be Amaya—but I felt the loss of my child's breasts viscerally.

With hindsight, I can see the similarity between my reaction to the idea of top surgery and my response years earlier to Amaya's request to wear boys' underwear. I was resistant then because allowing him these choices (to wear boys' underwear, to have top surgery) would have been an admission in part that my child was transgender. Further, while I've always been accepting, and open, and supportive, and all that, I've also been scared all this time because I know it's not easy to be different in our society. I was never upset about who my child was or is; rather I was scared how he might be treated. I was scared about his safety, his social life. I was scared for him. I wondered often, "What will his adult life look like?" "Whom will he marry?" "Will he have kids?" "*Who will love my child?*"

Some of these fears had a legitimate basis. There are tons (way too many) of documented cases of discrimination, harassment, and violence against transgender people. I do understand now that some of my fears were based on my own ignorance regarding transgender people. Healthy transgender people live healthy lives that can include great jobs, love, sex, family, and children. We have much to fear, but we have much to look forward to. Like all parents.

And now, back to the surgery:

As it turns out. we did run into a bit of a challenge with the insurance company. Our insurance was at that time provided by Gabriel's former employer. He'd been laid off just before Christmas by the firm that bought the company he'd worked at for 18 years. The company was based in California, but took advantage of an office in Reno to purchase its employees' medical insurance policy from a Nevada insurance company (so they could save a few bucks). We found out quickly that unlike California law, Nevada law at the time did not require coverage for top surgery for transgender people, and we panicked. How would we afford this? How could we tell Amaya now that we *couldn't* afford it. We tried to table the conversation about how we would proceed, knowing we would not disappoint Amaya in the end but fearing the deep financial impact.

Gabriel, hat in hand, went to his old employer and asked for a favor. As part of his severance package, the company was paying the bulk of our medical premiums for five months. He asked if we could quit the company plan and instead be reimbursed for an equal or less costly family plan offered on Covered California, the state's version of the "Obamacare" Affordable Care Act (ACA) exchange for individual insurance purchases. Whether they felt regret about terminating Gabe just before Christmas or not, we will never know, but we were pleasantly and certainly surprised that they agreed to help us out and fund our alternative insurance plan through the end of my husband's severance period.

The next step was to get the California insurer to approve the procedure. Dr. Crane presented our case, but still we had to call the insurer a few times to make sure a decision was made in time for us to proceed with our scheduled date of surgery. We were nervous for several days, but finally we got the call from Dr. Crane's office telling us we had approval.

Fast forward now to the days leading up to surgery. I was a mess. Worried. Unsure that it was the right decision, for the many reasons I described above. I was scared about the *what if's*, and of the very small, but nonetheless real, possibility that Amaya would regret the decision.

He assured me he would not. I was also reassured by the words his counselor, Cristin, offered; she said in 15 years of practice, she had not met one FTM trans person who expressed regret regarding their decision. She acknowledged there may be a few out there who held regrets, but not in her experience. I reminded myself Dr. Crane wasn't worried about the procedure, and that he had also told us that he'd never heard from any of his patients that they'd had second thoughts after they'd had their surgery.

Amaya, by contrast, was calm, impatient, and excited. He wanted the surgery *yesterday*, and his much-anticipated day under the knife could not come soon enough. Gabe was also calm by all appearances, though I know he shared some of the anxieties I was feeling. This was a huge step and there was no turning back. From one perspective, we could say that our healthy child was about to undergo elective surgery. However, that was not really the case. Our child was *not* completely healthy. He had long suffered from gender dysphoria. So was the surgery elective? No. This was a medically necessary procedure to address his gender dysphoria. The logic of this, the fact that my son *needed* this surgery, helped keep me focused.

EMAIL FROM CRISTIN BREW TO ME, 3/23/14

Thinking of you all and sending good vibes! Amaya spoke Thursday of how grateful he is to you and Gabe (and me) for supporting this decision.

Please do let me know when he is home from surgery.

Much love, Cristin

The day of surgery finally arrived. Amaya was calm with just a hint of nervous excitement. He was ready. He had his chest binder on as usual, and we celebrated the fact that it would be the last time he wore the contraption. I did my best to practice deep, calm breathing on the way to the surgical center. I felt an inner knowing and calm wash over me as we rode down the highway. No parent wants to see their child on the surgical table, but in my heart I knew it was the right thing.

Finally, after arriving at the surgical center and checking in, Amaya's name was called. Gabe and I gathered around Amaya, who had taken a seat on the edge of a hospital bed. Dr. Crane went over the surgical and recovery plan. He explained to us that he was about to make marks with a felt pen on Amaya's chest to denote where he was going to make his incisions. Amaya could have privacy during this "drawing" time, or he could have us present. He invited us to stay. I had not seen him naked for some time. It had been even longer for Gabriel, who says now that he thinks he only saw Amaya's developed chest at home perhaps once or twice, ever, once he'd started binding.

When Amaya took off his layers of binding, he exposed to us the heavy burden he'd been carrying around. I was shocked by the size of his breasts, as he'd hidden them so well. (I apologize for your DNA, Amaya!) I could tell Gabriel and Dr. Crane were surprised too. We all did our best to minimize our reaction. I felt it was so brave of Amaya to allow his parents to be there, especially his father, and I was glad we were able to bear witness. The doctor drew a few surgical circles and arrows on Amaya's chest with a Sharpie, and he and Amaya talked a bit about how high he wanted his nipples on his chest (top surgery allows for some preference about nipple placement,

within an inch or two). After that, it was time for the
doctor and his team to unburden Amaya, so we left him
with the doctor and let them get to work.

When Amaya woke, Gabriel was by his side. I was
just outside the building speaking on the phone with my
mom. A nurse came to find me and I was told Amaya was
asking, "Where's my mom?" "Awww," I thought, "Isn't
that sweet he needs me?!" (Amaya claimed later that he
wasn't *asking* for me; he insists he was just confused as
to why I wasn't there—where else would I be? I prefer to
think my initial impression was correct.)

Recovery was a gradual process, as expected. Amaya
healed well and improved day to day. As with any major
surgery, the first few days were the worst. Though we
were able to manage his pain, the tightly wrapped layers
of bandages were uncomfortably heavy, and they made
it difficult for him to breathe. Healing from surgery is
exhausting! Gabriel slept in the same room with him for
the first few nights to help him manage his comfort and
manage his pain medications. Through it all, Amaya kept
up his spirits as best he could, and he looked forward to
the day his bandages would be removed.

One special day during his recovery, a bunch of his
best friends came over with cards, gifts, balloons, and
ice cream. They lifted his spirits greatly. Their oversized
tag board get-well card read, "Congratulations on your
booblessness!" The best gift of all was their unwavering
acceptance and support for their friend.

The day his bandages were removed was one of
the most memorable days in my life as a mother. With
anticipation and excitement, we watched as a nurse
carefully removed the bandages. No longer hidden behind
mounds of unwanted flesh, and with no need to bind and

cover and hide, he bared *his* chest. His freshly scarred, flat, male chest. He was beaming, as were we all. I knew at that moment we had made the right choice to allow him to have this surgery. I was witness to no less than a rebirth of my child as *himself.*

✂

WITNESS

by Michael Krashes, a very dear family friend

Seeing Amaya become who he truly is has been an amazing and inspiring experience—something I am so glad I've gotten to witness.

I've known Amaya his whole life. Janna is one of my oldest and dearest friends, a truly special relationship in my life. We first met in ninth-grade Biology class and became instant friends. She helped me pass Chemistry by generously sharing correct test answers with me when I was lost, which was often. We visited each other in college, and soon after college she was amongst the first of my friends to get hitched, marrying the wonderful Gabe, whom I love like a brother.

Janna and Gabe were also the first of my friends to have a baby, the lovely Emily, with Amaya joining soon after. Though they were living on the west coast, I would see Janna every time she came back east to visit family, which was fairly often, at least several times a year. We would meet in Manhattan every time she was in town for lunch, and I remember her changing baby Emily on my desk while visiting me at work. We would have dinner at Leo's, a favorite neighborhood restaurant in Hoboken, where I live. Emily now lives in Hoboken a few blocks away from me, and I can't help but think a lifetime of visiting influenced her decision to live here.

A few years after Amaya was born, my wife Lisa and I had our own daughter, Zoe Tigerlily. I watched Emily and Amaya and Zoe grow up over plates of pasta at Leo's, and marveled as their personalities developed and they became themselves. Emily looked a lot like Janna, and Amaya like Gabe. Emily was a girl interested in fashion, and Amaya was a stereotypical tomboy, interested in baseball, playing drums, and wearing hoodies. I remember when Amaya was still quite young, perhaps six or seven years old, Janna said she thought Amaya was different than most girls her age. She did not use the word "transgender" at that time, but I knew what she meant. It would be several years before the term would become part of the cultural landscape, and several more before there would be a movement to acknowledge those who are transgender and encourage discussions about trans rights in our society. But discussing this early on with Janna, full of her unconditional love and understanding for Amaya, was a lesson for me in acceptance—and later on, a lesson in the ongoing battle that must be fought by and for transgender people, searching to be welcomed and understood in a society that often is not so understanding.

When Janna told me that Amaya was transitioning, I was incredibly happy for him. But nothing prepared me for the rush of emotion I felt when I saw him. Now, he seems like a flower that has bloomed. He has become his true self. I literally had a tear in my eye, seeing him as he should be, with his family, full of love.

Plus, he's one buff good-looking dude!

LOOKING FOR REFLECTIONS

It is important for each of us to see reflections of ourselves in our communities. I wanted this for my child. I also wanted it for myself.

As Amaya affirmed his gender identity and moved closer to living fully as male, I wondered what life would be like for him as an adult. I was curious and concerned. Who would love my child? I wanted to talk to adult trans men and ask them so many questions. Perhaps that seems inappropriate or even voyeuristic, but my intention was to educate and reassure myself. I didn't know anyone who identified openly as transgender. At the time, I knew quite a few people who identified as gay or lesbian, and for many years I have had a few female friends whose gender expression veers more toward the male side of the spectrum (although these friends still identify as female). As a mom, I wanted reassurance that I was doing the right things, that my son would be okay, that "it gets better." I wanted to meet trans adults.

In the spring of 2014, after Amaya had his top surgery, he and I attended a reading of the book *Manning Up*.[24] Though he was not thrilled with the idea when I asked him to join me, Amaya was willing to go. *Manning Up* is a collection of stories written by trans men who share their experiences of being male, and of being male community members: fathers, sons, brothers, husbands, boyfriends, friends, and mentors. Most of the people in attendance at the reading were adults, but there were a few young people. One of the other teenagers in the audience came up to us and introduced himself to Amaya, which I thought was pretty cool. We listened, and witnessed, as strong, courageous men of all ages told their heartfelt stories. The event was enlightening and uplifting, and it gave me comfort and hope. Amaya said it was interesting—and a little boring. He was a bit overwhelmed, I think. Still, it was a bonding experience for us and time well spent.

Several months later, Amaya and I went to hear a talk by actress Laverne Cox, a well-known transgender woman, trans rights activist, and dynamic speaker. Around the time Amaya was just beginning to transition, the Netflix television show *Orange Is the New Black* had become a hit. This comedy/drama series focuses on a wide cross-section of women sentenced to do time at an upstate New York jail. One of the main characters is a trans woman prisoner played by Laverne Cox, and to a great extent the show fairly depicts many of the significant challenges faced by transgender MTF people in our prison system. While I knew the show wasn't completely appropriate for a young teen (it is laced with profanity and features R-rated sex scenes, for one thing), I also saw the value of allowing Amaya to watch a show that dealt with transgender issues openly and with some sensitivity. To be honest, Gabriel and I were rather *laissez-faire* when it came to controlling what media Amaya took in (I've already recounted how he had ample time to explore his gender expression and research transgender-related topics online without our knowledge or oversight). But because I also watched the show, and Gabe started watching after a while too, it gave us an opening to talk with Amaya about topics related to gender and sexuality. The show served as an icebreaker and a connector.

When I first brought up the idea of going to see Laverne Cox, Amaya said he wasn't interested, but then he changed his fickle young mind and I bought some tickets.

The evening of the event, I could tell he was excited and nervous. I felt the same. When we arrived at the theater, I realized I was in the minority as a cisgender straight white middle-aged mom. It was the most gender diverse gathering I had ever been to. It was also the first event I'd ever attended where the bathrooms were labeled for "All Genders." I thought I detected a bit of ease and comfort when Amaya saw those signs and realized he could use a restroom without having to figure out which one would bring him the least attention in a public arena.

On stage, Ms. Cox told her story of growing up as a gender non-conforming youth alongside a cisgender twin brother in the South. She talked about finding a home in the performing arts world. She described her struggles as an actress wanting to be hired for all kinds of roles, not just for trans characters. (Note: She has since realized this goal, as she currently is cast as a cisgender woman on ABC's *The Trustee*.) She named many of the people who had inspired her along her journey, the women upon whose shoulders she stands. They include Sojourner Truth, late 19th-century abolitionist and women's rights activist; bell hooks, an author and social rights activist who focused on the intersectionality of race, economics, and gender; Miss Major Griffin-Gracy, veteran of the 1969 Stonewall Riots, a trans elder, activist, and community leader; and Janet Mock, a trans rights activist, writer, and television host. She quoted Simone de Beauvoir, from her 1949 book *The Second Sex*: "One is not born, but rather becomes, woman."[25]

Toward the end of the evening, Ms. Cox invited to the stage a young, gender-creative girl who had been teased often in her young life. On stage, Ms. Cox told her she was beautiful and loved. Turning to the crowd, she said,

"To really stop bullying, we need to create spaces for our children to be more gender creative, non-binary. We will *not* be the gender police today!" I was inspired. Amaya said it was cool to see so many diverse people gathering together. I think he was mostly excited to see a celebrity. One thing I know, he was rapt with attention when Ms. Cox spoke, and she definitely made an impression upon him.

I found another reflection of adult life as a gender-expansive person when I shared my mothering story with one of my yoga students over a cup of tea one afternoon. Upon hearing about my transgender child, the student told me about her partner, Aram, and she suggested that I reach out for a conversation. I did, and we agreed to meet over dinner. Aram identifies as gender queer and prefers to be referred to with pronouns "he"/"him" or "they"/ "them." They openly shared their story with me, specifically regarding their gender and sexuality. One piece of the story Aram shared really stayed with me: it was the way Aram described how their understanding about their own gender identity and expression grew during their college years. It gave me a deeper understanding of the difference between gender identity (one's inner-held sense of who one is) and gender expression (behaviors that clue others in about how we want to be seen and treated). Aram said, "I still presented mostly femme with tomboyish undertones, but I adopted the masculine counterpart because I felt more comfortable emulating the stereotypical protect-and-provide role assigned to male identity."

Aram sent me home with a book for Amaya in the hope that he might find value in it. *The Gender Book*,[26] by Mel Reiff Hill and Jay Mays, is an illustrated book for all ages that explores many facets of gender in an easy-to-read, encouraging, and lighthearted format. Aram also encouraged me to keep an eye out for local events and happenings planned specifically for transgender people, and they encouraged me and Amaya to get involved in community action. They told me they planned to attend the Trans March, part of the San Francisco Pride weekend held yearly in June to educate the public on LGBTQ issues and to commemorate, celebrate, and liberate LGBTQ people. Aram offered to meet Amaya and me at the march if we wanted to attend. Grateful for the book and suggestions, I was most appreciative of my new friend's willingness to share their story with me.

In June 2014, Amaya and I participated in the Trans March in San Francisco. This event is known to be one of (if not *the*) largest transgender events in the world. Still, it is much smaller than the weekend's marquee event, the San Francisco LBGT Pride Parade, and the Trans March feels more like an *action* than a *party*.

Amaya asked one of his best friends to come with us, and my good friend A– met us at the march. We gathered at San Francisco's Dolores Park, the starting point of the parade route. Always a place where diversity is the norm, the park on this day was a bright, beautiful rainbow of expression. There were people of all genders, races, cultures, and ages milling about and then gathering together to march in solidarity and support of transgender rights.

When the march began, Amaya took off his shirt and bared his chest. It was less than three months after his top surgery. The long scars across the curves that underscored his pectorals were still red and quite visible, quite obvious. I was blown away by his courage. To me, this was a big step in his coming out. He received multiple high fives and many a "You Go Dude!" from fellow marchers. It was clear that being in this crowd empowered him, and that he was proud to be himself. We marched together for a few miles along Market Street, closed to traffic for the event, a river of beautiful humanity.

As we walked, my friend A– told me a lot about her own gender identity and sexuality. I knew that A– considers herself bisexual or perhaps pansexual. I knew she identifies as *queer*. However, I didn't know that for years she'd harbored feelings of being anything other than female. Marching down Market Street that day, she revealed that at a young age, she'd had feelings of being different, of being "other." But she understood back then that it would be unacceptable to express anything other than femaleness. "When I was little and I had very short hair, I was often mistaken as a boy," she told me. "I was always horrified when this happened because it was as if they knew some secret about me that even I didn't know, some secret shame that others saw but I was blind to." She said she'd tried to express her maleness somewhat by dressing and acting "butchy" in high school, but her parents did not approve of nor quietly accept those behaviors so she squashed it down. Only recently had A– begun to uncover and explore some of these feelings. I think that was one of the first and only times she'd ever told anyone about those feelings; she'd come to the march in support of our family, and ended up finding support for herself.

The march ended in the Tenderloin district at the site of the 1966 Compton Cafeteria riot, which was one of the first recorded transgender riots in US history (a story for another day). It was a fitting commemoration at the end of a long march in the midst of an eternal journey toward acceptance and integration. Amaya and I interacted with many new people that day, and we learned and experienced many new things. Being part of the Trans March that year was an amazing experience, and I've attended every year since. San Francisco recently announced plans to designate part of the city's Tenderloin district to be the nation's first Transgender district. The area will be known as Compton's Transgender, Lesbian, Gay, and Bisexual (TLGB) District.

By the summer of 2014, my quest for reflections of, and information about, being a trans adult was morphing into a full-blown passion, driven as ever by my desire to understand and protect my child, and to provide for his happiness and security. Next on the docket: Gabriel and I attended our first Gender Spectrum Conference in July. Each year this conference offers programming for transgender, non-binary, and otherwise gender-expansive youth and their families. Led by experts in the field, the conference aims to provide a safe space for families to get informed, find support, and connect with others who may have similar experiences. (Some of these presenters identify as transgender or non-binary themselves.) We could not convince Amaya to join us, but we felt it would be valuable for us to go anyway. (Amaya told me he was glad we were going; I think it felt good to know that his parents wanted to learn more about transgender people and the challenges they face.)

Although I had known about the conference for some years, this was our first time attending. As soon as we got to the conference, I couldn't understand why I hadn't been there yet! Here were so many families with transgender and gender-expansive youth. There were many repeat attendees. The word "community" buzzed in my ears; we belonged here.

Gabriel and I were grateful for the company of our friend Anne at the conference. Anne, who was double-majoring in Psychology and Women, Gender, and Sexuality at the time, had been close friends with our daughter, Emily, during their middle and high school years. Today, Anne defines as a queer bisexual woman. We invited her to join us at the conference, thinking the experience would be informative and relevant to her education. As it turns out, having her come with us made me feel like I had my own tutor to help parse all the new information presented in the forums and workshops we attended. She was far ahead of me in terms of understanding gender. I learned a lot from her that day (and since), and I was comforted by how easily she spoke of her own exploration regarding her gender identity and sexuality.

One highlight of my first conference was learning about the brain science regarding gender in general, and specifically regarding being transgender. Another great experience was listening to young people on Gender Spectrum's Youth Council share stories about their lives and educate others about what it's like to be gender non-conforming in today's world. In addition to getting an education, Gabriel and I left the conference feeling validated and confident—*validated* in that we knew we were doing the right thing by supporting our transgender child, and *confident* that he was going to be okay after all.

PUBERTY, AGAIN?!

After top surgery, free now from the burden of his breasts, Amaya's mood and energy shifted greatly. He was visibly "lighter," holding his head high and meeting people's eyes with his own. He stood straighter and walked taller, no longer hunching over and folding his shoulders forward to hide his bound breasts. He was more comfortable in his clothes and took pride in his appearance. He started going to the gym regularly. He'd finished his sophomore year with good grades, and as the new school year loomed, he was back to interacting socially with friends.

At the same time, Gabe and I noticed he was still somewhat depressed, disconnected, and lethargic at home. His anxiety, lessened but not abated, was still present from time to time. He reported having no energy and he was often tired. Cristin Brew described his condition as "a lingering, low-grade depression, a brain fog."

So when Amaya came to us (once again in command of his needs) to discuss hormone therapy, we were hardly surprised. It was the logical next step on the road to his full transition. We were not without our concerns, however. Just as we were aware of the permanence of top surgery, the permanent effects of hormone replacement treatment for someone whose body was still maturing was potentially worrisome. Even though Amaya had already experienced puberty, he was still young and his body was still growing. We were concerned about long-term effects on our child's health, and concerned too about his fertility. It is only in recent years that transgender youth (those under age 18) have been medically treated with hormones as a component of their transition, and the effects on young bodies are still being studied. We do know that trans men who undergo hormone therapy are at higher risk for typical male risk factors such as hypertension, cardiovascular disease, balding, stroke, and weight gain.[27] (My husband points out that these risks are, unfortunately, just part of what it means to have a male body.) And yet, as we discovered through our family's research and exploration, even with these factors taken into consideration the long-term use of hormone therapy to treat gender dysphoria (under a doctor's care) is considered to be safe.[28]

When we spoke with Amaya's therapist, Cristin, she encouraged us to consider the request carefully. She explained that hormone treatment could very well clear Amaya's "brain fog" and depression. She told us how the latest research regarding gender dysphoria showed that his depression was very likely connected to his brain chemistry. Recent, peer-reviewed studies seem to show that for some transgender people, the difference lies not in hormone levels themselves, but rather in the hormone *receptors* in the brain.[29] The brain of a transgender person may have a biological variance—to be specific, they may have an atypically large number of hormone receptors for sex hormones of the gender that is opposite their natal gender. It is thought that this disparity causes that "brain fog" depression. People who have this brain characteristic are simply not receiving the correct chemical cocktail to match the receptors in their brains. "Brain fog" caused by this imbalance is often lifted and eliminated when a person takes hormones that align chemically with their affirmed gender.

Until recently, researchers thought transgender people may have a hormone imbalance that causes them to be transgender. However, this is not the current state of thinking among the experts working with transgender youth. A recent study conducted by Johanna Olson, MD, and her colleagues at Children's Hospital Los Angeles, found that, "Transgender individuals have sex hormone levels consistent with the gender they were assigned at birth." Olson's study documents the experience of 101 participants, aged 12–24, who had experienced incongruence with the gender they'd been assigned at birth. "We've now put to rest the residual belief that transgender experience is a result of a hormone imbalance," writes Olson. "It's not."[30]

With all this in mind, my husband and I decided to allow Amaya to try hormone treatment and see if it was the right path for him. The long-term use of cross-sex hormones has permanent effects, as I mentioned above. However, we'd learned that a person can undergo hormone treatment for a short period of time without the same risk levels associated with long-term use. A trial gives a person a chance to feel if the treatment is right for them. If it is not, a person can stop using the proscribed hormones, and their effects will taper off quickly with no long-term impact. On the other hand, when a hormonal treatment trial *does* produce positive results for an individual, that person can continue to explore and refine the dosage under medical supervision to find what works best.

The more we learned, the more we knew the risk of *not* allowing Amaya to start hormonal treatment would likely be worse than any possible side effects. If we didn't try the hormones, Amaya would continue to suffer from his depression and anxiety. Despite the lessening of those symptoms after his top surgery, ignoring them at this point was not a healthy option.

Gabriel and I accompanied Amaya to his first appointment with the specialist assigned by our medical group to monitor Amaya's health and potentially implement his hormone treatment. Amaya's primary care doctor had referred us to Jess Pinder, a nurse practitioner based in San Francisco who specializes in transgender health. Though he works mostly with adults, Jess felt upon meeting Amaya that he was "close enough" to adulthood (biologically speaking and also relative to his emotional maturity), and surmised that indeed our son would be a good candidate for testosterone treatment. We scheduled time to come back for his first shot.

Testosterone can be administered through an injection, a patch, or a cream. Injections are considered the most effective and consistently reliable method, so it is the default approach recommended most often by medical practitioners. I wondered how Amaya would feel about giving himself a weekly injection. It's an intramuscular shot and the needle must penetrate deeply. Some youth have a medical professional administer it weekly, while some have the help of a parent. I was willing to learn how to do it, but I was really hoping Amaya would take that on. Maybe I was the skittish one? I hoped he'd be stronger.

Though he said he wasn't thrilled with the idea of needles, Amaya faced the challenge of his first shot with courage, knowing this was likely to be a lifelong (and lifesaving) habit. As ever, he took matters into his own hands when we again visited Jess in his downtown San Francisco office. He knew what he needed and he was ready. With me and Jess watching, Amaya took that needle and plunged it deep into his thigh, pressing the plunger down to squeeze the testosterone into his bloodstream. I was blown away by his bravery, his determination; his *badassery*. He "took it like a man." (Pardon the gender stereotype, but I couldn't help feeling that way!)

Amaya began by taking a low dose of testosterone every other week. We did not notice any changes for a while; it takes a body some time to adjust to the hormonal impact, and results are different for everyone. Each person has to find the dose that is correct for them. It took over a month, during which Amaya took his first two or three shots, before we began to notice changes. For one thing, Amaya's moods were all over the map (he'd always been our most even-tempered child, despite his depression these past few years). For the first time in his life, acne appeared on his face. His energy level would go up and down; he seemed to have a full tank of gas in his belly for a few days or a week after each shot, but by the middle of the second week he would crash, and the fog would return.

We talked to Jess, who suggested Amaya try giving himself a weekly shot with a slightly higher dosage. It is common for practitioners to recommend starting slow and increasing dosage and frequency over time in order to find the optimal course of action. Indeed, increasing Amaya's dosage and frequency worked, and once this new pattern was set in place, his energy level stabilized at a healthy level, and any symptoms of depression became nearly imperceptible.

With testosterone coursing through his bloodstream at an appropriate level, Amaya's male puberty was now set in motion. His period stopped and he has not had one since—and likely never will again. Although he had not suffered a large amount of dysphoria around his menses outwardly, I knew he was quite relieved to be done with the monthly reminders of who he was *not*. On the other hand, on the path toward who he *was*, Amaya continued to experience the physical effects one would expect to accompany male puberty. Over a relatively short period of time, his voice cracked, then deepened. For the past year or two, it seemed to me and Gabriel that Amaya had been purposefully trying to train his voice to speak in the lowest possible tones so he would sound more "boy-like," but now his voice dropped to a true baritone. His jaw line became sharper, and he began to grow hair in places men grow hair. He asked his father to buy him an electric razor. He grew a bit taller and his feet got bigger. His hips narrowed, his shoulders broadened. He bulked up at the gym, the testosterone guiding his body to translate his weightlifting efforts into the sculpted pectorals and strong, bulging biceps one typically sees on athletic men. The sparkle in his eyes returned.

During this time of change, as his body attuned to the testosterone, Amaya was also more prone to frustration, anger, and even aggression. He felt agitated at times, and he told us he felt less in touch with his feelings than he had before he'd started the treatment. It was a different thing than the depression and anxiety he had felt previously, and certainly I was glad those symptoms had abated. But where was my level-headed kid? Then it dawned on me: I realized Amaya was also experiencing some of the typical *emotional* effects of male puberty. I expressed my concerns to Jess, and he worked with Amaya to refine the dosage and frequency a bit more. As my son's testosterone levels stabilized and built up in his system over time, he experienced fewer and fewer swings between shots, and the negative emotional effects diminished.

Over the next few years of hormonal treatment, I watched my boy become the young man he is today.

One positive effect I didn't quite expect was a change in the way Amaya relates to me. From his tween years on, he'd rejected most physical affection, generally shunning touches and caresses and certainly avoiding hugs from me, his father, his siblings, and pretty much everybody else. (He may have been a bit more physically affectionate with friends, but I don't think by much.) Being a very affectionate person myself, his physical distance had been difficult for me. As he became more comfortable in his own skin, he was more open to being touched. I now happily receive frequent hugs from Amaya, offered freely, and he doesn't recoil and twist away when my husband puts his arm around Amaya's shoulders.

My son's transition changed our relationship profoundly. I used to relate to Amaya as my daughter, one of my girls. It's noteworthy that we didn't want to know the gender of our unborn babies either of the times I was pregnant, despite the growing trend to identify a baby's natal sex via ultrasound imaging. (When asked during my pregnancies what we were going to have, implying a "boy or girl?" question, my husband would sometimes answer, "a scientist!" or "a mathematician!") But now Amaya is—and always was!—my son. He is the same person, the same being I carried in my womb. Before I ever held him in my arms, I *knew* this child, *my* child, on a deep level. Yet, though I always knew him so deeply, he had changed in some way as a result of the hormone treatments. There is something about the relationship between a mother and her son that is different than the relationship between a mother and her daughter. His transition, leaving me now with a son named Amaya and not a daughter, brought with it new characteristics that changed our interactions and helped clarify my inner knowing of my son's true nature.

My son is protective of me. He knows how to calm me down and talk me off a ledge. He supports and encourages me. He wraps his arm around my shoulder and offers me an elbow or a hand if the ground is slippery. These actions feel very manly to me, very adult and very masculine. Yes indeed, he's always been my son.

YOUR PAPERS, PLEASE!

After Amaya's surgery and the launch of his hormone treatment, I began the process of updating his government-issued documents to reflect my son's appropriate, male gender. It was an arduous process, and although there were some resources to help guide me, I wished many times that I'd had one, single roadmap to help navigate the many twists and turns involved in updating a birth certificate, a Social Security card, a US passport, and more. I hope to provide the rough outline of such a map to help other parents below.

Parenting a transgender minor inevitably leads to questions of legal identity. Legal documents are required to make one's way through the world, and I've discovered many reasons why a person's legal identity documents need to appropriately represent that individual's gender. Official identity documents are required in the United States to drive a car, to get on an airplane, to register to vote, sometimes even to obtain housing. Our ID documents ostensibly prove to others that we are who we say we are. They also provide a level of safety and security that helps ensure that others will recognize and respond appropriately to each person's gender. It is important for parents of transgender or non-binary youth to understand why legal documents such as driver's licenses and passports need to reflect their child's correct name and gender, and to know how to change these documents when their child transitions in the public sphere.

Confusing situations (to say the least) arise on occasion when a person's ID documents do not align with that person's gender identity. To compound this confusion, in many cases, a person's gender identity may not be apparent based solely on the way the person presents to others. In some cases, this confusion leads to transgender people being exposed to discrimination, harassment, and even assault. People who do not identify distinctly as either male or female (including non-binary, gender-fluid, and agender people) may experience even greater challenges than transgender people who identify clearly as male or female. For one thing, there are very few areas in the world that offer more than two gender choices on form checkboxes, making it difficult to have ID documents issued that can represent everybody accurately.

When Amaya was about 11 or 12 years old, we got caught in a confusing situation at the airport. Amaya had already started menstruating, and he'd begun hiding his developing chest under many layers of clothing. He presented as a boy to people who didn't know him. Until that time, we'd experienced no issues regarding his gender while going through airport security lines. (Amaya had flown a few times every year with us on vacations and holidays for his entire life.) I was not even conscious there even *might* be any issues—that is, until I saw a federal airport security agent feel up my child.

This was when airports were just beginning to implement the use of full-body scanners, now in airports everywhere. To use these machines, the federal Transport Security Administration (TSA) agents who operate them will press a button to reflect the gender of each traveler as they enter the scanner. Selecting a gender to mark the image allows the security agent reviewing an onscreen x-ray of each traveler to look for anomalies while accounting for gender differences. For instance, women are expected to have "shapes" detected where their breasts should be, while men are expected to have "shapes" where their testicles and penis should be. If the agents reviewing the onscreen images spot something in the image that does not align with gender norms (such as "shapes" where a male chest is expected to be flat, or "shapes" roughly representing a penis where a woman's genitalia are expected), the disparity triggers the agent's suspicion and likely leads to a security pat-down of the individual. But the agents who push the button on the full-body scanners to set the gender marker for each traveler do not ask to see ID documents nor ask any person their gender. Rather, they make a binary gender determination (male or female) based on an assumption of gender they derive from each person's clothing, hair, jewelry, mannerisms, etc. Those assumptions are hardly reliable, and can result in misgendering travelers as they enter a full-body scanner.

My child was misgendered by the TSA.

I didn't realize this had happened until after we went through the scanner. Amaya had walked through the scanner, and he was pulled aside before I knew what was happening. I looked over to see a TSA agent patting down my *girl* with his hands sweeping Amaya's developing chest. Quite alarmed, to say the least, I asked, "Why are you touching my child?!"

The agent told me that an anomaly had appeared on the screen. I realized right away what must have happened, that they assumed my child was a boy, and therefore a male agent would do any physical inspection. The agent confirmed my suspicion when I asked if he thought this was a boy. I told him they had made a mistake. They had read Amaya as male even though his ID was still marked female. They had misgendered my child. I was very upset, but I said calmly that my child was transgender. I whispered (so as not to embarrass Amaya and widen the circle of people in the security checkpoint area who were aware of what was happening) that my child appeared as a boy but has girl anatomy.

The agent apologized, and I suggested that he pass along to the Powers That Be at the TSA that they need to provide agents with some training regarding gender awareness.

The next time we went through an airport security line, I told Amaya that I would go through first so I could tell the TSA agent (quietly) that although my child looked like a boy, Amaya was a girl, and to make sure they mark the scanner correctly. He was comfortable with my offer of assistance. It worked perfectly, and I was thanked by TSA agents every time I did this.

I did this for Amaya whenever we flew anywhere until he'd had his surgery and we'd changed his government-issued documents.

Some people never feel comfortable disclosing their gender in public. Today, travelers in US airports may choose to be scanned by an agent with a handheld wand rather than enter a full-body scanner. However, it still may be necessary to disclose one's transgender status in order to ensure one's privacy will be respected. At the very least, anyone going through airport security can ask a TSA agent to take them to a private room for a discreet inspection. Personally, I think that approach would make it even more stressful for Amaya, who prefers to draw the least amount of attention possible. A quick whisper to an agent was all that was ever needed for Amaya.

As of this writing, TSA agents are (so we are told) trained how to work with people who are transgender, but confusion still abounds and problems still arise. I recommend parents of transgender children discuss their strategy before heading to the airport. Parents should include their child in the discussion about the strategy, as appropriate for the child's age, in order to understand the child's needs, set expectations, and clarify what will happen (and what may happen) in the security line.

Changing federal identity documents to reflect a person's appropriate gender and name is hardly a one-stop process. It is small comfort that those of us who live in the United States even have the ability to proceed with such changes; many countries have no protocol at all for gender changes on official ID documents, and others strictly and specifically forbid gender changes on birth certificates and other forms of identification. In the United States, a person will have to change documents one at a time by following each issuing entity's unique process. This complicated venture can be quite daunting for some people, and the fees required can be prohibitive.

Not every transgender person changes their name, and this is a bullet we dodged by giving Amaya a unisex moniker. To legally change a person's name with any state or federal agency, a person first needs to obtain a court order issued in the county where they live. From a legal standpoint, people generally can petition to change their name for any reason at all. In some states a petitioner needs to attend a court hearing to change his or her name, whereas other states allow a name change to be filed by postal mail. Many states have a publication requirement for a name change (meaning that a petitioner needs to place an ad in a local paper to allow for public input before a change is approved), and there is often a cost for publication. Currently, it seems some states are moving toward doing away with this publication requirement.

There are a number of limitations that often make it difficult for people to obtain a court order certifying their name change. Typically, a person must use a street address when petitioning for a name change. A shelter address *may* be sufficient in some courts, but often a PO box is not. It is therefore a greater challenge for homeless or transient people to comply with court requirements. There are also rules in some localities that rule out name changes for people with a history of arrests or convictions, or people who are currently under the jurisdiction of a state's Department of Corrections. There are also rules that prohibit name changes for anyone required by a court to register as a sex offender.

For minors, a parent or guardian must petition the court on their behalf. If a minor has two legal parents, they both have to agree to the change. If only one is present, then the other has to be notified. The Transgender Law Center advises that a minor who is close to 18 wait until they turn 18 as it can make the process much easier.

The process for gender changes to federal documents (primarily passports) and immigration documents (such as permanent residence cards) has been streamlined somewhat in the United States. As of today, the only requirement for a name or gender change to one's federal ID documents is an official letter from a physician stating that the person has had "clinically appropriate treatment" for gender transition. There is no specific treatment that is required by any federal statute. What is "appropriate" is whatever has been decided to be appropriate by an individual and their doctor. Activists have voiced concerns of late that the process of changing one's gender and/or name on federal documents may become more challenging, and the rules more restrictive, under the direction of the presidential administration voted into office in 2016. Likewise, the current Republican-led Congress also gives us cause for concern, as some representatives have sought to introduce legislation that will define and greatly limit what is deemed "appropriate treatment."

Laws concerning name and gender changes on state-issued documents (such as birth certificates and driver's licenses) vary from state to state. Some states allow name and gender-marker changes on original birth certificates, but others strictly prohibit any changes at all. Most will allow a gender-marker change on a driver's license. The National Center for Transgender Equality has a state-by-state guide available online.[31]

As I said above, I wish I'd had a roadmap to help me navigate these twisted avenues when it was time to change Amaya's gender on his "papers." Information seems to become obsolete quickly these days, but I hope the notes and links below remain accurate long enough to help a few transgender people and their families achieve their legal transition.

Let's start with a list of federal agencies in the United States that you will need to contact. I gathered the information here from the Transgender Law Center and the National Center for Transgender Equality. This is only a basic guide—your high-level road map rather than turn-by-turn instructions.

For the most up-to-date information, and for guidance on the document change process in the United States in particular, visit the website of either the National Center for Transgender Equality[32] or the Transgender Law Center.[33] You will also find a list of resources for legal, medical, and support help at the end of this book, as well as a list of recommended reading and informative websites.

UNITED STATES SOCIAL SECURITY ADMINISTRATION

» www.ssa.gov

» You will need to appear in person at a Social Security Office.

» To change your name in the Social Security system, you must first obtain a court-ordered name change.

» To change your gender in the Social Security system, you must submit *one* of these three documents:

- certification of a court-ordered gender change; or

- an updated US passport; or

- a declaration from a physician stating you have had "appropriate clinical treatment" for gender change. (See the following page.)

» You will retain the same Social Security number when the process is complete.

UNITED STATES PASSPORT

» https://uspassportonline.com

» You can appear on person OR submit an application online.

» To change your name on a US passport, you must first obtain a court-ordered name change.

» You are required to have a valid state-issued ID and proof of US citizenship.

» To change your gender, you must submit a US passport application with a letter from a physician stating you have had "appropriate clinical treatment" for gender change. (See the note below.)

» You will retain the same Social Security number when the process is complete.

IMMIGRATION SERVICE DOCUMENTS

» To change your name, it is best to *start* the immigration process with the correct or preferred "name." A court order should be obtained whenever possible.

» To change your gender, you will need one of these three documents:

• an amended birth certificate or passport; or

• certification of a court-ordered gender change; or

• a letter from physician regarding "appropriate clinical treatment." (See the note below.)

An important note about those physician letters: The Transgender Law Center advises that the wording of a physician letter is very important. These letters must include the exact words "appropriate clinical treatment" to ensure compliance with current agency policies. The National Center for Transgender Equality provides a sample letter online.[34]

For further assistance with the process, I urge transgender people and their families to reach out to the organizations below. I have availed myself of their help many times, and I have served as well as a volunteer for the Transgender Law Center in particular. Based on my experience, I can vouch unequivocally for the expertise and professionalism provided by these resources.

TRANSGENDER LAW CENTER

» http://transgenderlawcenter.org

» TLC helpline: (415) 865-0176

» TLC email: info@transgenderlawcenter.org

NATIONAL CENTER FOR TRANSGENDER EQUALITY

» www.transequality.org

» (202) 642-4542

LAMBDA LEGAL

» www.lambdalegal.org/about-us

» (212) 809-8585

In the United Kingdom, transgender and non-binary people are able to amend their legal documents. While I'm no expert on UK documentation, I understand the procedures vary slightly between England, Scotland, Wales, and Northern Ireland. Some introductory resources:

LEGAL NAME CHANGE

» UK deed poll website

» www.deedpoll.org.uk/AdviceForTranssexuals.html

LEGAL GENDER CHANGE

» In the United Kingdom, a legal gender change requires a Gender Recognition Certificate.

» The gov.uk website has information about how to apply for a Gender Recognition Certificate: www.gov.uk/apply-gender-recognition-certificate/overview

For help and information about government ID documents in the United Kingdom:

UK TRANS INFO

» https://uktrans.info/namechange

THE GENDER TRUST

» http://gendertrust.org.uk

PRESS FOR CHANGE

» www.pfc.org.uk

THE LAY OF THE LAND: CURRENT MEDICAL — PRACTICES FOR TRANSGENDER YOUTH —

To kick off this chapter, I want to emphasize that I am not a medically certified professional. Anything I write about medical practices comes from a layperson's point of view. Also, please note that the information I offer here is current as of this moment, and remember that the landscape is shifting constantly.

Until recently, the consensus in the medical community (and in society in general) was that children cannot be transgender. Today we see that, based on current research, attitudes and practices have shifted among medical and psychological professionals. There are now quite a few medical gender centers in the United States and abroad that have been established to serve the needs of gender-variant children, adolescents, and their parents and families. Doctors now see children as young as two-and-a-half who have expressed gender behaviors not typically associated with their birth sex. Some announce their inner-held sense of their gender identity at a young age, such as Jazz Jennings, who said "I girl" when she was just 18 months old. As more information becomes available, more parents are seeking advice and support when they begin to notice their child behaving outside of perceived gender norms.

One leading resource for parents is the San Francisco-based Child and Adolescent Gender Center (CAGC), a collaboration between the University of California, San

Francisco (UCSF) and community organizations. From the CAGC website:

> [CAGC] offers comprehensive medical and psychological care, as well as advocacy and legal support, to gender non-conforming/transgender youth and adolescents. A central component of this program is the UCSF CAGC Clinic, housed in the Division of Pediatric Endocrinology.
>
> Gender non-conforming/transgender youth and adolescents feel a strong conflict between their gender (inner sense of who they are) and their physical sex characteristics. The CAGC team believes that being transgender is a normal variation in gender identity. As of May, 2013, the American Psychiatric Association has replaced the term "gender identity disorder" with the term "gender dysphoria."
>
> Medical treatment may include administration of gonadotropin-releasing hormone agonists (GnRH-A). These hormones can safely suppress puberty by blocking the production of the principal sex hormones: estrogen and testosterone. Fully reversible, this treatment gives young people time to achieve greater self-awareness of their gender identification. If and when appropriate, our experts may administer cross-gender sex hormones.[35]

Notice the word "may" in the statement above. Not all gender-questioning or gender non-conforming children receive administration of puberty-suppressing blockers, and not all will receive cross-gender sex hormones. Those decisions, and all medical decisions, are made in confidence between a patient, the patient's parents, and their doctor. The benefit most often cited as an argument for using blockers is to extend a child's time prior to entering puberty and thereby allow for more learning, understanding, and decision making. Puberty blockers can help a child avoid going through the "wrong" puberty (a puberty that doesn't match the person's gender identity) and avoid the development of secondary sex characteristics (e.g., growing facial hair, a typically male characteristic). In most cases, this is a completely reversible intervention for tweens, and discontinuing blockers results in resumption of pubescent changes.

The next step for many children after going on puberty blockers is, essentially, to wait. Eventually, after much counseling and exploration, it may be determined by child, parent, and doctor that the time is right and the patient is ready to move forward with their transition. At this point, perhaps following a family's lead, a doctor may indeed recommend a course of hormones that correspond with the patient's affirmed gender. The hormones are introduced, the dosage and frequency are established, and the patient then undergoes puberty changes that align with their affirmed gender.

Until recently, puberty-blocking treatment was not available. Most transgender people had to go through the puberty predetermined for their natal sex, and subsequently many transgender people have had to live with bodies that do not match their inner sense of gender identity. Many suffer from dysphoria as a result. Such was the case for our son. When Amaya was going through the early stages of puberty (when blockers are most effective), the use of puberty blockers for this purpose was only just beginning to come into practice. Until then, these drugs were only prescribed for those children who were diagnosed with precocious (i.e., early onset) puberty. Had this treatment been available to us, we might have taken that road. Certainly, we would have given great consideration to blockers if Amaya had asked us about it. But the treatment was still novel, and without it my child experienced female puberty. Because we did not find that path, he later had to have surgery to align his body to his gender identity.

It should be noted that not all transgender and gender non-conforming people seek medical intervention, nor do they undergo surgery. Each person has their own needs regarding what interventions they may need to relieve the gender dysphoria they experience.

It is also interesting to note that not everyone who has gender-related surgery considers themselves to be transgender. I hope I'm not belaboring the point by saying again that there is not just one definition of "transgender." Each person has their own needs regarding what interventions they may need to relieve the gender dysphoria they experience.

The availability of medical support for transgender children has expanded exponentially in the last several years, but for many in the United States, United Kingdom, and elsewhere, resources are still limited. Many people have to travel great distances to access specialists in the field (which precludes many people from access for financial reasons). The topic of transgender medicine today is controversial and politically charged. Not all doctors and insurance companies are on board yet to cover necessary procedures and interventions. Many medical doctors report they lack instruction when it comes to care for transgender patients. This needs to change.

In May 2016, the US Department of Health and Human Services (HHS) finalized a new rule to ensure equal treatment for all patients. The new rule was issued to reinforce the non-discrimination clause of the 2010 ACA, and it specifically provides protection for gender-identity patients. According to the HHS website:

> Under the rule, individuals are protected from discrimination in health care on the basis of race, color, national origin, age, disability and sex, including discrimination based on pregnancy, gender identity and sex stereotyping.
>
> The rule forbids health care providers who take funding from the HHS from denying health care based on gender identity or denying patients treatment for sex-specific ailments like ovarian or prostate cancer simply because an individual identifies as a different sex.[36]

According to the National Center for Transgender Equality:

> [The rule] means that in every state, almost every insurance company cannot exclude transition-related care from coverage. And, in every state, most health care providers can't treat you differently because of your transgender status or refuse to treat you according to your gender identity.[37]

So what does this mean in practice? To start with, enforcement of this rule will ensure that transgender people have legal protection from discrimination based on gender when seeking health care. For example, if an insurance plan covers pap smears for women, under this rule that plan must also cover pap smears for transgender men who have a cervix. Likewise, a transgender woman who has a prostate gland must be provided the same medical care that would be provided for any man with a prostate gland. Transgender and gender non-conforming people have not had access to the medical care they need for far too long. The finalization and clarification of the *non-discrimination clause of the ACA* was welcomed as a huge step forward.

To be sure, the topic of discrimination relative to health insurance coverage in the United States has been mired in legislative and legal controversy for the past several years. As of 2016, 13 US states and the District of Columbia had laws in place prohibiting insurance companies from discriminating based on sexual orientation and gender. Six US states have *some* protections and 31 states have *no* explicit protections for transgender people in place at all.[38]

Medicaid coverage for transgender health care also varies widely from state to state. Although it is a US government program funded in part with federal grants, Medicaid is administered at the state level, and states are allowed much latitude to develop policies for coverage. Under the ACA, if they do not abide by the rule that affords protections for transgender people, states are at risk to lose federal funding for their programs.[39]

On August 23, 2016, Texas, North Carolina, and three other states filed suit against the Obama administration to challenge the HHS rule. These states claimed the anti-discrimination rule would force medical professionals to provide service that was contrary somehow to their morals, and therefore the rule placed a burden on their free exercise of religion. Soon after it was filed, North Carolina withdrew its participation in the suit. The *Texas Tribune* (1/17/17) reported that the state's Governor cited "substantial costs to the State" as one reason for dropping the lawsuit, adding that it did not serve the "interests of judicial economy and efficiency."[40] It was a practical if not ethical withdrawal. The legal battle is waged in the courts to this day while medically necessary care is being withheld from many in need.

Securing medical coverage for gender transition-related surgery for people under 18 remains even more challenging. While there are some areas in the United States where medical care is available for gender-questioning youth, most parents find they have access to little, if any, of the medical support they need. Many families travel long distances to find a doctor versed in the care of gender-questioning and transgender youth (and of course, not everyone can afford to do that). Doctors are often ill-equipped to care for gender-variant patients, to offer support to their parents, to answer the questions both parents and children may have. Many doctors I have spoken to report that they did not learn about transgender-specific medical care in medical school nor have they since. They recognize they certainly are not prepared to work with transgender youth. (Our current doctor told us that much of what she has learned came on the job from her interactions with transgender patients.) Once parents find a doctor with the experience and knowledge to provide care for a transgender child, they still face hurdles. Parents often must appeal to the review board of their health insurance company on a case-by-case basis to gain coverage for each procedure or prescription.

It is difficult to say with certainty if the current federal and state protections will remain in place. The political climate in the United States has shifted now that Donald Trump has been elected to replace Barack Obama as President of the United States. The fate of the ACA (a.k.a. "Obamacare") as a whole, and of the HHS's transgender-specific rulings in particular, is in jeopardy. At the very end of 2016, a federal judge issued a temporary injunction against the regulation, and today, barely a month later, already I've heard news of people who have had their coverage stripped.

Organizations such as the American Civil Liberties Union (ACLU) and Transgender Law Center are currently working hard to preserve and further the protections afforded to transgender people under the ACA. As I was writing this chapter, the ACLU filed a motion to stay the court order issued by the judge in Texas. The motion quoted Kate Parrish, president of the River City Gender Alliance based in Omaha, Nebraska: "The judge's court order [is a] direct attack on the transgender community's right to function normally and safely in everyday life. Our access to medically necessary health care treatment is being restricted simply because of who we are."[41]

In contrast to the current practices in the United States, the United Kingdom today provides all citizens with comprehensive, free national health care administered by the National Health Service (NHS). Transgender adults have a full suite of services available to them, including mental health, hormone therapy, and surgical options. The NHS has a center that works specifically with gender-expansive and transgender youth. If a child is under 18, the NHS will refer them to the Gender Identity Development Service. A multidisciplinary team at the Gender Identity Development Service will assess the needs of the child and provide appropriate treatment and support, including family or individual child therapy, support groups for children and parents, and hormone therapy.[42]

The NHS website states that, in practice, most youth will receive only psychological support rather than medical intervention. The NHS says a very small percentage of children *may* qualify for hormonal treatment at the onset of puberty, but most will have to wait until they are 17 to receive care from the adult clinic. According to the NHS: "Most children with suspected gender dysphoria will not have the condition once they enter puberty."[43] The same reason is often used to deny hormonal treatment and other care for minors in the United States as well, but it is currently considered an outdated theory among the leading experts in the field.

According to Dr. Johanna Olsen of the Children's Hospital of Los Angeles, this notion is most likely based on one particular study that relied on unsound research. Dr. Olsen has decades of experience working with transgender children and she is seen in her profession as a leader in the field. When I heard her speak at the annual Gender Spectrum Conference in 2015, Dr. Olsen described a 2008 study conducted in The Netherlands that showed 80 percent of children who identified as transgender youth later reverted to identify as cisgender adults. The study tracked a cohort of youth who identified as transgender and sought care from a particular clinic. However, some of these people never returned to the clinic for follow-up care, and therefore did not report later on whether they identified as transgender adults. These youth were included in the study and counted among those who reported reverting back to their assigned gender. Their inclusion contributed to the high rate noted in the flawed study.

Dr. Olson went on to say that she has not seen anything in her practice over many years to support those flawed statistics. Among those she has met who have insistent, persistent, and consistent gender dysphoria, the rate of those who have reverted to their cisgender identity is close to zero. To the contrary, Dr. Olsen told us about research that shows children who receive care early in life have the greatest chance of successful treatment (psychological, medical, surgical, or some combination of the three) for their dysphoria.

While there has been much progress in both the United States and the United Kingdom, clearly there is much work to be done to provide appropriate care for transgender adults and children in the United States, the United Kingdom, and worldwide. The medical community must acknowledge its responsibility to keep up with the most recent best practices regarding gender. Transgender people must be assured they will receive the medical care they need, and that their medical care will be covered by insurance or national health care. No one should be denied medical coverage or treatment based on gender. It is unethical, and it is dangerous.

BIG SISTER, LITTLE BROTHER

by Emily Barkin, Amaya's sister, 5 years older

"No, that is not my brother, that's my sister." This was always an uncomfortable thing to say to any person who was unaware of Amaya's gender. Something about that sentence always made me feel awkward. Not only did this statement prove to be false, but even before we knew that, it just didn't *feel* right. I was never embarrassed, rather it was just exhausting having to correct people about something that inevitably confused them. The follow-up reaction from the inquirer was always one or more of the following (in no particular order): excessive apologies, shocked expressions, and/or extensive vocal confusion. None of which I enjoyed. This predictable charade, along with the displeasure I took participating in it, is now part of a time I look back upon with the same feelings one gets when looking back at a world before modern technology: I cannot believe we used to do *that*.

Amaya had his top surgery in May 2014. That same weekend, I was in Los Angeles for a spur-of-the-moment Universal Studios "let's be tourists!" trip with a good friend. It seems odd to me now that I did not even consider how the dates I'd scheduled for this trip would mean not being home the day of his surgery. I can only attest that this must be because my brother had exuded extreme confidence in the weeks leading up to his surgery, and I can't recall seeing him express any nervousness about it. It is obvious to me that, in his mind at the time, this surgery was the *one thing* standing in the way of him feeling like his true self: a teenage boy. Though he never spoke directly to me about it, I know that binding his chest daily had been such an upsetting and horrible experience, and the anticipation of not having to do that anymore must have eclipsed the fears that anyone might have preceding a surgical procedure.

At Universal Studios, I bought souvenirs for my family. In one of the souvenir shops, I saw fake Academy Award trophies with a variety of award titles to choose from. One of them said, "Best Brother." I could not think of a better gift to give Amaya after his surgery! His procedure was scheduled for the next day, and that evening I flew back from my trip. I walked in the door of my parents' house (I lived in the next town over at the time), and he was heavily medicated, half asleep on the living room couch. I gave him the trophy, and he thanked me. Although he didn't show much emotion (he seldom does), I could tell it made him so happy that I'd supported his decision to have surgery and to be the person that he is. I like to think that he sees the trophy as validation of my support.

Accepting Amaya for who he is has always been simple for me. In so many cases, a transgender person first presents as their gender at birth, and then seemingly (to observers) makes a sudden switch at a later age when they transition to become the gender that they truly are. Amaya certainly did not wait a long time to begin his transition from female to male appearance. Almost as soon as he was able to speak for himself, he began to make his own decisions regarding clothing, etc. He refused to wear clothes that presented him as a girl. He would throw fits about wearing dresses, and his wish lists for birthdays and holidays became filled with things related to sports, action figures, and other things that are primarily marketed to boys and not girls. Of course, anyone can be interested in anything they like, regardless of gender, but the reality is that even to this day, certain toys are marketed for boys and others for girls. Amaya's interests rotated, but one thing was for sure—his interests always reflected those of a stereotypical boy rather than a girl.

Because of his clothes and interests, nothing about his transition seemed out of the ordinary to me. In fact, I would barely even call it a "transition" as far as his personality is concerned. I cannot think of any one moment where he made a dramatic shift. Gradually, he grew older and his wants became more and more apparent. However, I do remember one particular time when I noticed Amaya's gender on Facebook had changed. Facebook allows users to list family members and link them to one's profile. I had linked all my family to my profile, and Amaya's profile was listed as my sister, as we all knew him to be. One day, I happened to notice that Facebook identified him as my "brother." My mom and I casually brought it up with Amaya, asking why he made the switch. He told us at first that someone must have hacked his account and changed it. At this point, we were aware that some people would talk about him and express curiosity because his appearance did not match his gender (according to what they were used to seeing). So when Amaya said his Facebook account was hacked, we asked him if he knew who it was and if he thought someone did it to be mean. He said he didn't know, and he added that he didn't care about changing it back either. He later admitted to my mom that indeed he had changed it himself. This was the first time I know of that he expressed being a boy outwardly. I can only imagine how good it must have felt for Amaya to see himself (even if only online) portrayed with the correct gender assignment.

My relationship with Amaya has always been typical as far as siblings go. We shared a room at one point, even shared a bunk bed. Road trips were always a pain because we could never figure out how to leave each other alone. Sharing a back seat, we would sass each other, mock each other, and generally drive each other (and our parents) up the wall. As most siblings do, we have grown out of these behaviors and into a wonderful brother–sister relationship, which I truly cherish. Although most sibling relationships mature as the people themselves mature, I cannot help but think that Amaya's transformation has vastly improved his ability to show himself and demonstrate his love outwardly. I fully believe that Amaya's ability to finally live as his true self is not limited to physical attributes. His personality, strength, and knowledge have always lived inside him, and it's about time we got to enjoy it too! I am so proud to call this guy my brother.

— *Part 5* —

COMPLETE

Complete. In this phase of transition, a person has made the necessary adjustments to live comfortably as their authentic, affirmed self. It is up to each individual to decide when their transition is complete—and for some people this feeling of completion may change at some point in the future, perhaps leading to yet another process of transition and a different sense of completeness. As I have said many times throughout this book, each person's transition path is unique. Equally true, each person gets to decide for themselves if and when their transition is complete. Some people feel complete at one point, but their gender dysphoria arises again later in life, and they find that they need to take further or different steps to live authentically. Some people may never feel their transition is complete, or even that it needs to be. Others may be satisfied to say their transition is complete. For now.

✺

THE "TALK"

by Gabriel Barkin, Amaya's father

My wife and I were talking last night about the "Talk." Birds and bees, genital responsibility, sheaths and raincoats, and a Johnny on every Jimmy—did I ever discuss such things with our boy?

I never got the Talk myself. I can't think of a single thing either of my parents ever said to me that might have touched, even just a tad, on any topic that might be part of a typical Talk. (My mom said to me once upon a time that their parenting style was "benign neglect.") But I suppose in theory that it's a parental chore one mustn't shy from when the time comes and opportunity presents. So, yes, did I ever discuss such things with our boy?

We were in the car, just me and my son, perhaps about a year ago when he was 17. I said to him, "So I guess I'm supposed to give you the *Talk*." A silent sense of doom filled the air; we'd both known this conversation *might* come someday, but we'd probably both guessed the odds of that actually happening were slim. And yet, here we were. I felt that calling of fatherhood, words spilled out. But not too many: "I suppose since you don't have a penis, what I would have to say just boils down to this: Be nice to women and respect them. Don't be a dick just because you don't have one."

Or something like that. It was probably less droll, less dramatic. But it was short and sweet. I think he replied that Mom had talked with him about "stuff."

And that was that. We drove onward to dinner and talked about cars and school.

COMPLETE, FOR NOW: AN
——— INTERVIEW WITH THE BBC ———

Amaya, Gabriel, and I were interviewed by the BBC's Louis Theroux for a television documentary in April 2015. Theroux's documentary, *Transgender Kids*, was broadcast in the United Kingdom and other countries. It was not shown in the United States because some of the other families whose children were interviewed on camera did not want to run the risk of being recognized and "outed" in their community.

In this documentary, viewers are introduced to several children aged 5–16 who are gender-questioning or define as transgender or non-binary. Theroux interviews the children and the parents, and we learn about a wide variety of circumstances. We meet one child whose parents are divorced; interviewed separately, we learn the mother and father do not see eye to eye regarding what is best for their gender-questioning child. The child lives as a boy at one house and as a girl at the other. Another child is a young teen transitioning from male to female. She is supported and accepted at home, but she cries when she talks about the bullying she suffers at school.

Theroux's program also explores some of the medical options available to prepubescent children, and discusses how those options differ from the options for tweens and teens who have experienced puberty. I've discussed previously how puberty blockers, for instance, are an option for kids who have not yet entered puberty. Use of this medical approach is increasing in the United States, but not in the United Kingdom, where an outdated national health policy assumes most transgender youth will "grow out of it." Since Theroux's documentary was geared primarily toward a UK audience, I was glad to see he presented a positive depiction of the appropriate use of puberty blockers to give children, and their families, time to explore their gender identity before they go through what may be the "wrong" puberty. Featured in contrast to the children were interviews with trans and gender non-conforming adults who had undergone some type of surgery to align their body with their gender identification. At 17, Amaya was the youngest interviewee among this group.

Here is an excerpt from Amaya's interview with Louis Theroux.[44] We met at the surgical center where Dr. Crane had performed the surgery. Dr. Crane was in the room with us as the cameras rolled, and Gabriel and I have brief cameos in the corner of the frame—we were interviewed by Louis Theroux as well, but all of our comments were left on the cutting-room floor. That's okay, Amaya had *much* more interesting stuff to say!

INTERVIEW WITH LOUIS THEROUX, APRIL 2015

Louis Theroux (LT): Before you grew breasts you weren't having dysphoria? To do with your body?

Amaya Barkin (AB): No, not that I can remember. At least at around 11 or 12 is really when I started to develop and when all those dysphoric issues started to come up. And then progressed from there.

LT: What was that like?

AB: It was tough. (Long pause) It definitely kind of hurt my own mental health a little bit I guess you could say.

LT: Why?

AB: It didn't make me want to be very social and kinda gave me a bit of an anxiety issue. It just didn't help anything, in terms of me going out in public and having to deal with it. It definitely made me have a bit of a struggle in that sense.

LT: It just didn't feel like it was you or you didn't like the way it felt or looked?

AB: I didn't like mainly the way other people were perceiving me. And so it was a lot of how I was perceiving myself, plus how others were seeing me, just on the street. How others were seeing me, people that didn't know me, and how they would think of me.

The interview went on, and Theroux asked Amaya if he felt he needed to do anything more. Amaya said he felt "complete, for now." He was asked if he wished he hadn't had to go through female puberty, and he replied, "All that I have gone through has made me who I am today."

Many of us take years or even a lifetime before we can come to this place of acceptance. Some never do. "Complete, for now" seems like a good place.

ROCK ON!

by Weston Walls, a very dear family friend

November 25, 2016

Hello Amaya!

This is your friend Weston. I'm writing this to let you know how much I admire and appreciate you! To witness your evolution over the years has been nothing short of astounding.

Your mother told me about you before I met you. I had been out of touch with Gabe and Janna for a few years. As we were getting reacquainted, Janna mentioned that her younger daughter looked, dressed and acted like a boy. She said strangers usually mistook you for a boy. After a few minutes of conversation, I asked what Gabe and Janna would do if their daughter eventually wanted a sex change. This was the early 2000s, and terms like "gender reassignment" were not yet part of our national vocabulary. Janna said something like, "Well, we'll deal with that when the time comes." It felt really good to me to know that my longtime friends were open and willing to be as supportive as possible in response to this potential challenge.

For the first few years I knew you, I saw an adolescent who was withdrawn and moody. It was tough to get you to string together more than two or three words at a time. There are people who would say that was typical adolescent/teen behavior, and they wouldn't be completely wrong. However, you seemed even more committed to being downcast and terse than most teens. But over time, you gradually opened up to me, little by little. Your parents commented on our budding friendship multiple times. I would drive up from LA for a visit, and as I sat in the kitchen catching up with Gabe and Janna, you would come out of your room and join us for a bit. Your parents were always surprised and pleased to have you join us; it was rare for you to be social with them and their friends.

I recall giving you a ride one afternoon to go meet the rest of your family somewhere. Knowing you were into hip-hop, I played a song I thought you would like. That was the moment when we started to grow more deeply connected. I'm imagining now you were thinking, "Cool, Weston likes stuff other than that hippy-folk-jam-band shit my parents listen to all the time!" (Full disclosure: I like that stuff too.) I might be wrong to assume we had such a "moment." Only you can tell me.

One day a few years ago I was getting ready to drive north to surprise your father at his 50th birthday celebration. I was texting with your mom and she mentioned that you'd told the family you wanted to be referred to with masculine pronouns. I asked if you would want me to do the same, and your mom replied that you would love that!

I'm not going to lie, it was a little challenging to change pronouns at first. I just wasn't used to it. I found it easier to say things like "dude" and "brother" than it was to use "he" and "his." I had to start from my own comfort zone. But what I saw that weekend was a very different person than the one I'd seen in visits over prior years. You were walking more upright. You seemed more confident and grounded. You were definitely more comfortable in your own body. Dare I say it, you had a bit of a glow about you!

Time moved forward, and your mom told me you'd decided to go ahead with the procedures to have your breasts removed. I remember feeling a mix of excitement and apprehension. New territories were being explored, what would be found there? It was several months before I saw you next, and when I did, I was blown away. You were sitting on your bike in your driveway. A group of your friends was with you. One of the girls put her arm around you and her head on your shoulder for a moment. You were acting like it was nothing. For me, it was *everything*! I hadn't yet seen you being that social with anyone, ever! With your friends, parents, sister, anyone at all. I was thrilled!

Since then, I've watched your confidence grow, heard your voice deepen, seen your body develop. (Those abs! Jesus Christ! Ah the low bf% of youth.) The evolution from your cocoon days to the opening of your wings has been an inspiration. I know for sure that you will continue to inspire others for the rest of your life. I'm excited to watch those stories as they unfold!

Rock on!

THERE HE GOES!

I wrote this on Amaya's first day of his senior year of high school (August 20, 2015):

> Amaya, my son, my youngest child starts his senior year of high school today. I feel a combination of excitement, concern, and mostly pride. The first days of school in previous school years were filled with trepidation and anxiety, but this year is different: Amaya transitioned from female to male during his high school years, and although he's told me in the past that transition for transgender people is "often an ongoing process," he considers his own transition to be "complete, for now."
>
> A snapshot of *before* and *after* [transition] would reveal many changes. His shoulders are broad now, and he stands tall. He has a deep voice and an Adam's apple. He shaves his face!
>
> A deeper look reveals even more:
>
> - the un-slouching of shoulders no longer hiding unwanted breasts
> - the brightening of eyes no longer dim from depression associated with gender dysphoria
> - the general lightness of a heart no longer heavy with the weight of the ultimate secret.
>
> My boy is becoming a man. He is clear who he is, and equally important he is seen by others as he sees himself.
>
> I believe, as my own mother taught me, that one of a mother's most important tasks is to raise her child to be independent. A momma bird has to teach her baby bird

to fly. (My mom occasionally bemoans how successful she was at this task, as I left her behind one day and moved all the way to California from New York. But that is another story.)

As I watch my son go out the door today, a senior headed off to his last year in high school, I can feel it: he is ready. While he will have to continue to navigate the many challenges transgender people still face on every day, he is ready. And so am I.

There he goes!

WHO'S "SHE"?!

The years of being in-between are long gone, and it seems Amaya has always been my son in both my mind and my heart. So it really takes me by surprise when someone misgenders Amaya. *She*?! Who is *that*!?

These days, when I see someone at the grocery store who has not seen me or Amaya for a long time, they often misgender him. They may ask me innocently, "How is she?" Sometimes it's a person who knows Amaya has transitioned but has not yet become well practiced in using the correct pronouns. Sometimes it's a person who just has not heard that my child has transitioned. So in those moments at the grocery store, I am faced with a choice: Do I take the time to tell about Amaya's transition? Do I even have the *time* it would take to tell this person, here in the grocery store checkout line, about this sensitive subject, and in a respectful way? Is it important that *this person* knows? And now that Amaya is an adult, isn't it really *his* story to tell?

Sometimes I do share Amaya's story, our story, my story. And sometimes it's just easier to say something gender neutral ("Amaya is doing great!") and move on. As one mother of a gender-creative child said recently, we moms often feel like "I just don't have the energy today, or the time or the desire, to defend my child to this person."

When I spoke with Cheri Stein, another mom to a transgender child, she said this:

> Living in a small tourist town, my family, all these years later, still makes a choice whether to inform, educate, or just smile and say something vague when asked how our daughter is doing by someone who doesn't know about my son's transition. At first, we felt we were betraying our son not to explain our new situation—but we are far more comfortable now and realize standing in the grocery line isn't always the best place for meaningful conversation. Especially when others naïvely ask uneducated and insensitive questions about sexual orientation or plumbing—we're still working on how to patiently educate about regular privacy norms without adding eye rolls on this one!

It is up to each family to decide to whom they want to reveal any information about a child's gender variance and transition. The decision to come out, or to let people in, can be affected by many circumstances. First and foremost, it is always up to the individual. It is a matter of utmost respect for our individual rights; no one should ever "out" anyone without their permission. In the case of minor-aged children, parents are often the ones who communicate to others about gender changes, certainly when their children are in the pre-teenage years. However, in any case, parents should not do so without agreement from their children, even if a child is very young. (Let me be clear again: If my child was not willing to let me share our story I would not be doing so.) A parent's decision to reveal information about their child's gender to a specific individual may be based on many factors, including safety and health concerns, emergent need-to-know situations, and the relative balance of family and community support needed *vis-à-vis* the level of acceptance and tolerance in one's community. It can be helpful for families to discuss individual preferences for such scenarios with their gender-variant children, and to agree upon a plan for how parents will respond and what they will reveal when confronted with people who may misgender their kids.

COLLEGE UNBOUND

Amaya attended NOVA, the self-study high school program in our town (while also enrolled concurrently at the traditional high school close to our home for math and language classes) until he graduated in 2016. He stayed engaged in his learning and continued to earn high grades. Toward the end of junior year, he began his college search. We only considered schools with a high rating with Campus Pride,[45] a non-profit organization that works to create safer college environments for LGBTQ and ally students. We also made sure there was an active LGBT Center on all of our target campuses.

In December of his senior year, Amaya received an early acceptance letter to Portland State University, where his high marks qualified him to participate in the Western Undergraduate Exchange (WUE) program. WUE allows qualified undergraduates from some western US states to attend school in other states with a deep discount on the out-of-state tuition. So his grades actually did pay off!

Amaya graduated from NOVA with high academic honors, including the school's Principal's Award and the President's Education Award signed by President Obama. He also received several scholarships awarded by our local Rotary Club. We were so proud of our guy! The Rotary presented him with a scholarship bestowed in recognition of my boy's "perseverance and success in overcoming obstacles in his life." We were surprised at the scholarship award luncheon when the Rotary called Amaya's name for a *second* scholarship, one we had not been told about in advance.

In addition to the academic awards he earned, he received a unique award from his senior year NOVA teacher Ms. Julie Adams, who called him to the stage with these words:

> The Renaissance was a time of great discovery and advancement in many areas of art and culture. From that time period has risen the concept of "The Renaissance Man," which Dictionary.com describes as: "An outstandingly versatile, well-rounded person." A lot to live up to by high school, but some traits come to mind: willing to explore and challenge oneself; pursuing a diversity of interests both academically and personally; measuring where you are against where you wish to be and doggedly moving toward the person you wish to become.
>
> NOVA's Renaissance Man: Amaya Barkin.

❋

REFLECTIONS:
A LETTER TO MY BELOVED
by Linda Masia, Amaya's maternal grandmother

July, 2016

Dear Aaron,

I have a very interesting story to tell you. Of course, I've already told you, but now I will write it down.

When you suddenly and sadly left us in 1997, Janna was seven months pregnant. We had suffered Dad's loss just two years prior, not so sudden but also so sad. After you died, Janna stayed with me for about a month. She needed to leave and go back home to California to have her baby, but also she needed to be with me and mom, her dear Gramma. Since Janna had planned another home birth, she did not know if a boy or girl would be arriving, but she decided with Gabe that this baby, if a son, would be named Aaron Joseph in memory and honor of you and Dad. If a girl, still would be named for both of you, but using just the A and J initials.

A little over three months go by and Janna delivers—a girl! She is named Amaya Jael. Emily, your first and only grandchild (whom you loved beyond loving), loves "her baby," and life goes on. Emily was such a girly girl, loving the skirts and tights, fancy socks and hair stuff, and angel wings. Amaya, at an early age, perhaps two-ish, began to show a preference for coveralls, jeans, trucks, nothing with ruffles or bright colors, no skirts or tights, no angel wings. A couple of years go by and we are thinking, wow, Amaya is surely a real tomboy, not liking anything feminine, not clothes or toys or activities. The family would come to New York to visit, and I'd see Emily choosing to wear the same kind of outfit Janna was wearing, but Amaya would check to see what Gabe was wearing and dress like her dad.

2001 arrives and brother Shawn is getting married. Shawn and Val invite Emily and Amaya to be flower girls. Oh, wonderful for Emily, pretty dress and shoes and a flower basket. Not so much for Amaya, who also did wear a pretty dress and shoes and carry a flower basket but did not at all wear a smile. Of course, we can look back *now* and understand, but at the time, we did not "get it." Incidentally, Mom would call Amaya "he," and I would say, "Mom, Amaya is a girl!"

As it will, time goes by, and I see Janna, Gabe, and the kids a couple of times a year, once here on the East Coast and once there on the West Coast. I see Amaya growing taller and developing a feminine body, but insisting on a short, boy haircut, and boy sneakers, and boy clothes purchased in the boys' department. I see a kind of moody kid, yet sweet and loving, plays sports, does well in school. But joyous, no. I hear and see Emily pushing Amaya in the back to encourage her sibling to "stand up straight" and I don't understand why Amaya won't stand up straight myself.

Perhaps it just took a really long time to find the words, but Amaya thankfully did, and told his truth: "I am a boy!" Janna tells Emily that he wants to be called her brother, not her sister. Emily is fine with that and so the journey begins. So many people, upon meeting Amaya, already thought he was a boy, never thought they were meeting a girl.

Amaya is 16, physical changes continue, and he looks more and more like a boy. I notice that when we eat out, he is always drumming on the table. The family comes east for a visit, and as usual I invite the East Coast family to dinner to see the West Coasters. Everyone here now knows that Amaya is transgender. The nieces and nephews, aunts, uncles, and cousins are here. Everything is normal, everything is fine and warm. We are all respectful of pronouns, Amaya doesn't mind if there is an occasional slip, we are all learning. What a great family we have. No doubts, only acceptance.

The youngest cousin, perhaps he is three, puts both hands on Amaya's face and says, "Amaya, I just love you!"

Amaya is 18. I attended his high school graduation. He earned several honors and a small scholarship and will start college in the fall. He is tall, handsome, funny, fun, and smart. He has his dad's gift of sarcasm, his mom's gift of kindness, and hopefully, his Grampa Aaron's gifts of patience and unwavering, unconditional love.

Love, Linda

MY AMAYA

by Elaine Barkin, Amaya's paternal grandmother,
September 2014, Valley Village, CA

Editor's Note: In this piece, female pronouns are used to talk about Amaya when he was younger.

Amaya's birth in January, 1998, occurred three months after the premature death at age 58 of Aaron Masia, Janna's beloved dad, which brought great sadness to the Masia-Barkin households. "This baby was not supposed to be an 'A' baby," cried Janna, but alas, Amaya was an "A" baby. [Janna's note: An "A" baby because in our family we name new babies after our loved ones who have died. This baby would be named for my recently departed father whose name started with "A," hence, an "A" baby. The baby was not supposed to be an "A" baby because my father died very late into my pregnancy, and until then we were not going to name the baby after him.] And she was, thought I, a second girl with loads of clothes awaiting her, including a bunch of pretty batik dresses I had bought for her sister Emily during my many summers spent in Bali and Java.

On Amaya's third or fourth birthday, we drove to a toy store at the Northgate Mall and I asked her to pick out whatever she wanted. After a few moments, she—rather sheepishly I thought—pointed to a large toy Ford F-150 pickup truck. "Are you sure?" I asked. "Yes," she said, and home we went with the truck. Admittedly, I was a bit surprised; maybe the truck choice was some sort of statement, but if so, it wasn't totally out of character. And why shouldn't girls play with trucks?

So let's fast forward a few years, by which time Amaya not only had refused the pretty batik dresses but also had begun wearing boys' underwear and pants and kept her hair cut short. Okay, I thought, a tomboy, like me— although I'd worn girl's underwear.

Before I continue, I want to say something about my own history and awareness of gender and sexuality issues. I was born in the Bronx in 1932 and by age 12 had read Radclyffe Hall's *The Well of Loneliness*. During my teens, I spent time in Greenwich Village, where being with homosexuals was just part of the scene. As a young musician and college student in the 1950s, I hung out with dancers and theater people and had several gay and lesbian pals. That was the way the world was in New York: loads of minorities of all stripes and colors, way before the March on Washington, Stonewall, *La Cage aux Folles*, and AIDS. Homophobic police harassment and physical violence were an everyday occurrence, as were suicides.

But also—*voila!*—there was the revelation in 1952 that someone called Christine (born George) Jorgensen had undergone sex reassignment surgery in Denmark, not a procedure much known or used back then! She was a worldwide sensation and tabloids had a field day: "Former GI becomes Blonde Bombshell!" Transgender was a new word for me, even if I had visited lesbian bars with friends where many women and men cross-dressed, but in later decades I read about cultures in which "third gender" persons have long been integral members of communities from Albania to India to Polynesia to several Native American tribes.

Back again to my erstwhile second granddaughter, after a look through photograph albums from Amaya's birth to the present.

As Amaya grew up it became more than evident that "tomboy" was a totally inadequate description. Basically, I didn't care much insofar as the most critical factor was for Amaya to feel comfortable with who she was or who she was becoming. The disconnect between what was going on in Amaya's mind and what was perceived or assumed externally by others must have been near breaking point for Amaya, but many of us were unaware of any inner turmoil. Maybe Rocco knew. (When she was a young child, Rocco was one of Amaya's secret-pretend pals and confidants. I once overheard a one-way conversation with Rocco coming from Amaya's bedroom, and when I asked whom she was talking to, there was a sly smile but no answer.)

In 2007, my husband George and I celebrated our 50th anniversary, and Amaya, now nine, decked herself out in a long-sleeved print shirt, long pants, and (if I recall) a tie. In restaurants, waiters would ask Amaya, "What would you like, young man?" Her parents had stopped correcting waiters and waitresses; Amaya didn't seem to mind. For me, no matter what she looked like to strangers, I thought of Amaya as a girl, a she. And if Amaya had to go to the bathroom while we were at the movies, I would go along to be sure that she wasn't hassled or told to use the men's room. (Designated, non-unisex, public bathrooms are ground zero for the trans community!)

Insofar as I didn't live with Amaya and her parents, all I could do was speculate: maybe Amaya was going to be a very butch lesbian, or perhaps she was some sort of third-gender person. Amaya was the only girl on her Little League team, and many of the boys didn't even seem to know that she was a girl—while those who knew didn't care as long as she played well. Moreover, there were/are role models aplenty: Ellen DeGeneres, Rachel Maddow, Robin Roberts for starters.

When Amaya did "come out" at 15 as a trans FTM, none of us was surprised, but the full implications of transition would take a while to be assimilated and understood. Amaya hadn't changed. Who she was, and who he had announced he was becoming—both were totally recognizable as the Amaya we had always known, or at least the Amaya that we were permitted to know. Whatever perplexity had been brewing inside for over a decade had mostly been externalized only via short hair and boy's clothing, not such a big deal I'd thought. She had characteristics that reminded me of my son Gabe (knuckle-cracking, a loping walk), and of my brother Bill (quivering knees). But the desire at 15 to minimize the appearance of breasts suggested a bigger deal; alas, menstruating isn't as safe to modify or do away with, not yet at least. If the medical community was more certain about long-term effects of hormone replacement therapy, I'd have been less anxious.

One of my concerns was, and still is, the fear of an antagonistic response or bullying from classmates and strangers. Teenagers can be brutal; social media can be deadly. I wished for the best and feared if not the worst, then damaging negativity. Brandon Teena's story frightened me, and Michel Foucault's 1980 retelling of the memoirs of intersex person Herculine Barbin saddened me. The latter was hardly the same circumstance but worrisome nonetheless.

And yet, whenever I told a friend or my two sisters-in-law about Amaya, I was told similar stories: of Andrew who'd lived in Paris for a year and returned home at 18 a beautiful and happy Andrea; of a friend's FTM child who transitioned and is now a married orthodox Rabbi;

and Amaya's maternal grandmother, Linda, is close friends with the grandmother of well-known MTF teen trans activist, Jazz Jennings. In a recent *LA Times* "Dear Amy" column headlined, "Nephew Wants to Be Niece," a letter from a confused aunt led to Amy's compassionate advice: be supportive. (Several days later the column's headline read, "Disclosing One's Sexuality," and contained a letter from a bisexual person asking if and when it's okay to disclose one's sexual identity in new relationships. Amy's practical advice: wait until the third date!) FTM and MTF personae now appear on network TV and cable regularly, comparable to the slow-but-steady appearance in the 1970s of people of color on TV and in ads, and also comparable to the ongoing increase of women in politics. And regarding politics—in Oklahoma recently, the state's first openly trans MTF candidate for state legislature lost by just 22 votes.

Back in my old days, LGBs were slowly, in many instances painfully, finding acceptance. Nowadays it's the T's "outing" their way in.

For sure, hundreds more LGBTQ people of all ages remain closeted and fearful for personal, religious, financial, professional, and political reasons. A large number of my UCLA colleagues were closeted gay men; several were married, several were alcoholic. Not until the early 1990s did most of them fully come out. My dear friend and colleague Paul came out at age 75!

In New Zealand, Georgina Beyer (born George Bertrand) of Maori heritage became the world's first trans MTF Member of Parliament in 1999, representing the Labour Party. She had had sexual reassignment surgery in 1997, at age 30. (Among New Zealand's other world firsts was giving the vote to women in 1893.) In the

United States, among many others there's Jennifer Finley Boylan and Martine Rothblatt, both of whom came out as MTFs in midlife, both of them married with children and wives. And then there is, perhaps more pertinently and certainly more famously, FTM Chaz Bono!

In the early 1990s, music historians and theorists began organizing *ad hoc* sessions to discuss Queer Music Theory, a then-new concept and field exploring the intersection of musical and LGBTQ spheres. They met, at first timidly, at national annual conferences, and now such sessions are a regular feature at such events. In 1994, I was asked to co-edit a collection of essays concerning composing women, feminist music theory, and gender. My co-editor for this project, Lydia Hamessley, is a musicologist and a lesbian active in the field of Queer Music Theory. Our book *Audible Traces*, was published in 2000, and joined a spate of similar collections. I had, and still have, doubts about the audibility of gender or sexuality in music—for if one accepts such a premise, one also accepts narrow and limited definitions and boundaries. Nowadays, courses and programs on gender and sexuality in music are widespread. Academicians love jumping on new bandwagons.

But back again to Amaya. For him, fortunately, there is today a community of similarly conflicted or decisive youths and adults with whom each can share experiences, doubts, and support via YouTube and social media websites. He has access to meet face-to-face with dedicated counselors, and some of them are also trans people. None, or few at best, of these support groups were available to the LGBTQ community 60 years ago when many of my friends could have benefited from empathic advice or commiseration. Doubly fortunate for Amaya, the Bay Area is one of the better places in the

United States for a trans person to find simpatico voices and counselors and doctors and lawyers and insurance coverage. Most significantly, Amaya's family, the entire Barkin-Masia clan, fully supports him.

But the shift of pronoun has been a bitch. At the start, I told Amaya that if I put a quarter into a jar every time I said "she" instead of "he," Amaya would soon be able to buy a completely new wardrobe. Gradually and self-consciously, I have tried to use male pronouns whenever speaking of, about, or to Amaya. But it still seems weird to say "he," or "him," or "his" when I speak about or think of Amaya as a very young child, when she was still wearing dresses and had longer hair. And I can no longer casually ask Gabe, "How are the girls?" (I try to ask "How are Em and Am?")

Fact is, the shift of pronoun brings with it the shift of reality, the acceptance of a new reality. The welcoming, the acknowledgment. Along with the awareness that Amaya might be gay, straight, or bi, just like the rest of us. That there are multiple ways of being.

What might seem to be a set of confusing statements expresses an enrichment of sexual-gender identification, all referring to Amaya's relationship to me and vice versa:

- She is my youngest grandchild.

- He is my youngest grandchild.

- She is my youngest granddaughter.

- He is my youngest granddaughter.

- She is my youngest grandson.

- He is my youngest grandson, or transgrandson.

After his disclosure, it didn't take anyone in Amaya's family long to accept his decision and ultimately be proud of him for transitioning at such a relatively young age. Teen years are tough any way they're sliced, but to overcome compounding issues of sexuality and gender identification takes confidence, strength, and a sense of what's real and how one wants to live one's life.

Of course I worry about physical and physiological issues. I never imagined that a grandchild of mine would opt for a double mastectomy at 16! But I think it was a mature decision. He has comrades and is rather calm when facing the confusion of strangers. I suppose I wish Amaya would change his first name or add a name to it, but that's my problem and none of my business.

And then at some point there's hormone replacement therapy, and I worry about that as I do about any medical procedure. I worry that nasty brutes out there will make trouble for him. A recent *LA Times* article describes the many problems facing LGBTQ youths in foster care, reporting that "Gay foster youths are twice as likely to report being treated poorly by the foster care system than their straight counterparts, according to a new study of Los Angeles County's foster care system."[46] Amaya will never face this issue, but homophobia and transphobia will never disappear. So I remain anxious. "What, me worry?"

To all LGBTQ's and the rest of us, I close with Miranda's words from *The Tempest* by William Shakespeare:

> *O wonder!*
> *How many goodly creatures are there here!*
> *How beauteous mankind is!*
> *O brave new world,*
> *That has such people in't.*

POSTSCRIPT: MY AMAYA 2, DECEMBER 2015

It has been more than a year since I wrote the words above. Amaya is now preparing to go to college in Portland, Oregon, a milieu he says is congenial to the LGBTQ community. Now post-double mastectomy, now taking testosterone, Amaya's voice has deepened, his chest is flat—and as I wrote above, he has remained the same person but not the same person. That's the odd rub. More self-assured, as independent as always, valuing his privacy and yet perhaps a tad more sociable. And the pronoun shift has become easier for me.

2014 and 2015 have been the years of T-conscious-raising! Pundits and politicians and presidents of the United States have all referred to trans people in public commentaries. Documentaries, books, and websites are available for those who want to learn more. A spate of midlife adults and seniors have come out publicly. All of which, we hope, has been good for Amaya and the rest of us. Confusion, negativity, and nastiness will remain among various individuals and entire nations. But Amaya has a lot to look forward to and I am confident he will live a full, productive, and fantastic life.

POST-POSTSCRIPT: MY AMAYA 3, JUNE 13, 2016

Today is one day after the horror in Orlando (where a mass-shooting took place in a gay club) and five days after Amaya's graduation from Nova Independent Study High School in Novato. George and I flew up, Burbank to Oakland, to be at his graduation and to spend time with family: Amaya, his dad Gabriel, our no. 3 son; Amaya's mom Janna, sister Emily, maternal grandma Linda Masia, and Jesse, his uncle, our no. 2 son. The contrast between the two events cannot be more stark, the graduation an outpouring of love and acceptance, Orlando an embodiment of hate and malevolence. For many days after Orlando, the lyrics of Oscar Hammerstein II's "You've Got to Be Carefully Taught" from *South Pacific* (which I'd seen 67 years ago) ran through my head, something about how we are *taught* to be afraid of people with different eyes and skin shade.

The graduation was special in many ways: a relatively small group—ca. 60 graduates, about 20 in Amaya's Indie program and 40 in Marin Oaks High School. The group comprised a Crayola-like array of flesh-tones from pale pinks—aka "white," definitely in the minority at this graduation—through various ochres, siennas, and umbers, encompassing a wide age range. Several teachers took turns speaking personally and directly to each student as each mounted the steps to receive her/his degree, with yowling, clapping and stomping—from folks in chairs on the floors and benches in the bleachers— accompanying each graduate. Amaya's shiny royal blue gown was bedecked with medals: the Principal's award for academic achievement; for being a Renaissance Man, the latter my favorite; an Honors award and two scholarships from the Rotary Club ($$$$!). Afterwards we went out for dinner and all were very proud! Amaya looks wonderful, a handsome 18+-year-old with loads of friends. He now stands fully up straight, smiles a lot and is so obviously more comfortable with himself and the rest of the world and is himself a supportive person. At dinner that night all was so much more comfortable and the annoyance I experienced years back when waiters said to Amaya, "And what will you have, young man?" was gone. Now young manhood is what Amaya is in the midst of and will be for a bunch of years to come.

Whether the Orlando killer was motivated by a dedication to ISIS or an act of homophobia doesn't matter; it was probably a combination of both with a mix of self-hatred. That it happened around the time of the annual nationwide PRIDE celebrations has only increased awareness, for better and for worse, of LGBTQs, their presence and their legal problems. I write "for worse" because such "publicity" is not always beneficial for a minority population, in this instance maybe ca. 2½ percent of Americans. But Amaya, I write again, has love, support and many friends of all stripes!

Amaya will be going to Portland State University in Oregon (and is probably there as you read this), currently planning to major in clinical psychology and enrolled in a cohort freshman year program. Portland is said to be a congenial city for the LGBTQ community, for vegans, masseurs and yoga teachers, for flower adults, yuppies, hippies and housing developers who are gentrifying like crazy.

So again with deep wishes for a future marked by love (which is not "all you need" but always a boon), inclusivity, intelligence, good-will, a caring community and enjoyment of life and life's work.

PPPS: MY AMAYA 4, JUNE 30, 2016

Today, June 30, the US Military has decided to allow transgender men and women to serve openly in all of the armed forces—another notch in the transgender belt, so to speak, although I hope that Amaya will never want or have to serve. Moreover, in recent primaries for

Congress—Colorado—and the Senate—Utah—two openly transgender women, both Progressive Democrats, have won and will run against Republican incumbents in November. Misty Plowright in Colorado and Misty K. Snow in Utah!! Politics may not be in Amaya's future but so much is possible these days. Ya never know.

PPPPS: MY AMAYA 5, DECEMBER 16, 2016

This is my final comment, written after Amaya's first semester, which ended with the peaceful protest in the streets of Portland after the results of the 2016 election and Amaya's first time as a participant in the American election process. He will have much to protest against and be in favor of supporting. We are all so very proud of him and his ever-evolving development as a caring, intelligent, thoughtful person, looking for and defining his own way in a knotty world.

— *Part 6* —

NOW (AND BEYOND)

Now is the time. Amaya is complete, for now. Can any of us say more?

FROM ALLY TO ACTIVIST

As Amaya settled into himself and matured, I found I wanted to put what I had learned to use for a bigger purpose. Starting in 2014, after my first experience attending a Gender Spectrum Conference, I began to seek ways to serve the broad community of transgender people and their families as an ally and activist. I learned (through a Facebook post) that the Transgender Law Center (TLC) in Oakland, California, was looking for volunteers for their helpline. From the TLC mission statement: "Transgender Law Center changes law, policy, and attitudes so that all people can live safely, authentically, and free from discrimination regardless of their gender identity or expression."[47]

Volunteering at the TLC gave me a way to contribute my time to help transgender people in need. It also gave me an opportunity to interact with some amazing people, people whom I respect greatly and who have served as role models for my own activism. It was a "win–win" situation. Among those employed by the TLC are many people who define as something other than cisgender; the great majority of people I have worked with at the TLC are openly transgender, gender non-conforming, and/or queer. As I've gotten familiar with these new friends and heroes, I've been told more than once that they are grateful for parents like me who "get it," who want to contribute time and energy to work for transgender rights. I tell them I am grateful to be part of their community, and I thank them for being positive role models for me and others.

──────── A BLOG WAS BORN ────────

Facebook is great for making connections. Around the same time I started volunteering at the TLC, I stumbled onto a blog written by Roz Gold Keith. A woman who continually inspires me, Roz is also mom to a son who is FTM. Through her blog I learned about her Detroit-based organization Stand with Trans[48] and its mission to support transgender youth. She also started Ally Moms,[49] a volunteer group with a mission to provide an understanding mother's ear and a shoulder to lean on for transgender youth who find themselves without support from their own family. An *Ally Mom*, that's me! When I reached out to Roz, we felt an instant connection. I signed on right away, and as a volunteer I helped create a database of all the registered Ally Moms. I also took on the role of processing new applications to be an Ally Mom, and I help Roz market our group on social media— we want to spread the word far and wide so people know Ally Moms are here to help transgender youth and their families. We have Ally Moms in many states, and we are proud of the help we provide.

Meeting Roz and reading her blog empowered and inspired me to write my own. Reading her story about mothering her son Hunter reflected to me how powerful it can be to share our stories with others. In particular, Roz led a writing workshop at the Gender Spectrum Conference in the summer of 2015, with a co-presenter named Sandra Collins. Another Ally Mom, Sandra is mother to a trans child, and she founded the Bay Area Rainbow Day Camp. She also founded enGender,[50] a national organization that supports gender diverse youth and their communities. Sandra and Roz's workshop, titled "Telling Your Story, One Moment at a Time," was intended to encourage people to write about their experiences and provide them with some tools for sharing stories.

The workshop began with each presenter sharing her own experiences of parenting a transgender child. Next the presenters discussed different tools and avenues writers can employ to share their stories. They told us how the writing and sharing process can be cathartic and healing, and encouraged us to pick up the practice. Among the tools Roz and Sandra discussed was blogging, which they described as an easy, quick, accessible method for sharing stories.

Following some discussion, the workshop attendees were given time to write. We then had an opportunity to read our stories out loud. The stories were all personal, powerful, and poignant. There wasn't a dry eye. We learned that by sharing our stories, we can develop empathy, we can find commonality in our experiences, we can develop respect for our differences.

The workshop sparked my desire to blog about *my* experiences.

I published my first blog in August, 2015. When I first launched my blog, I didn't realize how cathartic writing would be for me, or how well it would be received by others. I've been pleasantly surprised: many people have read my posts, have reached out in support, have shared my blog with others. I have been touched by the stories friends and strangers have shared with me as a result of reading my stories. I have been surprised by the number of people who have contacted me looking for the same support I had sought in the not-too-distant past.

I was struck by the response from people who lived nearby in Marin and Sonoma Counties. Parents were reaching out to me with questions, or they just wanted to talk to someone else with a transgender child. I recalled my experience at Joel Baum's Gender Spectrum parents' group: how Gabe and I found there were no other parents with kids Amaya's tween age in the group. I remembered feeling frustrated that there was no connected community of families with older transgender kids in our county at the time. I felt it was time to help other parents and provide some of the local community support we never found. It was time to start a local support group in Marin County for parents of gender-alternative children.

In December, 2015, I launched a support group for parents and caregivers of transgender, gender non-conforming, and gender-questioning youth. Inspired by Roz, Gender Spectrum, and others, I intended to provide a local space where people could meet, get information, and support each other. I contacted Spectrum of Marin, which by this time had become part of the Spahr LGBT

Center in San Rafael. The Director told me Spectrum of Marin recently had been receiving an unprecedented number of calls looking for information or support related to gender. The Director welcomed my proposal to host a monthly group meeting at the Spahr Center. Meanwhile, I discovered that Cammie Duvall (who had taken over from Cristin Brew as facilitator of Amaya's teen group a few years earlier) still facilitated the center's teen group, and that she was starting a private practice as well. Sensing an opportunity to add her expertise and experience to the mix, I reached out to Cammie, and she agreed to co-facilitate the group with me. We have gathered monthly for over a year now, always a mix of new and continuing participants. Each month, 8–12 people gather looking for information, support, and community. Cammie and I hope to expand our reach in the years to come and provide a wider circle of parents and caregivers with community, support, and information.

Last summer I co-presented a workshop, my first time in that role, at the annual Gender Spectrum Conference. Roz and Sandra had been scheduled to present their writing workshop again. I'd signed on as a volunteer, but Roz was not able to make it, and I found myself in the co-presenter seat next to Sandra. The group was diverse. There were a few teens with their moms. Two grandmothers were there to support their granddaughter. Two or three young adults who defined themselves as non-binary attended on their own. There were a few lone moms, and one mom-and-dad couple. Again, each person was encouraged to write and then read their story. Some were hesitant at first, but by the end everyone had read their story. Emotions were stirred, we shed tears, and we laughed a lot too. Although writing was the primary focus of the workshop, the sharing of the stories in the group was equally important and impactful.

I look forward to presenting the writing workshop again in the future. Everyone has a story to tell, and we have so much to learn from each other. And that's why I blog.

HE'S SO LUCKY

People say, "He's so lucky he has you two as parents."

I feel mixed emotions when I hear that. Part of me takes it as a compliment. "Thank you," I say. "I feel lucky to have him as my son; he is always teaching me." But another part of me wonders why I hear this so often. Is it because people know so many children do not have the support of their families or communities? Perhaps. Is it because people somehow think Gabriel and I are doing something most others wouldn't do? Well that makes me wonder, would they not accept a transgender or LGB child of their own?

Perhaps he is lucky. We are so grateful to have Amaya as our child, as we are grateful to have his siblings too. Neither Gabriel nor I feel it is any sad or bad or terrible thing to have an LGBT child. I personally think it is an absolutely beautiful way to be a human, and to me it is illogical to think any other way. I just don't see what the problem is. I do not mean to imply that the experience has not had its challenges, but I have never wished my child to be anyone who he is not.

Gabriel and I embrace each of our children and love them each for who they are. Of course we experienced some confusion regarding Amaya as he grew up, and we needed to learn how best to care for our gender-questioning child—just like we needed to learn how to care best for each of our other children. Each child needed their own support. When my stepson Travis was going through a very hard time in his young life, we did our best to provide him with the things he needed, including counseling and special schooling. When our daughter Emily was four years old and in need of speech therapy, we reached out to all the resources we could find to get her the therapy she needed. Raising my transgender child has had its own set of challenges, but in many ways it has been no more difficult than raising either of our other children. Each came with their own gifts but also their own challenges, and we met *all* of those challenges with love.

Does this type of parenting make my transgender child "lucky"? According to the Human Rights Campaign's (HRC) 2013 survey of 10,000 LGBT identified youth,[51] it seems indeed he may be lucky. Transgender people experience verbal and physical abuse at far higher rates than the general population. This HRC study reported that 42 percent of youth say the community they live in is not accepting of LGBT people. Evidence reported in the 2012 study conducted by TransPulse in Toronto, Canada also suggests that the number one factor that can greatly reduce these factors for trans youth is parental and family support.

[O]ur findings show clear associations between the support that trans youth experience from their parents and numerous health outcomes. The most significant differences show that trans youth who have strong parental support for their gender identity and expression report higher life satisfaction, higher self-esteem, better mental health including less depression and fewer suicide attempts, and adequate housing compared to those without strong parental support. These findings draw a direct relationship between strong parental support and the reduction of significant risk factors for trans youth.[52]

I just cannot imagine how a parent can turn their back on their child when what the child needs *most of all* is their parents' understanding and acceptance.

Maybe Amaya *is* lucky. And that makes me sad.

❀

WHO'S THE LUCKY ONE?

by Gabriel Barkin, Amaya's father

I happened to meet a young man recently who was scheduled to have genital reassignment surgery in the near future. He told me this was the last step in his physical transition; he'd undergone top surgery a few years earlier. My son had his top surgery at the same surgical center, and this man, who'd flown out from Chicago for the procedure, was looking for reassurance that he'd chosen the right place. Were the staff supportive? Responsive to patient needs? Sensitive and encouraging? He was worried; this was literally a life-changing event he'd signed up for, and he was looking for every ounce of security he could find.

I told him about our family's solid agreement that my son's surgical center experience was very positive and successful. I talked a bit about how Amaya had come to his decision to have surgery, how we supported him from the get-go, and how careful and considerate we were when selecting a surgeon and a surgical center. I painted a picture that reflected our truth—the results were everything we'd hoped for. While my son had a different surgeon, I vouched for the staff and the level of care at this center. I told my new friend that he was in good hands.

At one point, after hearing me talk about Amaya and our experience, he said I seemed like a great dad, and that my son must be very lucky. He said he'd transitioned publicly only a few years ago, already well into his twenties, and he was sad that his father was having a very hard time coming to terms with the fact that his "daughter" was now his "son." The new name and new pronouns were not yet forthcoming when he talked to his dad. He felt it was important to praise and thank me for supporting my son.

To reflect on such praise: I've been honored and humbled before on occasion by such kind words about our parenting, but I am certainly not bringing it up here to pat myself on the back. My response is always the same—I say, "Thank you," but then I feel I need to explain that I never thought I was doing anything hard or unusual. I just loved my son, and I tried to let him have a lot of room to be the person he wanted to be. (I've joked that all my kids grew up to be amazing people *despite* my best intentions to provide complete inattention. My parents jokingly called their parenting style, which I inherited, "benign neglect.") It's hard for me to understand why any parent would not honor his or her children and respect them as we did our kids. And of course, it makes me sad to think that something so easy for me is so hard for so many people.

When people tell me my son is lucky for having us as parents, I thank them and remind myself how lucky we are to have three wonderful children.

WITHOUT UNDERSTANDING

by Travis Owen, Amaya's brother, 11 years older

Amaya was three years old the last time I saw him wear a dress. It was at our uncle's wedding in New York in 2001. It was a fairly traditional wedding with formal wear required, and it was around 90 degrees outside in the sun, humid as hell. Amaya was expected to wear a dress. At the time, Amaya had fairly short hair and didn't mind being misconstrued for a boy at the playground or anywhere else. As far as anyone could tell, Amaya was a tomboy. The dress took no fewer than three people to get on—poor little Amaya kicking and screaming the entire time. It seemed to take an hour (though surely it was less) due to the struggle that ensued. It was a scene reminiscent of a bank robber being subdued by the guards, it was epic. So yes, Amaya wore a dress for the wedding, but it was the last dress he would wear.

Personally, I couldn't care less what Amaya wore, then or ever. Amaya was extremely fortunate to be born into this era and to grow up in the Bay Area with loving family, friends, and community. He could wear what he wanted. But for most people, social pressures demand conformity while offering the illusion of choice—and one must choose wisely, lest the chooser become chastised.

Many people I have conversed with seem either to reject the notion of gender identity or to be ignorant of it altogether. Religion and blind faith have roles to play here, as things that are misunderstood by followers are too often deemed "wrong" or sinful by their holy texts and religious leaders. I recently had an earnest discussion about gender identity with a close Christian friend of mine who said he believed homosexuality and transgender identity were "wrong," although he conceded that he just did not understand much about such things. His argument was that God had made us the way he wanted, and we should not tamper with God's plan. I challenged my friend's beliefs by suggesting that his children might turn out to be gay or transgender, and I got the expected response: "That would never happen to me." I suggested he tell that to every parent of a gay or trans youth and see what they'd say. He thought deeply about this while I assured him that he would still love his children even if he didn't understand them. This is, in essence, the result we hope for everyone with non-conforming gender identities or sexual preferences: that it doesn't matter if they are *understood* as much as that they are *loved*.

I am a straight white male. I cannot truly understand what it is like to be anything else. What I do know is that to be open and honest about a non-conforming lifestyle takes a type of bravery and courage that I can only speculate about. It seems funny in a society that apparently loves people who take risks (both physical and otherwise) that a huge risk such as coming out as gay or trans is not appreciated as an act of bravery and courage. People who come out as gay or trans risk losing relationships, even risk their lives, just to be who they are.

Amaya, figuratively speaking, has balls. I am proud and inspired to call Amaya my brother and I will continue to fight ignorance and dogma to make the world better for him and those like him.

───── HE'S ALWAYS BEEN A TEACHER ─────

Amaya has been challenging gender norms since he was very little. From an early age, to meet him was to "see" a boy only to be told the child you were looking at was a girl. Most people, upon learning "he" was a "she" (though now we know Amaya was always a "he"), would show a surprised or even shocked look on their face. It was rare that someone would take the information in their stride without missing a beat. Everyone who met him found their notion of gender had been challenged. Myself included.

I never really knew anyone like my son. By this I mean that I had not ever met anyone who looked *so much* like a boy but was a girl. I didn't have any friends whom I knew at the time to be transgender. In over a decade teaching preschool, I had not once come across a child who was a "tomboy" as thoroughly as my child was. I was ignorant in many ways about gender identity and what it means to be transgender. I had to learn along the way. I had to let go of who I thought my child *should* be, and paid close attention instead to my child. He always showed me exactly who he was. I often said, "My child is always teaching me."

Amaya *has* always been teaching me, and he has taught many people simply by being himself. Regardless of whether he wanted the role of *Teacher* or not, he has taught our family, our friends, and many people in our community about gender and what it means to be transgender (or at least one way to be transgender). Those who have known Amaya for many years have had to undergo an individual process to understand and accept him as transgender, or more specifically as male. First, we had to accept the notion of a "girl" who was very boy-like. And then we had to let go of the idea that this "girl" was female and accept his maleness, and that he is transgender. It's been a lot to take in!

Many people ask me questions about Amaya, and sometimes these questions seem to question the validity of Amaya's identity. Sometimes it feels like what's being questioned is our parenting. One person asked me, "Why can't Amaya just be a butch lesbian?" Another asked, "If he is changing his gender, why doesn't he change his name? I just think it would be so much easier to remember to use 'he' if he also changed his name." Another comment I've heard many times: "How can you be sure? Isn't he too young to know he is transgender?"

For the answers, I draw on what I learned from parenting my transgender child:

Q: *"Why can't he just be a butch lesbian?"*

A: He cannot "just be a lesbian" because that is not who he is. His inner sense of his gender is male. He is not a girl.

Q: *"Why doesn't he change his name? If he wants to be a boy, why doesn't he use a more masculine name?"*

A: He is not changing his name because he likes his name and does not want to change it. It's not his job to make it easier for you. And I like his name, I gave it to him!

Q: *"How could you be so sure? Isn't he too young to know he is transgender?"*

A: To this I say, "How do you know you are your gender?" I knew I was a girl from a very young age. My body and my gender expression and my inner sense of who I am have always aligned. For my son this was not the case. The latest thinking is that what we call gender is actually a complex paradigm comprised of a combination of biological, social, and psychological factors.[53] The more I have learned about what it means to be transgender, the more confident I have become knowing that my child always knew who he was. He just needed to make a few changes so that he could align himself physically, mentally, and emotionally, and be seen by others as the male person he knows himself to be.

Gabriel and I trust we did the right thing by following our child's lead, and the evidence today supports this. Amaya is free from the dysphoria, depression, and anxiety he suffered for many years. He is a happy, healthy individual leading a productive life. What more can a parent ask for?

MISTAKES, I'VE MADE A FEW

Amaya does not have any regrets whatsoever about his transition, and recently he told me I should have no regrets either. I asked him if, looking back in hindsight, there was anything along his journey toward completeness (for now) that he would have done differently, or wished his father and I had done differently, and he said, "All that I have gone through has made me who I am today."

Still, I wish I'd known more, done more, approached some things differently. If I knew *then* what I know *now*, I might have been more open-minded about what makes someone a boy or a girl earlier in Amaya's life. When my young child said, "I wish to be a grandpa," perhaps I could

have said, "Tell me more about that?" Instead, I told him
girls grow up to be grandmas and not grandpas. Perhaps
if I had been more receptive when my child said things
like this—words that effectively screamed "I am a boy!"—
he might have felt more and more comfortable referring
to himself as a boy, *thinking* of himself as a boy. Perhaps
he might have come to terms with his dysphoria earlier.
Perhaps with earlier recognition and acknowledgment
of his inner male self, we might have put Amaya on
hormone blockers in his tween years and forestalled his
female puberty. Who knows how different things might
have been? But alas, my logical explanation, that girls
have vaginas and boys have penises, squelched that world
of "perhaps." The signs were there at an early age. My
child tried to show the world the boy named "Amaya"
that he felt himself to be. He was persistent, insistent, and
consistent with his behavior.

I also wish now that I hadn't corrected people who
used male pronouns and masculine descriptive words for
Amaya. Certainly, Gabe and I could have stopped doing so
sooner than we did. I feel now that we were misgendering
own child, albeit unwittingly. We consistently told him,
both directly and by correcting others, that he was a
girl. Yes, a girl who could do anything she wanted, be
anything she wanted. Except she couldn't be a boy.

I want to go back in time and tell myself: Yes, she can
even be a boy!

Many trans people are misgendered on a regular
basis. The constant disparity between one's own gender
identity and other people's *perception* of gender can cause
anxiety and depression. Simple things like encounters
with someone using the wrong pronoun or pointing
someone to the wrong bathroom can add up to a barrage

of dysphoric experiences each day. Some transgender people feel it is an act of violence when someone knowingly misgenders someone; at the very least, to do so knowingly is rude and cruel.

I feel sad when I think about Amaya going through that time in his life when people who actually got it *right* were corrected by his parents all the time; when his own mother and father were telling others he was someone he was not. Oh if only I could have a do-over! If I could talk to that young child again, I would tell him he is seen and heard. I would tell him that as he grows he will get to have the body he needs to match his gender identity, that we will help him on his journey and support every step. I would tell him he will grow up be a happy, healthy man. If I knew then what I knew now, I certainly wouldn't have corrected people for seeing him as the male person he truly was.

Another wish: I wish we had been able to get Amaya to go to counseling sooner. In his middle school years, our kid was resistant to any suggestion of counseling, even though it was clear he was struggling with symptoms of dysphoria. He had to reach a point of despair before he would let us help him at all. Then at long last, with Cristin Brew as his counselor and guide, Amaya was able to explore his gender identity and find a way to describe and define it. With support, Amaya was able to express his needs to us—to visit friends in Texas, the first people he befriended as a male; to change his pronouns; to undergo top surgery. With guidance and support, we were able to take steps that helped him transition and live a complete life.

Amaya again: "All that I have gone through has made me who I am today."

Despite my wishes, Amaya's confidence today feeds my own. Writing this book has led me back through time, through all the moments that in turn led us forward and brought us to this point, this chapter, these words. As parents, Gabe and I did the best we could during those moments, given our understanding of what was best. Mostly we watched, waited, supported, listened, and followed our child's lead. He always knew where he was heading. And without a doubt, he's always been my son.

$\maltese$

SHIFTED

by KB, a very dear friend, and "Aunt KB" to our children

Knowing Amaya has shifted my understanding about what it means to be transgender.

I can recall the first time I heard anything about transgender people. When I was a child in the mid-70s, growing up on Long Island, my mom had a friend who would take my brother and me for drives into Manhattan just to get us out of the house. I have a vivid recollection of my mom's friend pointing out streetwalkers near Times Square and telling us, "Those are 'trannies,' men who dress up as women." I was about ten years old at the time, and that made me chuckle, amused at the absurdity, like they were wearing clown suits or some other funny costume. Changing their appearance for a silly effect.

Once I was old enough to understand sexual relationships, I thought of "transgender" as if it were a choice, a sexual deviation, a fetish. Or maybe, I thought, being queer was just a rebellion against the norm for some people. In my narrow view at the time, it was weird, and it was hard for me to understand why someone would be into being queer, unless it was just to scream for attention. Maybe they were just confused. Perhaps I got my thinking by hearing the term "gender-bender," which to me meant someone experimenting with all sides of human sexuality. I assumed all people must ultimately be either 100 percent heterosexual or homosexual. To me there was no separation between gender and sexual orientation.

My impressions, and the words I used to describe people, came from what I heard from other kids or relatives say, including derogatory terms that seemed normal, common. To me, using these words didn't imply judgment, rather they inspired my curiosity. I've always respected people's freedom to do what they want with whomever they want. In high school, I became aware that I had friends who were gay. It was kept quiet, nobody really talked about it (at least not with me), and I remember feeling that the knowledge anyone was gay was always a secret by default. I also remember wondering if being transgender was a way for a gay person to not be gay. But despite my limited exposure to, and knowledge about, gender-alternative people, I felt empathy for anyone who had to suppress who they were, or worse, to live in hiding and fear of their true self being exposed.

Moving to San Francisco after college propelled me to learn more about diverse cultures and to develop a more accurate understanding of the distinctions of LGBTQ people—starting with the revelation that there are a wide variety of distinctions among people—not just "gay" or "straight." The most important lesson I've learned living in the Bay Area is that one's gender identification and sexual orientation is innate, regardless of any perceived "deviation from the norm."

Which brings me to Amaya, whom I've known since he was born. I've said since he was very young that I'd never met anyone more sure of who they are. I recognized this trait of his years before Amaya was able to articulate that he was not a girl; certainly before I realized that he was in fact a transgender person.

It took me some time to shift to referring to Amaya as "he" and not "she." Choosing words carefully as I spoke and learning the proper utilization of words in regards to Amaya, especially pronouns, created a mental shift in and of itself. Through this process, I've learned it is important to understand how words make people feel. "He-she" for example, which I have heard throughout my life in reference to some transgender people, is not acceptable anymore as a pronoun in my opinion. It feels derogatory (unless of course a person *asks* to be referred to with that pronoun construction). I've also learned to distinguish between gender identification and sexual orientation.

I no longer feel bad for transgender people. I no longer think, "Poor them, born in the wrong body." I know now that the world is full of diversity, and that each person deserves to feel right and good and whole in their own body.

THERE HE GOES, FOR REAL!

My boy just left for his freshman year of college. He is not here, and I miss him. Wow, how to express in words all the feelings that come with sending my youngest child off to college, this child of mine who has shown me so much about courage, inner knowing, ways of being, trust, and hope?

So many feelings. The first is a huge sense of accomplishment. Our family has come so far. When Gabriel and I got married, we were very young, he was 27 and I was 24. We had our first child, Emily, barely more than a year later. Gabe was already a father to my stepson Travis, who came to live with us when he was 14, many years after our wedding. Amaya was born in 1998.

We've been at this parenting thing for a while.

I remember all those times I'd said to myself (as I imagine so many mothers do), "I can't wait until they're all grown up and I have time to myself!" But now I realize how quickly time flies. Sometimes I wish I could talk to my younger self, to tell her, "Even though it feels really hard right now, it's going to go really fast." I would tell her to remember that each moment is to be treasured. I would tell her there will be challenges, and that she won't always make the right choice, but that so much of what she is doing *is* right. I would urge her to be confident. I'd tell her that when she's older and looking back, she will forget many of the day-to-day things, but she will always remember that she was there for her kids. She will remember giving them baths, taking them to school, to baseball games, to girl scout camp, and to gymnastics classes, soccer practices, horseback riding, science camp, and all those other places. She'll remember special family days, all those times she and Gabe took them camping and hiking, all those family trips to New York and Los Angeles and Hawaii and Mexico and Cuba. But most of all, she will remember she loved with all her heart and always did her best.

I would tell her it seemed to take a long time coming to get where we are. But it wasn't long at all. In the end, it went too fast.

Now Gabriel and I are in that empty nest phase. I don't feel it to be "empty" as I feel my kids are with me all the time. I feel tethered to the children, just as a baby is tethered to its mother physically at first. Even after the umbilical cord is cut, the lifelong, energetic cord between a mother and her child is unlike any other connection in our lives. Anyone who has given their heart and energy to raise his or her child knows these emotional/energetic tethers exist, even for mothers and fathers who never had an umbilical connection to their children. My children will always be a part of me, and I can feel their tugs.

With our empty next comes a chance for Gabriel and me to reconnect with and rediscover each other. I am grateful to have all this space and time in my life to be with my husband, to be alone in my house, to not have to include everybody in my thoughts about what I want to eat for dinner. Of course I miss our family dinner times, and I also enjoy this focused time with my husband. It feels natural. (Regarding our empty nest, my husband says, "I always wanted my kids to move out as soon as they grew up—but I hoped they'd just move up the block.")

People have asked me how I feel about sending my transgender child to college, to live away from home for the first time. Sure, we've been separated for brief times;

I've been on vacations away from my family for as long as ten days, and Amaya has been on some school trips that lasted four or five nights, but that's about it. With Amaya living out of our home during school sessions, this will be a time of growth and expansion for all of us.

I believe he is in a perfect place for a transgender college freshman. He chose Portland State University because of its progressive, urban feel (and its distance from home may have been a factor, as it is for many kids seeking independence and experience). On moving day, he discovered signs had been posted on all the doors in his dorm hall so each student could write their name and preferred pronouns. This was a great way for the kids to introduce themselves to each other and avoid misgendering. As it turns out, there are people of many genders and variations living on his dorm hall, and his first roommate was gay. A friend of mine, hearing all this, asked if Amaya's dorm was in an LGBTQ-specific housing unit. Actually no, he's not, it's just that Portland State's culture welcomes and includes all people in all of its dorm situations. I appreciate the welcoming and affirming culture the university provides; it makes me feel confident my son is in the right place.

I am also confident Amaya will find his way, as he always has. And really, my son has led the charge along. From the time he was two years old, and increasingly as the years went by, he led us to the places he needed to go. He taught us by behaving and dressing in the manner he felt was appropriate for himself from an early age. He was out in front when he told us he needed to go to a self-study high school, when he told us about the medical adjustments he needed to make. It was always Amaya who showed us what he needed in order to live and thrive.

I have no doubt he will continue to be a teacher and a leader—that's just who he is.

Photo courtesy of Zoe Davis

I AM WORRIED, I AM HOPEFUL

It is now January, 2017, and the United States is about to inaugurate Donald Trump as President. Trump's electoral victory is concerning for so many reasons, especially when it comes to the rights of transgender and gender non-conforming people. A Republican administration combined with Republicans in charge of both houses of Congress does not bode well for the advancement of LGBTQ rights. I am full of worry.

Until there is more acceptance and safety in our land and our world for trans people, I will worry. I worry that my child will encounter discrimination or rejection. I worry that he might be the victim of violence. I worry not only for my own child, but for transgender people in general, and for all people whose gender does not fit into the male/female binary system. There is a lot to be worried about.

Indeed, these concerns drove me to write this book. Our entire family agreed it was time for me, for all of us, to share our story of love, support, and acceptance so that we may help to educate and inspire others. We share so others will know they are not alone on this journey. We share because we know acceptance increases with familiarity. According to a study done by the Pew Research Center: "In the eyes of LGBT adults, greater social acceptance has come as a result of more Americans knowing someone who is lesbian, gay, bisexual or transgender as well as the efforts of high-profile public figures."[54] This book is my and my family's attempt to foster more familiarity, understanding and acceptance.

I am called to action, but sometimes I hesitate. I know there is risk in sharing our story; visibility does not guarantee a unanimously positive response. Media attention these days is hyper-focused on transgender people, their rights, and the challenges they face. *Time*, *Newsweek*, and *National Geographic* all have featured transgender people and issues as cover stories in the past year. Transgender people are the focus of several current reality TV shows that are, on the whole, honest, positive portrayals of their subjects' lives. *I Am Jazz* follows well-known transgender teen activist Jazz Jennings. *Strut* focuses its lens on a modeling agency that features trans models. The Emmy award-winning comedy-drama series *Transparent* tells the story of a transgender woman who transitioned late in life. Janet Mock's *Trans List* celebrates influential transgender people throughout history. Some people have pointed to Hollywood's portrayal of gay people on the hit series *Will and Grace* as a turning point in national levels of acceptance; perhaps these shows will have some similar impact.

There certainly are many positives that may result from having transgender people represented on television. However, when I read the "Comments" sections below any online news story about transgender people, I am reminded that this nation is still stocked with ignorance, hatred, and bigotry. And the danger is real: Jazz Jennings has reported receiving death threats. When her family first chose to share their story, they could not have imagined what would come of it. Her family chose to go public with their story in the hope that they could increase understanding and acceptance and thereby make the world safer for their child. They could have stayed silent, but they didn't. They took their story public in order to make the world better for their own child—and in doing so, they have helped many others feel at least a bit safer. The Jennings family is an example of acceptance and love. The non-profit organization they started, TransKids Purple Rainbow Foundation,[55] is an invaluable resource and a force for positive change.

Like them, I feel called to tell our story. And again, making the decision to go public was a challenging one. I certainly don't want to put my son, myself, or anyone in danger. But I know my silence would not make the world safer for transgender people. My silence would not provide comfort to other parents, nor tell them they are not alone. And it's more than that: by sharing our stories, we can give voice to the voiceless. Our family is fortunate for what we have, for where we live, and we are grateful. We have the strong support of our extended family and a wide circle of friends, a great number of loved ones who fully accept our transgender child. We have good jobs and good medical coverage. We are white. We live in an accepting community.

I am humbled to remember *every day* that not everyone shares these privileges.

It is my sincere hope that our stories will contribute to real change that has positive impact for everyone, with the greatest and most positive impact upon those who need it most. These stories are for anyone and everyone who needs to hear them.

RESOURCES FOR TRANSGENDER PEOPLE AND THEIR FAMILIES

When our family was first looking for support, it was difficult to find information about children who did not conform to gender norms. Today there is a wealth of resources available for parents who have children that are gender creative, gender questioning, or transgender. Here is a partial list of resources that are currently available.

Many of these resources are organizations I have interacted with. A few have been recommended for this list by colleagues or friends. To find something in your area, try searching online and use key words such as the name of your city and phrases such as "transgender resources," "transgender children," or "transgender parenting." Another option: seek out the nearest LGBTQ center in your region and ask if they offer, or perhaps they know of, support groups for parents and/or trans children.

Most of the resources below are based in the United States, but I have also included some UK resources. *To find resources specific to your region in the United States, please consider contacting someone through Ally Moms.* Ally Moms is a group of mothers of transgender youth who want to make a difference in the lives of gender-expansive kids who do not have supportive family by providing listening ears, calm understanding, and information on local and national resources. Ally Moms are also available to help family members and friends of trans youth. Ally Moms volunteers are available throughout the United States in many states, and our moms can be reached via phone or text. I invite and encourage my readers to visit our Ally Moms page on the Stand with Trans Website at http://standwithtrans.org/ally-moms.

US RESOURCES

I. Legal Guidance

Transgender Law Center (TLC)

Organizational Mission (from their website): "Transgender Law Center changes law, policy, and attitudes so that all people can live safely, authentically, and free from discrimination regardless of their gender identity or expression. We envision a future where gender self-determination and authentic expression are seen as basic rights and matters of common human dignity."

http://transgenderlawcenter.org
(415) 865-0176

National Center for Transgender Equality (NCTE)

Organizational Mission (from their website): "The National Center for Transgender Equality is a national social justice organization devoted to ending discrimination and violence against transgender people through education and advocacy on national issues of importance to transgender people. By empowering transgender people and our allies to educate and influence policymakers and others, NCTE facilitates a strong and clear voice for transgender equality in our nation's capital and around the country."

www.transequality.org
(202) 903-0122

Human Rights Campaign

Organizational Mission (from their website): "HRC works to improve the lives of LGBTQ people worldwide by advocating for equal rights and benefits in the workplace, ensuring families are treated equally under the law, and increasing public support around the globe."

www.hrc.org
(800) 777-4723

American Civil Liberties Union (ACLU)

Organizational Mission (from their website): "For almost 100 years, the ACLU has worked to defend and preserve the individual rights and liberties guaranteed by the Constitution and laws of the United States."

www.aclu.org
(212) 549-2500

Lambda Legal

Organizational Mission (from their website): "Lambda Legal is the oldest and largest national legal organization whose mission is to achieve full recognition of the civil rights of lesbians, gay men, bisexuals, transgender people and those with HIV through impact litigation, education and public policy work."

www.lambdalegal.org/about-us
(212) 809-8585

Sylvia Rivera Law Project

Organizational Mission (from their website): "The Sylvia Rivera Law Project works to guarantee that all people are free to self-determine gender identity and expression, regardless of income or race, and without facing harassment, discrimination or violence."

https://srlp.org
(212) 337-8550

GLAAD

Organizational Mission (from their website): "GLAAD is a non-governmental U.S. media monitoring organization founded by LGBT people in the media. As a dynamic media force, GLAAD tackles tough issues to shape the narrative and provoke dialogue that leads to cultural change."

www.glaad.org
(323) 933-2240

National Center for Lesbian Rights (NCLR)

Organizational Mission (from their website): "NCLR is a national legal organization committed to advancing the civil and human rights of lesbian, gay, bisexual, and transgender people and their families through litigation, legislation, policy, and public education."

www.nclrights.org

Asaf Orr, Esq. Transgender Youth Project Staff Attorney:
(415) 392-6257 ext. 326
AOrr@NCLRights.org

II. Identity Document Changes
National Center for Transgender Equality

State by State Guide: www.transequality.org/documents

Transgender Law Center

Identity Documents Resources: https://transgenderlawcenter.org/resources/id

Lamba Legal

State by State Guide: www.lambdalegal.org/know-your-rights/article/trans-changing-birth-certificate-sex-designations

Help Desk: www.lambdalegal.org/helpdesk

III. Families and Students

Gender Spectrum

Organizational Mission (from their website): "Gender Spectrum helps to create gender sensitive and inclusive environments for all children and teens." Gender Spectrum focuses on transgender children/teens and their families. The organization presents an annual conference for family and professionals, and also provides trainings to educators and schools.

www.genderspectrum.org
(510) 788-4412
info@genderspectrum.org

enGender

Organizational Mission (from their website): "Our mission is to support gender diverse youth, their families and communities by strengthening self-determination through direct services and programming."

www.engendernow.org
sandra_collins@rainbowdaycamp.org

Human Rights Campaign (HRC)

Organizational Mission (from their website): "As the largest national lesbian, gay, bisexual, transgender and queer civil rights organization, HRC envisions a world where LGBTQ people are ensured of their basic equal rights, and can be open, honest and safe at home, at work and in the community."

www.hrc.org/resources

Stand with Trans

Organizational Mission (from their website): "The mission of Stand with Trans is to provide the tools needed by transgender youth so they will be empowered, supported and validated as they transition to their authentic life."

http://standwithtrans.org

Ally Moms

Ally Moms are parents to trans youth who want to make a difference in the lives of others by providing a listening ear, understanding, and resources to transgender youth who may not have supportive family. Ally Moms are also available for families and friends of trans youth. (I am a proud Ally Mom!)

Ally Moms are listed by state and are reachable through phone or text: www.standwithtrans.org/ally-moms

TransKids Purple Rainbow Foundation (TKPRF)

Organizational Mission (from their website): "TKPRF is committed to the premise that Gender Dysphoria is something a child can't control and it is society that needs to change, not them. Families need to support their children and be encouraged to allow them to grow-up free of gender roles. Founded by the family of Jazz Jennings, TKPRF is committed to enhancing the future lives of Trans Kids by educating schools, peers, places of worship, the medical community, government bodies, and society in general, in an effort to seek fair and equal treatment for all trans youth."

www.transkidspurplerainbow.org

TransActive Gender Center

Organizational Mission (from their website): "TransActive Gender Center provides a holistic range of services and expertise to empower transgender and gender diverse children, youth and their families in living healthy lives, free of discrimination."

www.transactiveonline.org
(503) 252-3000

Trans Students Educational Alliance (TSER)

Organizational Mission (from their website): "Trans Student Educational Resources is a youth-led organization is dedicated to transforming the educational environment for trans and gender nonconforming students through advocacy and empowerment. In addition to our focus on creating a more trans-friendly education system, our mission is to educate the public and teach trans activists how to be effective organizers."

www.transstudent.org
tser@transstudent.org

Campus Pride

Organizational Mission (from their website): "Campus Pride serves LGBT and ally student leaders and campus organizations in the areas of leadership development, support programs and services to create safer, more inclusive LGBT-friendly colleges and universities. It exists to develop, support and give 'voice and action' in building future LGBT and ally student leaders."

www.campuspride.org

Trans Family Support Services

Organizational Mission (from their website): "Works with families on the gender journey all over the US. Aid with parent coaching, medical transitions and insurance coverage, guide to resources and the legal and educational systems."

www.transfamilysos.org

Parents, Families, Friends, and Allies of LGBTQ People (PFLAG)

Organizational Mission (from their website): "PFLAG is committed to advancing equality through its mission of support, education, and advocacy."

www.pflag.org

Center on Halsted Street (Chicago, IL)

Organizational Mission (from their website): "Dedicated to advancing community and securing the health and well-being of the Lesbian, Gay, Bisexual, Transgender and Queer (LGBTQ) people of Chicagoland."

www.centeronhalsted.org

Mazzoni Center (Philadelphia, PA)

Organizational Mission (from their website): "Quality comprehensive health and wellness services in an LGBTQ-focused environment, while preserving the dignity and improving the quality of life of the individuals we serve." Mazzoni Center provides health care, advocacy, and support for LGBTQ people and also presents an annual conference.

www.mazzonicenter.org

Jim Collins Foundation

Organizational Mission (from their website): "The Jim Collins Foundation is a community-based initiative promoting the self-determination and empowerment of all transgender people. The Jim Collins Foundation raises money to fund gender-affirming surgeries for those transgender people who need surgery to live a healthy life, but have no ability to pay for it themselves. We recognize that for those people who require surgery for a healthy gender transition, lack of access to surgery may result in hopelessness, depression, and sometimes, suicide."

www.jimcollinsfoundation.org

IV. Suicide Hotlines
The Trevor Project

US: 1 (866) 488-7386
www.thetrevorproject.org

Trans Lifeline

Staffed by transgender operators.

US: 1 (877) 565-8860
www.hotline.translifeline.org

V. Gender Clinics in the United States

There are quite a few Gender Clinics in the United States that offer care to transgender and gender non-conforming youth. The list continues to grow as more and more parents seek care for their transgender and gender questioning children. Among the leaders are:

The Center for TransYouth Health and Development at Children's Hospital Los Angeles

Under the leadership of Dr. Johanna Olson.

www.chla.org/the-center-transyouth-health-and-development

Q&A with Dr. Johanna Olsen: www.chla.org/blog/ physicians -and-clinicians/transgender-community- questions-answers-johanna-olson-md-chla-s

UCSF Benioff Child and Adolescent Gender Center

Under the leadership of Stephen Rosenthal MD, Diane Ehrensaft, PhD, and Joel Baum, MS.

www.ucsfbenioffchildrens.org/clinics/child_ and_adolescent _gender_center/index.html

Callen-Lorde Community Health Center & Health Outreach to Teens (HOTT)

Located in New York, NY, under the direction of Manel Silva, MD, MPH.

www.callen-lorde.org

Susquehanna Family Practice

Located in Oneonta, NY under the direction of Carolyn Wolf-Gould, MD.

www.bassett.org/medical/locations/regional- health-centers/susquehanna-family-practice

Duke Child and Adolescent Gender Care Center

www.dukehealth.org/locations/duke-
child-and-adolescent -gender-care

Human Rights Commission (HRC)

The HRC has a more extensive list of gender clinics:

www.hrc.org/resources/interactive-map-clinical-
care-programs-for-gender-nonconforming-childr

VI. Research Surveys, Studies, and Reports
NCTE 2015 U.S. Transgender Survey

www.ustranssurvey.org/report

The Williams Institute—UCLA Law School

Latest Study: "Age of Individuals Who Identify as Transgender
in the United States."

http://williamsinstitute.law.ucla.edu/research/
transgender -issues/new-estimates-show-that-150000-
youth-ages-13-to-17-identify-as-transgender-in-the-us

Trans Pulse Project Youth Report 2012

http://transpulseproject.ca/wp-content/
uploads/2012 /10/Impacts-of-Strong-Parental-
Support-for-Trans-Youth-vFINAL.pdf

Human Rights Campaign LGBT Youth Report 2012

www.hrc.org/youth-report

VII. Support for Schools
Gender Spectrum

This is listed here again to underscore that Gender Spectrum has free training and educational resources available.

www.genderspectrum.org

Creating Gender Inclusive Schools
A film created by The Youth and Gender Media Project and Gender Spectrum. Directed by award-winning filmmaker Jonathan Skurnik.

Schools in Transition: A Guide for Supporting Transgender Students in K-12 Schools
A free download written by Asaf Orr, Esq. and Joel Baum, M.S.

www.genderspectrum.org/staging/wp-content/ uploads /2015/08/Schools-in-Transition-2015.pdf

VIII. Books

Here are a few of my favorites:

The Transgender Child: A Handbook for Families and Professionals by Stephanie Brill and Rachel Pepper (Simon and Schuster, 2008)

The Transgender Teen: A Handbook for Parents and Professionals Supporting Transgender and Non-Binary Teens by Stephanie Brill and Lisa Kenney (Simon and Schuster, 2016)

Gender Born Gender Made: Raising Healthy Gender Non-Conforming Children by Diane Ehrensaft (Workman Publishing, 2011)

The Gender Creative Child: Pathways for Nurturing and Supporting Children Who Live Outside Gender Boxes by Diane Ehrensaft, PhD, with a foreword by Norman Spack, MD (Workman Publishing, 2016)

Manning Up: Transsexual Men on Finding Brotherhood, Family & Themselves edited by Zander Keig and Mitch Kellaway (CreateSpace Independent Publishing Platform, 2014)

Trans Bodies, Trans Selves: A Resource for the Transgender Community by Laura Erickson-Schroth (Oxford University Press, 2014)

The Gender Book (a picture book for all ages) by Mel Reiff Hill and Jay Maya (Marshall House Press, 2013)

I Am Jazz (a children's picture book) by Jessical Herthel and Jazz Jennings (Dial Books, 2014)

Being Jazz: My Life as a (Transgender) Teen (a memoir written by well-known transgender teen Jazz Jennings) by Jazz Jennings (Ember 2017)

I'm Jay Let's Play (a joyful picture book about play that reflects and celebrates kids of all genders) by Beth Reichmuth (self-published, 2017)

It's OK to Sparkle (written by a transgender youth) by Avery Jackson (Debi Jackson, 2016)

IX. Television Programs

These programs may be available for viewing online or via your cable company's "on demand" service:

Gender Revolution (documentary) (National Geographic Channel 2017)

Louis Theroux: Transgender Kids (BBC 2015) (note that Amaya is interviewed in this documentary, and Gabe and I have brief cameo appearances)

The Trans List (documentary) (HBO 2016)

I Am Jazz (reality TV series) (2015)

Orange Is the New Black (drama) (2013)

UK RESOURCES

Britain

Gendered Intelligence

This is a community interest company that works predominantly with the trans community and those who impact on trans lives. They particularly specialise in supporting young trans people aged 8–25. They also deliver trans youth programs, support for parents and carers, professional development and trans awareness training for all sectors, and educational workshops for schools, colleges, universities, and other educational settings. Youth groups meet across England, and training and school presentations are offered across the United Kingdom. An online forum is available for parents who are unable to attend in person.

Gendered Intelligence, 200a Pentonville Road, London N1 9JP

020 7832 5848
www.genderedintelligence.co.uk

Gender Identity Research and Education Society (GIRES)

This is a national organization which was set up to improve the lives of trans and gender non-conforming people, including those who are non-binary and non-gender.

The Gender Identity Research and Education Society (GIRES), Melverley, The Warren, Ashtead, Surrey KT21 2SP

01372 801554
www.gires.org.uk

The Beaumont Society

This is a UK self-help body run by and for the transgender community. They welcome all transgender people and their partners, regardless of gender, sexual orientation, race, creed, or color, and all varieties from the nervous newcomers to those who are experienced and confident in their preferred gender.

The Beaumont Society, 27 Old Gloucester
Street, London WC1N 3XX

01582 412220
enquiries@beaumontsociety.org.uk
www.beaumontsociety.org.uk

UK Trans Info

This is a national charity focused on improving the lives of trans and non-binary people in the United Kingdom.

UK Trans Info, PO Box 871, 109 Vernon
House, Friar Lane, Nottingham NG1 6DQ

info@uktrans.info
www.uktrans.info

Trans Media Watch

This is a charity dedicated to improving media coverage of trans and intersex issues. It aims to assist people in the media to understand these issues and produce clear, accurate, respectful material. It also helps trans and intersex people who are interacting with the media to get results they are comfortable with.

Trans Media Watch, London WC1N 3XX
www.transmediawatch.org

Press for Change

This is a key lobbying and legal support organization for trans people in the United Kingdom. It provides legal advice, training, and research to trans people, their representatives, and public and private bodies.

Press For Change, BM Network, London WC1N 3XX

0844 8708165
office@pfc.org.uk
www.pfc.org.uk

The National Trans Youth Network

This is a network of trans youth groups across the United Kingdom. They represent young trans people up to the age of 25 across all areas of the United Kingdom, with groups from England, Scotland, Wales, and Northern Ireland.

www.ntyn.org.uk

Mermaids

This is a UK charity set up by a group of parents whose children experienced gender identity issues. It has evolved and grown to meet demand and offer appropriate resources to young people, up to the age of 19, their families and carers, and professionals working with gender-variant young people.

Mermaids, BM Mermaids, London WC1N 3XX

0844 3340550
www.mermaidsuk.org.uk

Wales
LGBT Cymru Helpline

This offers a free and professional caring service for transgender people in Wales, aiming to offer support and information to trans men, trans women, and non-binary people, as well as their partners, parents, families, and friends. They offer a free telephone helpline and a low-cost counseling service.

LGBT Cymru Helpline, c/o 92 Corporation
Avenue, Llanelli, Wales SA15 3SR

0800 840 2069
www.lgbtcymruhelpline.org.uk

Scotland
Scottish Transgender Alliance

This assists transgender people, service providers, employers, and equality organizations to engage together to improve gender identity and gender reassignment equality, rights, and inclusion in Scotland. They strive for everyone in Scotland to be safe and valued whatever their gender identity and gender-reassignment status and to have full freedom in their gender expression.

Scottish Transgender Alliance, Equality Network, 30 Bernard Street, Edinburgh EH6 6PR

0131 467 6039
sta@equality-network.org
www.scottishtrans.org

Transgender Support Programmes (within LGBT Health)

This provides social groups, confidence-building workshops, and one-to-one support for transgender people.

Transgender Support Programmes, LGBT Health and Wellbeing, 9 Howe Street, Edinburgh EH3 6TE

0131 523 1100
admin@lgbthealth.org.uk
www.lgbthealth.org.uk

Northern Ireland
Transgender Northern Ireland

This is a website that provides general information, advice and confidential support in many areas of life and around various issues that people might experience. Their qualified staff and trained volunteers are able to help any caller with gender identity issues.

www.transgenderni.com

GenderJam

This is a community group for the young transgender community in Northern Ireland, mostly in the Belfast area. They bring young transgender, non-binary, questioning and intersex people together and create resources to help the community in Northern Ireland. They also provide individual support for young people experiencing difficulty with housing, education, health care, and other issues that affect the trans community in the region.

GenderJam NI, Belfast LGBT Centre, 9–13 Waring Street, Belfast BT1 2DX

028 90 996 819
www.genderjam.org.uk

Republic of Ireland
Transgender Equality Network Ireland (TENI)

This is the leading trans organization in Ireland. It seeks to improve conditions and advance the rights and equality of trans people and their families throughout the Republic of Ireland.

Transgender Equality Network Ireland (TENI), Unit 2, 4 Ellis Quay, Dublin 7, Ireland

(01) 873 3575
info@teni.ie
www.teni.ie

National Health Service (NHS)

Download this guide for parents looking for support:

www.nhs.uk/Livewell/Transhealth/Pages/
local-gender-identity-clinics.aspx

UK Non-Profit Organizations
UK Trans Info

Organizational Mission (from their website): "UK Trans Info is a nationwide charity focused on improving the lives of transgender and non-binary people in the UK."

https://uktrans.info/namechange

The Gender Trust

Organizational Mission (from their website): "The Gender Trust is a listening ear, a caring support and an information centre for anyone with any question or problem concerning their gender identity, or whose loved one is struggling with gender identity issues."

http://gendertrust.org.uk

Press for Change

Organizational Mission (from their website): "Press for Change has been a key lobbying and legal support organization for Trans people in the UK since its formation in 1992."

www.pfc.org.uk

Gendered Intelligence

http://genderedintelligence.co.uk

NOTES

1. Haas, A.P., Herman, J.L., and Rodgers, J.L. (2014) *Suicide Attempts Among Transgender and Gender Non-Conforming Adults.* The Williams Institute. Accessed on 04/02/17 at https://williamsinstitute.law.ucla.edu/wp-content/uploads/AFSP-Williams-Suicide-Report-Final.pdf

2. Human Rights Campaign (2015) *Growing Up LGBT in America.* Washington, DC: Human Rights Campaign. Accessed on 04/02/17 at http://issuu.com/humanrightscampaign/docs/growing-up-lgbt-in-america/3?e=0

3. Gender Spectrum: www.genderspectrum.org

4. University of California at San Francisco Child and Adolescent Gender Center Clinic: www.ucsfbenioffchildrens.org/clinics/child_and_adolescent_gender_center/index.html

5. Kellaway, M. (2017) *Facebook Now Allows Users to Define Custom Gender.* New York, NY: Advocate. Accessed on 04/02/17 at www.advocate.com/politics/transgender/2015/02/27/facebook-now-allows-users-define-custom-gender

6. Flores, A.R., Herman, J.L., Gates, G.J., and Brown, T.N.T. (2016) *How Many Adults Identify as Transgender in the United States?* (p.2). Los Angeles, CA: The Williams Institute. Accessed on 04/02/17 at https://williamsinstitute.law.ucla.edu/wp-content/uploads/How-Many-Adults-Identify-as-Transgender-in-the-United-States.pdf

7. Haas, A.P., Herman, J.L., and Rodgers, J.L. (2014) *Suicide Attempts Among Transgender and Gender Non-Conforming Adults.* The Williams Institute. Accessed on 04/02/17 at https://williamsinstitute.law.ucla.edu/wp-content/uploads/AFSP-Williams-Suicide-Report-Final.pdf

8. Human Rights Campaign (2015) *Growing Up LGBT in America.* Washington, DC: Human Rights Campaign. Accessed on 04/02/17 at http://issuu.com/humanrightscampaign/docs/growing-up-lgbt-in-america/3?e=0

9. Human Rights Campaign (2017) *Violence Against the Transgender Community in 2017.* Washington, DC: Human Rights Campaign. Accessed on 04/02/17 at www.hrc.org/resources/violence-against-the-transgender-community-in-2017

10. Brill, S. and Pepper, R. (2008) *The Transgender Child: A Handbook for Families and Professionals.* San Francisco, CA: Cleis Press.

11. Ehrensaft, D. (2011) *Gender Born, Gender Made: Raising Healthy Gender Non-Conforming Kids*. New York, NY: The Experiment.

12. Travers, R., Bauer, G., Pyne, J., Bardley, K., Gale, L., and Papdimitriou, M. (2012) *Impact of Strong Parental Support for Trans Youth*. Ontario: TransPULSE. Accessed on 04/02/17 at http://transpulseproject.ca/wp-content/uploads/2012/10/Impacts-of-Strong-Parental-Support-for-Trans-Youth-vFINAL.pdf

13. Huston, M. (2015) "None of the above – An emerging group of transgender people is looking beyond 'man' and 'woman.'" *Psychology Today*. Accessed on 04/02/17 at www.psychologytoday.com/articles/201503/none-the-above

14. Pew Research Center (2013) *A Survey of LGBT Americans* (p.3). Accessed on 04/02/17 at www.pewsocialtrends.org/2013/06/13/chapter-2-social-acceptance

15. Pew Research Center (2016) *Where the Public Stands on Religious Liberty vs. Nondiscrimination* (p.1). Accessed on 04/02/17 at www.pewforum.org/2016/09/28/where-the-public-stands-on-religious-liberty-vs-nondiscrimination

16. Oxford University Press (2017) *Oxford Dictionaries*. Oxford: Oxford University Press. Accessed on 04/02/17 at https://en.oxforddictionaries.com/definition/transition

17. Merriam-Webster (2017) *Merriam-Webster Dictionaries*. Springfield, MA: Merriam-Webster Inc. Accessed on 04/02/17 at www.merriam-webster.com/dictionary/gender%20dysphoria

18. Ehrensaft, D. (2016) *The Gender Creative Child*. New York, NY: The Experiment.

19. Human Rights Campaign (2017) *Violence Against the Transgender Community in 2017*. Washington, DC: Human Rights Campaign. Accessed on 04/02/17 at www.hrc.org/resources/violence-against-the-transgender-community-in-2017

20. Suicide Prevention Resource Center (2008) *Suicide Risk and Prevention for Lesbian, Gay, Bisexual, and Transgender Youth*. Newton, MA: Education Development Center, Inc. Accessed on 04/02/17 at www.sprc.org/sites/default/files/migrate/library/SPRC_LGBT_Youth.pdf

21. Durso, L.E. and Gates, G.J. (2012) *Serving Our Youth: Findings from a National Survey of Service Providers Working with Lesbian, Gay, Bisexual, and Transgender Youth who are Homeless or at Risk of Becoming Homeless*. Los Angeles, CA: The Williams Institute with True Colors Fund and The Palette Fund. Accessed on 04/02/17 at https://williamsinstitute.law.ucla.edu/wp-content/uploads/Durso-Gates-LGBT-Homeless-Youth-Survey-July-2012.pdf

22. Human Rights Campaign (2015) *Growing Up LGBT in America*. Washington, DC: Human Rights Campaign. Accessed on 04/02/17 at www.hrc.org/youth-report/view-and-share-statistics

23. Trans Students Educational Resources: http://tser.org

24. Keig, Z. and Kellaway M. (2014) *Manning Up: Transsexual Men on Finding Brotherhood, Family & Themselves*. Oakland, CA: Transgress Press.

25. Beauvoir, Simone de (2011, c.1952) *The Second Sex* (C. Borde and S. Malovaney-Chevallier, trans.). New York, NY: Vintage Books.

26. Hill, M.R., Mays, J. and Mack, R. (2013) *The Gender Book*. Houston, TX: Marshall House Press.

27. Deutsch, M. (2015) *Information on Testosterone Hormone Therapy*. San Francisco, CA: University of California at San Francisco (UCSF) Transgender Care Navigation Program. Accessed on 04/02/17 at https://transcare.ucsf.edu/article/information-testosterone-hormone-therapy

28. Louden, K. (2014) "Largest study to date: Transgender hormone treatment safe." *Medscape Medical News*. Accessed on 04/02/17 at www.medscape.com/viewarticle/827713

29. Celec, P., Ostatníková, D., and Hodosy, J. (2015) "On the effects of testosterone on brain behavioral functions." *Frontiers in Neuroscience 9*, 12, doi: 10.3389/fnins.2015.00012. Accessed on 04/02/17 at http://journal.frontiersin.org/article/10.3389/fnins.2015.00012/full

30. Children's Hospital of Los Angeles (2015) *Transgender Youth Have Typical Hormone Levels*. Los Angeles, LA: Children's Hospital of Los Angeles. Accessed on 04/02/17 at www.chla.org/press-release/transgender-youth-have-typical-hormone-levels

31. National Center for Transgender Equality (2017) *ID Documents Center*. Washington, DC: National Center for Transgender Equality. Accessed on 04/02/17 at www.transequality.org/documents

32. National Center for Transgender Equality (2017) *ID Documents Center*. Washington, DC: National Center for Transgender Equality. Accessed on 04/02/17 at www.transequality.org/documents

33. Transgender Law Center (2016) *ID Please: Quick Guide to Changing Federal Identity Documents*. Oakland, CA: Transgender Law Center. Accessed on 04/02/17 at https://transgenderlawcenter.org/resources/id/id-please-quick-guide

34. Visit www.transequality.org/know-your-rights/social-security

35. UCSF Benioff Children's Hospital San Francisco (2017) *Child and Adolescent Gender Center Clinic*. San Francisco, CA: University of California San Francisco. Accessed on 04/02/17 at www.ucsfbenioffchildrens.org/clinics/child_and_adolescent_gender_center

36. Office for Civil Rights (2017) *Section 1557 of the Patient Protection and Affordable Care Act*. Washington, DC: Office for Civil Rights. Accessed on 04/02/18 at www.hhs.gov/civil-rights/for-individuals/section-1557/index.html

37. National Center for Transgender Equality (2017) *Know Your Rights – Health Care*. Washington, DC: National Center for Transgender Equality. Accessed on04/02/17 at www.transequality.org/know-your-rights/healthcare

38. National Center for Transgender Equality (2017) *Map: State Health Insurance Rules*. Washington, DC: National Center for Transgender Equality. Accessed on 04/02/17 at www.transequality.org/issues/resources/map-state-health-insurance-rules

39. National Center for Transgender Equality (2017) *Know Your Rights – Health Care*. Washington, DC: National Center for Transgender Equality. Accessed on 04/02/17 at www.transequality.org/know-your-rights/healthcare

40. Satija, N., Carbonell, L., and McCrimmon, R. (2017) *Texas vs. the Feds – A Look at the Lawsuits*. Austin, TX: The Texas Tribune. Accessed on 04/02/17 at www.texastribune.org/2017/01/17/texas-federal-government-lawsuits

41. Hersher, R. (2016) *North Carolina Governor Drops "Bathroom Bill" Lawsuit Against US*. Washington, DC: National Public Radio. Accessed on 04/02/17 at www.npr.org/sections/thetwo-way/2016/09/19/494573314/north-carolina-governor-drops-bathroom-bill-lawsuit-against-u-s

42. Gender Identity Development Service (2016) *England: National Health Services*. Accessed on 04/02/17 at http://gids.nhs.uk

43. National Health Service Choices (2016) *Gender Dysphoria – Treatment*. England: National Health Service www.nhs.uk/Conditions/Gender-dysphoria/Pages/Treatment.aspx

44. BBC (2015) *Louis Theroux: Transgender Kids*. Documentary for BBC Two, directed by Tom Barrow.

45. Campus Pride (2016–2017) *Campus Pride Index*. Accessed on 04/02/2017 at www.campusprideindex.org

46. Branson-Potts, H. (2014) "Gay youths more likely to report trouble in foster care study finds." *LA Times*. Accessed on 04/02/17 at www.latimes.com/local/countygovernment/la-me-lgbt-foster-youth-20140827-story.html

47. Transgender Law Center (2017) *About-Mission, Vision, Values*. Oakland, CA: Transgender Law Center. Accessed on 04/02/17 at https://transgenderlawcenter.org/about/mission

48. Stand With Trans: www.standwithtrans.org

49. Ally Moms: http://standwithtrans.org/ally-moms

50. enGender: www.engendernow.org

51. Human Rights Campaign (2015) *Growing Up LGBT in America*. Washington, DC: Human Rights Campaign. Accessed on 04/02/17 at http://issuu.com/humanrightscampaign/docs/growing-up-lgbt-in-america/3?e=0

52. Travers, R., Bauer, G., Pyne, J., Bardley, K., Gale, L. and Papdimitriou, M. (2012) *Impact of Strong Parental Support for Trans Youth*. Ontario: TransPULSE. Accessed on 04/02/17 at http://transpulseproject.ca/wp-content/uploads/2012/10/Impacts-of-Strong-Parental-Support-for-Trans-Youth-vFINAL.pdf

53. Gender Spectrum (2016) *Understanding Gender*. Oakland, CA: Gender Spectrum. Accessed on 04/02/17 at www.genderspectrum.org/quick-links/understanding-gender

54. Halloran, L. (2015) *Survey Shows Striking Increase of Americans Who Know and Support Transgender People*. Washington, DC: Human Rights Campaign. Accessed on 04/02/17 at www.hrc.org/blog/survey-shows-striking-increase-in-americans-who-know-and-support-transgende

55. TransKids Purple Rainbow Foundation: www.transkidspurplerainbow.org